Wooley

Kentucky Nature Studies: 4

Trees & Shrubs
of Kentucky

Trees & Shrubs of Kentucky

Mary E. Wharton
& Roger W. Barbour

The University Press of Kentucky

ISBN: 0-8131-1294-X

Library of Congress Catalog Card Number: 73-77257

Copyright © 1973 by The University Press of Kentucky

A statewide cooperative scholarly publishing agency
serving Berea College, Centre College of Kentucky,
Eastern Kentucky University, Georgetown College,
Kentucky Historical Society, Kentucky State University,
Morehead State University, Murray State University,
Northern Kentucky State College, Transylvania University,
University of Kentucky, University of Louisville, and
Western Kentucky University.

Editorial and Sales Offices: Lexington, Kentucky 40506

for Lucile & Bernice

Contents

(*Continued*)

Preface

With the hope that more people will come to recognize and appreciate woody plants, we have organized this book so as to enable the layman to identify an unknown tree, shrub, or vine as easily as possible. The whole picture section replaces conventional dichotomous keys, which a lay person tends to avoid. Because the photographs are grouped for ease in identification, not all illustrations of a given species are together. For example, bittersweet flowers are placed so that they may be distinguished from other small white flowers; the fruit is distinguished from other red and yellow fruits; and the vegetative characters, including leaves, are placed to contrast them with those of other deciduous vines. Cross-references connect the illustrations and discussions of each species.

The text was written by Mary E. Wharton; the photographs, except those specified below, are by Roger W. Barbour. Most of the photographs were taken expressly for this volume, the great majority in 1971 and 1972. Many tasks in the preparation of the book were shared jointly.

We wish to express our appreciation to the following persons for the use of their photographs in this volume:

Carol Baskin: pp. 111, 139, *Forestiera ligustrina.* E. Lucy Braun: pp. 19-20, virgin forest scenes (ca 1932), used by permission of Dr. Annette F. Braun. E. W. Chester: p. 70, *Bumelia lycioides.* Jim Conrad: p. 221, *Viburnum nudum,* form and twig; p. 273, *Alnus serrulata,* form; p. 289, *Styrax americana,* form; p. 307, *Fraxinus tomentosa,* form and bark; p. 344, *Carya aquatica,* bark; pp. 348–49, *Carya laciniosa,* form and bark; p. 365, *Nyssa sylvatica,* form; p. 373, *Diospyros virginiana,* form; p. 391, *Populus heterophylla,* form and bark; p. 453, *Quercus michauxii,* form and bark. R. W. Henley: p. 132, *Aronia arbutifolia;* p. 134, *Aronia melanocarpa;* p. 139, *Viburnum molle.* W. S. Justice: p. 43, *Philadelphus hirsutus;* p. 57, *Lonicera sempervirens;* p. 68, *Aristolochia durior;* p. 84, *Lyonia ligustrina;* p. 104, *Castanea pumila;* p. 123, *Cocculus carolinus;* p. 127, *Lonicera dioica.* J. B. Varner: p. 136, *Menispermum canadense;* p. 138, *Viburnum rufidulum;* p. 426,

Ulmus rubra, form. Mary E. Wharton: p. 31, woodland scene in the Bluegrass region.

Many friends have contributed to this volume; to all of them, named and unnamed, our thanks. We should like especially to express our gratitude to the following:

Raymond Athey, a self-taught botanist, freely shared with us his unsurpassed knowledge of the flora of western Kentucky. He was our guide on many delightful excursions and pointed out numerous species that we would not otherwise have seen. In addition, he collected and sent us several specimens.

The staff of Bernheim Forest was most congenial and cooperative. Clarence E. Hubbuch was our capable and gracious guide during many pleasant hours there.

Jim Conrad waded in winter swamps in western Kentucky, taking photographs to our specifications and collecting specimens for us.

E. C. Hale, Jr., and Faith Hershey did many of the line drawings; William Petrie led us to *Castanea pumila*; John Tierney was our guide to many species in Carter Caves State Resort Park; and the Kentucky Wilderness Preservation Society contributed some funds, through the Kentucky Research Foundation, which helped defray expenses.

Bernice L. Barbour was especially helpful, spending long hours in the darkroom helping process prints, accompanying us on field trips, and aiding in the selection of the color photographs. R. W. B. would like to add a more personal thanks—she tolerated me in times of stress and encouraged me always.

Introduction

PURPOSE

Trees enrich man's life, yet the march of civilization has needlessly been accompanied by sylvic ignorance and apathy. With the conviction that knowledge precedes appreciation, the authors present this book to the layman.

On a hot summer day one is grateful for a shade along a city street or in a residential lawn, and livestock clustered under trees in a pasture benefit from the coolness of shade and often from greener grass. Trees and shrubs, with beauty of form and color, soften the landscape, and without trees our parks would not be havens of serenity to relieve the tensions of modern life. Trees in a forest dominate a living community which includes many animal creatures and countless other plant species, and are guardians of soil and water, without which man cannot live.

Unfortunately many Kentuckians who appreciate trees and shrubs in general do not realize the great beauty and variety of our native species. The more one knows about them the fuller is his enjoyment of them, and the more persons there are with such knowledge, the more likely will our nature heritage be perpetuated. Therefore this book is as complete and nontechnical as possible. It is designed to enable the layman to identify our native and naturalized woody plants in different seasons—in flower, fruit, or leaf, and most species in winter dormancy—and to understand their environmental relationships, their values in ornamental planting, and their commercial uses. The information here will be useful likewise to the botanical student. The book will be helpful also in surrounding states.

The method of identification is to follow a grouping of photographs, a simpler and less technical means than the use of a dichotomous key. With this system one need only look through a particular group or subgroup of plates in order to identify an unknown. Technical terms are held at a minimum; the indispensable ones are explained by a glossary and diagrams (pp. 569-74).

SCOPE

This volume covers 282 species of woody plants. There are 260 color photographs and 914 black-and-white photographs. The species included are virtually all those known to occur wild in Kentucky, with the exception of the taxonomically complex genera *Crataegus*, the hawthorns, and *Rubus*, the blackberries and dewberries. (The distinguishing of species in these genera has no place in a book for the amateur naturalist; even the general taxonomist usually consults a *Crataegus* or *Rubus* specialist for species determination.) Most of the naturalized foreign species are included, but as time goes on, more introduced species may escape from cultivation and become part of the wild flora.

PLAN AND ARRANGEMENT

Procedure in Identification

For convenience in identification the plates and descriptions (Part II) are divided into nine series; the arrangement in these series is outlined on pages 37-38. The first two series, constituting the color section, picture colorful or otherwise showy flowers and fruits. The seven series in the black-and-white section deal with leaves, trunk, winter twigs, and general form, as well as some fruits. Each species pictured in the color section is also included in the black-and-white section.

After deciding to which series of plates your specimen belongs, turn to the first page of that series and select the group, then the subgroup, with the characteristics of your plant. Check the plates and descriptions in that subgroup. After using the book a few times you will be familiar with the composition of each series and can turn directly to the correct one. When you have identified a plant, turn to Part III for its classification and for an account of its habitat, distribution, frequence, and uses. Cross references are given to all other pages where a species is illustrated and/or discussed.

Although no absolute distinctions are possible between trees and shrubs and between shrubs and woody vines, in most instances there is no question. In general, trees are larger than shrubs, both in height and in stem diameter; and a typical tree has a single trunk, whereas a typical shrub is bushy with several stems from the ground. However, some shrubs may occasionally be twenty feet or more tall with a stem diameter of three or four inches. And a tree may sometimes have multiple trunks, while a shrub may have a single stem. The dividing line between a sprawling shrub and a woody vine is also indefinite. Nevertheless, since the borderline plants are relatively few and the categories of trees, shrubs, and vines are usually obvious, we believe that more will be gained in convenience and rapidity of identification by separating these than will be lost in occasionally having to check two series for a borderline case.

If a small plant has a perennial woody stem above the ground, it is technically a shrub, regardless of its size. However, diminutive shrubs, other small semishrubby plants, and vines woody only at the base were included in the authors' *A Guide to the Wildflowers and Ferns of Kentucky* (1971). For these, such as *Chimaphila maculata, Gaultheria procumbens, Ascyrum hypericoides, Vinca minor, Mitchella repens, Pachysandra procumbens,* and *Clematis virginiana,* the reader is referred to our earlier book.

Names Used

For most species the scientific names used follow *Gray's Manual,* Eighth Edition, by M. L. Fernald. When another scientific name is used, the synonym in *Gray's Manual* is given in brackets in Part III. Only the common names in widest usage are included although several common names may be applied to a single species. Calling a plant by a name different from the one given here is therefore not necessarily incorrect.

Frequence and Distribution

The terms used in Part III to denote abundance and frequence are as follows, in descending order: abundant, common, frequent, infrequent, and rare. "Abundant" and "common" indicate, for example, not only that a plant is frequently

PHYSIOGRAPHIC DIAGRAM OF KENTUCKY

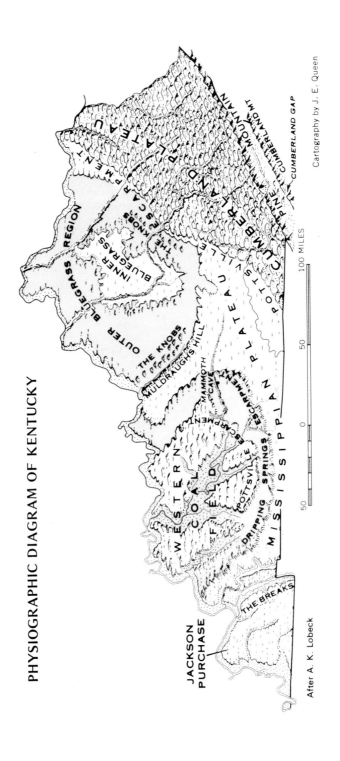

After A. K. Lobeck

Cartography by J. E. Queen

found but that it occurs in considerable quantity. The rating applies only within the habitat; for instance, a species common in climax forests and one common on roadsides and in fence-rows would differ in their overall occurrence.

Range of a species is given only for Kentucky. To learn the total range in the United States consult general manuals. Species distributed throughout the state can be expected also in adjacent states, and species restricted to a particular section may occur in an adjacent portion of another state. The frequence, however, given only for Kentucky, may vary in other states.

In citing the range of a species in Kentucky, often the physiographic region is mentioned; this can be located on the map on page 4.[1] Often, however, general geographic sections are mentioned and these are delimited approximately as follows:

Eastern Kentucky:	*The Cumberland Plateau, Cumberland Mountains, and eastern Knobs*
Southeastern Kentucky:	*Pine Mountain, Cumberland Mountain, Black Mountain, and Log Mountain, which collectively are called the Cumberland Mountains, and adjacent areas*
Western Kentucky:	*The lower two-thirds of the Green River basin northwest to the Ohio River and westward to the Mississippi River (approximately all the state west of Mammoth Cave)*
Southwestern Kentucky:	*The Jackson Purchase, west of the Tennessee River, and the area between the Tennessee and Cumberland rivers (now impounded lakes)*

[1] Lobeck is followed in designating all of the Appalachian Plateau in eastern Kentucky as "Cumberland Plateau"; some authors call the portion drained by the Big Sandy and Licking rivers "Allegheny Plateau," restricting the term "Cumberland" to that portion drained by the Kentucky and Cumberland rivers.

Southern Kentucky: *The basins of the Cumberland and Barren rivers*

Central Kentucky: *The Bluegrass region, the eastern part of the Mississippian Plateau, and the intervening Knobs*

Northern Kentucky: *The northern portion of the Outer Bluegrass region*

The term "Pennyroyal" or "Pennyrile," a popular name for the southern and western part of the Mississippian Plateau, is also sometimes used.

PRINCIPLES OF NAMING PLANTS

Common names for plants sometimes lead to confusion and misunderstanding, both because one species may have several names and because the same name may be applied to different species. Common names are frequently local and vary from place to place. Hence the naturalist or amateur botanist would do well to familiarize himself also with the scientific nomenclature.

Scientific names are not as difficult as many persons believe and can be learned by anyone seriously interested in plants. The scientific name of a species is a binomial composed of the genus name followed by the specific epithet. A genus is a group of closely related species; therefore the binomial indicates relationship, much as a person's surname denotes relationship to his brothers or cousins. The words in scientific nomenclature are Latin or latinized and are adopted throughout the world regardless of spoken language. Following the Latin binomial is the name, usually abbreviated, of the botanist who named the species; if two botanists are responsible for the binomial combination, the first is placed in parentheses.

International rules govern the naming of plants, and no two species in the world can have the same binomial. According to this code of nomenclature, there would be but one valid name the world over for any single species. However, occasionally there is difference of opinion regarding the application of the rules to a given species or regarding rank in classification, such as whether certain species should be grouped with others in a large genus or placed in a separate one by splitting the original genus. Also new knowledge sometimes necessitates some taxonomic revision. Although these situations result in *synonyms* in scientific nomenclature, there is nevertheless no ambiguity as there is with common names.

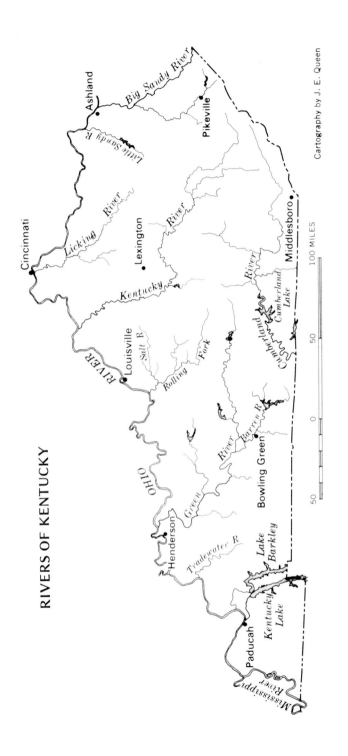

RIVERS OF KENTUCKY

Cartography by J. E. Queen

100 MILES

Part I.

The Woody Vegetation
of Kentucky in
Ecological Perspective

Geology, Climate, and Plant Geography

The woody flora of Kentucky, as well as the herbaceous, contains a variety of geographical elements. It has many Appalachian species which are also found in the Appalachian sections of adjacent states; it contains some southern species which extend northward only into our southern tier of counties. Also it contains some northern species occurring at the highest elevations, our coolest climates, located in southeast Kentucky, and occurring also in a few other relict colonies remaining from the time of Pleistocene glaciation when the southern Appalachians provided refuge for northern plants. The Purchase region, which is part of the Mississippi Embayment, has many Coastal Plain species. In addition, many species in the Kentucky flora are wide-ranging throughout the eastern half of the United States.

Many factors related to geology affect plant distribution in the state. Geologic structure determines what rock will outcrop in a given area, and the nature of the outcrop affects the physiography, as will be noted in comparing the geologic map (p. 16) and the physiographic diagram (p. 4). Soil chemistry, especially whether the soil is basic, neutral, or acidic, is often significant, and the location of calcareous and noncalcareous rock can be seen on the geologic map. Topography is important; for example, species found on a cliffside are not likely to be found on an alluvial flat. The role of physiography is a complex one which includes past vegetational history and plant migration as related to the development of the present topography. Geology and physiography also affect the pattern of land use, and this drastically affects our flora.

The climate of Kentucky is continental—with wide range between the heat of summer and the cold of winter—and humid and warm temperate, as shown by the maps on pages 13-14. The average length of minimum growing season (from latest killing frost in spring to earliest killing frost in autumn) is between 190 and 200 days in approximately the western half of the state (200 and over in the extreme southwest); most of central Kentucky has between 180 and 190 days, and most of eastern Kentucky has between 170 and 180 days.[1] Microclimates are also important in plant distribution; that is, certain small local situations for plant growth, such as rocky ridgetops, are hot and dry, and certain others, such as coves in north slopes, are cool and moist.

KENTUCKY'S FORESTS

Present Status

Pioneers coming to Kentucky in the late eighteenth century found luxuriant forests stretching over the entire state, with the exception of a small amount of grassland in the Mississippian Plateau. To the early settlers these forests were a hindrance to travel, an obstacle to homebuilding and farming and a hiding place for hostile Indians. Large-scale clearing was therefore embarked upon, not to utilize a resource but to rid the land of nature's bountiful production. The Bluegrass was settled first and hence lost its natural vegetation first, and for the most part other somewhat level lands were settled before the hilly areas. As migration to Kentucky was rapid, so was destruction of her vegetation. During the first century of statehood, when Kentucky ranked high nationally in iron production, wood from her forests furnished charcoal for blast furnaces, eight-tenths of an acre of trees per ton of iron.[2] Commercial lumbering grew and by 1900 had reached mammoth proportions in the mountain and hill sections.

Thus destruction of the great mixed forest which prevailed in eastern Kentucky and adjacent states was in full swing before there was an inkling of its significance. The fact that this forest was a lineal descendant of the mixed forest of the Tertiary period millions of years ago was first suggested by Harshberger in 1904, but it was not studied for another decade and was first termed "mixed mesophytic" by E. Lucy Braun in 1916. While timber exploitation continued unabated for

---

[1] U.S. Department of Agriculture, *Climate and Man*, Yearbook of Agriculture, 1941 (Washington, D.C.: Government Printing Office, 1941), pp. 884-85.

[2] A. M. Miller, *The Geology of Kentucky* (Frankfort: Kentucky Department of Geology and Forestry), Ser. V, Bull. 2, 1919.

AVERAGE MONTHLY TEMPERATURE IN KENTUCKY

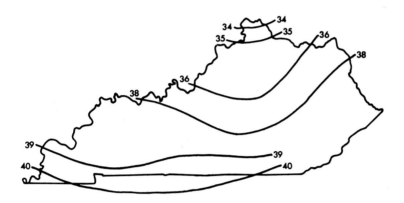

December, January, and February; 1931-1960 inclusive.
(Data not available for the highest mountains in the southeast.)

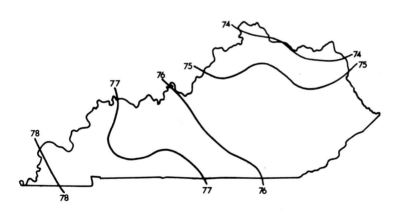

June, July, and August; 1931-1960 inclusive.
(Data not available for the highest mountains in the southeast.)

AVERAGE MONTHLY RAINFALL IN KENTUCKY

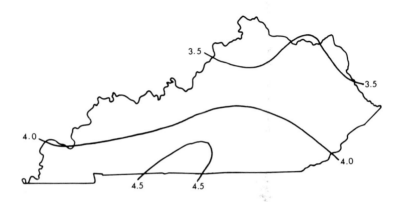

December, January, and February; 1931-1960 inclusive

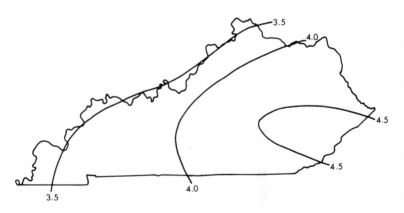

June, July, and August; 1931-1960 inclusive

several decades more, Dr. Braun was almost alone in deciphering the story of the* most complex forest type in North America. Her ecological research in Kentucky was published as five papers between 1935 and 1942 and culminated in her monumental work *Deciduous Forests of Eastern North America* in 1950.[3] Many of the virgin mixed mesophytic forests she analyzed and photographed were cut even before her work was published, and now, of those she studied, only a few small fragments remain that even resemble primary forest. Today no absolutely untouched virgin forests are left in the state. The few scattered fragments of essentially primary or original forest which have been acquired by the federal government and the Commonwealth will, we hope, be preserved.

Although there is much woodland in Kentucky today, most of it does not resemble the original forest type. Since our climate favors forest growth, cut-over woods and abandoned farmland are soon covered by woody vegetation. However, a plant community following man's disturbance of the environment is not of the same composition as that which he removed. Cutting and burning contribute to soil loss; farming practices often lead to leaching and erosion. The result is that the land to be reoccupied by trees has less soil, poorer soil, and drier soil than it had previously, and the former forest type cannot live on it.

Forest Types[4]

Kentucky is centrally located in the Deciduous Forest Formation of eastern North America. It contains parts of two forest regions, the Mixed Mesophytic in eastern Kentucky (east of the Pottsville Escarpment) and the Western Mesophytic in the rest of the state.

The *Mixed Mesophytic Forest* region includes the Cumberland Mountains and the Cumberland Plateau and extends into southeastern Ohio, southwestern Pennsylvania, West Virginia, and eastern Tennessee. However, it was more elaborate in

---

[3] For all the references here cited, see the bibliography in E. Lucy Braun, *Deciduous Forests of Eastern North America* (Philadelphia: Blakiston, 1950).

[4] For a more detailed explanation, see Braun, 1950.

GENERALIZED GEOLOGIC MAP OF KENTUCKY

Alluvium (narrow strips not shown)

Tertiary

Cretaceous

Pennsylvanian: mostly noncalcareous

Mississippian: mostly calcareous

Devonian: mostly noncalcareous

Silurian: calcareous

Ordovician: calcareous

Lake

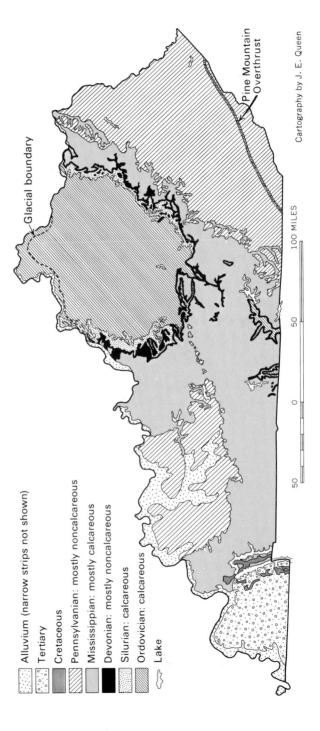

Glacial boundary

Pine Mountain Overthrust

Cartography by J. E. Queen

50   0   50   100 MILES

Kentucky than nearer the periphery of the region. Originally the Mixed Mesophytic association covered most of the land in this region except on the dry ridge tops and upper south-facing slopes, the flood plains, and certain peculiar physiographic features, such as the southeast slope of Pine Mountain. For the region it is the climatic climax, the ultimate in vegetative production that the existing climate will support; physiographic climaxes occur when physiographic features hold up vegetational development and stabilize it at a less mesophytic level, such as the oak-chestnut, oak-pine, and pine communities on the ridge tops. The Mixed Mesophytic is the most complex and the oldest association in eastern North America, and from it probably all other climax associations of deciduous forest have arisen. In this region mixed deciduous forest continued · uninterrupted for millions of years, although elsewhere it was killed off by geological upheavals and resultant drying in some places, by submergence in others, and by glaciation in still others. In the Cumberland Mountain section of southeastern Kentucky it attained its grandest development in number of species and size of individuals, "one of the finest deciduous forest areas of North America," according to Dr. Braun (1950, p. 50).

This association develops on moist well-drained sites with deep soil and a thick layer of humus. Instead of a few dominant species, as in the simpler associations derived from it (for example, beech-maple and oak-hickory), dominance is shared by twenty or twenty-five species, especially tulip tree, sugar maple, beech, basswood (three species, but not *Tilia americana*), yellow buckeye, red oak, white oak, red maple, hemlock, black walnut, black cherry, shagbark hickory, white ash, and formerly chestnut. Also there are characteristic understory trees, shrubs, and herbaceous plants. A specific mixed mesophytic community may not have all twenty or twenty-five species in the canopy, and different communities may have them in different proportions; there is a blending as some species drop out and others are picked up.

The secondary forests which we have today are more xeric than the original, since soil erosion occurred between removal and regrowth. The oak, oak-hickory, and oak-pine forests now prevalent resemble climatic climaxes in other regions more than they resemble the climax in this region. Also forest communities differ from one another in relation to slope, exposure, and underlying rock more than when the climax prevailed. The secondary mixed mesophytic communities of the present, less mixed than the original, are restricted to coves, ravines, and lower north-facing slopes.

The *Western Mesophytic Forest* region includes the Bluegrass, Knobs, Mississippian Plateau, and Western Coalfield, and the Kentucky portion of the Mississippi Embayment known as the Jackson Purchase. In adjacent states it includes southwestern Ohio, southern Indiana, the southern tip of Illinois, and central and western Tennessee. This region has a wide variety of upland forest types and extensive alluvial swamps. The forest communities, showing a pronounced influence of underlying rock, form a mosaic of vegetational types including oak-hickory, mixed mesophytic, and swamp forest. The region is transitional between the Mixed Mesophytic and the Oak-Hickory Forest region, which is situated primarily in the Ozarks.

The Inner Bluegrass section, according to Braun (1950, p. 124), is "the most anomalous of all vegetation areas of eastern United States." Here where the land is gently undulating and undissected away from the streams, no organized plant communities remain, but the large estates which have not been intensively farmed have many old trees, from 200 to even 400 years old. The most characteristic are bur oak and blue ash, but other old ones are chinquapin oak, Shumard's red oak, white oak, white ash, hackberry, sugar maple, black walnut, black cherry, coffee tree, American elm, shagbark hickory (both species), and bitternut hickory. Their widely spreading branches (except in the blue ash, which never spreads) indicate that they have always been well spaced. Early descriptions of this section were sketchy but they mention especially the undergrowth of cane in many places. Though forested, the region unquestionably would have been somewhat savanna-like with a very open canopy; in fact, bur oaks cannot grow in dense forest. The earliest surviving description of the area was written by James Nourse, who in May of 1775 traveled a buffalo road from the vicinity of Frankfort toward the present site of Lexington. "[On the plateau] it is light with timber,

Virgin mixed mesophytic forest, with tulip tree, beech, and sugar maple predominating, as it appeared in the early 1930s before cutting. Near Lynn Fork of Leatherwood Creek, Perry County.

Virgin mixed mesophytic forests (hemlock, beech, and
sugar maple above, tulip tree and beech below) in
the 1930s before cutting. Near Lynn Fork of Leatherwood
Creek, Perry County.

[consisting of] little oak—mostly sugar tree[s], Walnut, Ash, and buckeye. . . . The surface of the ground [is] covered with grass. . . . the ash very large and high, and large locusts of both sorts, [and] some cherry. The growth of grass under [the trees is] amazing; [there is] blue grass, white clover, buffalo grass, and reed pines . . . and what would be called a fine swarth of grass in cultivated meadows; and such was its appearance without end in little dells."[5]

The gorges of the Kentucky River and its tributaries, always of a different vegetational type from most of the Bluegrass, would have been densely wooded, and today they have second-growth woods.

The rugged area encircling the Western Coalfield, including the Dripping Springs and Pottsville escarpments, has several Appalachian species in its flora and has the same rock formations as the western edge of the Cumberland Plateau. River valleys in the Western Coalfield are thickly alluviated and swamps are frequent.

In the Mississippian Plateau section some areas were originally prairie—tall grasses in open country—which the early settlers inappropriately called "barrens." Any of these lands which now are abandoned after farming become wooded, in harmony with a forest climate. Here the original prairie grassland was a relict community which remained from a drier interglacial or postglacial time and had been perpetuated partly by herds of bison and partly by Indians who periodically burned it·to encourage grass and thus attract game.

In the Purchase region, which contains many southern and Coastal Plain species, the uplands have oak-hickory forests in which the southern red oak is often the dominant tree. The alluvial valleys have forests of swamp chestnut oak, willow oak, pin oak, overcup oak, swamp cottonwood, pecan, sweet gum, water tupelo, and bald cypress. Ravines in the loess hills which rise above the Mississippi alluvial plain contain mixed mesophytic communities.

5 "Diary of James Nourse, Sr.," Durrett Codex 142, Special Collections, University of Chicago Library, quoted by permission. Editorial additions are by Mr. Neal O. Hammon of Louisville, who kindly brought this material to our attention.

GROWING WOODY PLANTS

Use of Native Species in Ornamental Planting

There is a quirk in human nature that attaches glamour to the faraway. In selecting plants for landscaping Americans often choose an exotic species from Europe or Asia in preference to a native one, even though the native is as good or better. Similarly, many American species are appreciated and cultivated more in Europe than they are here. In the beautification of our highways with landscape planting, native species would be more appropriate than the exotic species frequently used.

The planting public, however, is only partly responsible, for they plant what the nurseries propagate and promote. It seems that our local nurseries would do well to propagate and feature more of our beautiful native woody plants.

Trees and shrubs should not be dug from the wild but should be planted from nursery-grown stock. One does not have the legal right to dig plants except on his own land or with the permission of the owner. But even if he obtains permission, there is little chance for their survival unless they are extremely small and dormant. In nature a root system is long and straggling, often intertwined with roots of other plants and sometimes growing around a rock or in a crack in a rock. The amount of root system that can be dug up is usually insufficient for survival. In contrast, a nursery-grown plant has a compact root system which results from root pruning due to several transplantings while small.

Care of Trees and Shrubs

The anatomy and physiology of woody plants figures so little in the thinking of the average person that incorrect handling and treatment of them is common. For instance, lawn mowers break the protective bark of many a young tree, thereby admitting fungi and bacteria.

Marking a trail through the woods by breaking and bending down the "leaders" of small trees ruins these trees forever, permanently deforming them and preventing their ever growing into straight and dignified forest monarchs. Saying there are "plenty more" is no excuse; they may be the most desirable species and the owner may have definite plans for those individuals to grow.

For pruning a branch off a tree there is a correct way which will permit healing and an incorrect way which will inevitably lead to decay. A major branch should always be cut flush with the trunk, and a secondary branch flush with the larger branch from which it grows, never leaving a stub. For healing there must be food transported from leaves beyond the cut; there is no source of food or enough living cells to grow over the cut at the end of a stub. Severe pruning of trees by cutting back all large branches is always inadvisable because it invariably results in decay of the trunk as well as the branches and produces an ugly form in the meantime. If a tree is actually too tall, it would be better to remove it and substitute a smaller one.

In pruning shrubs, ends of young stems should be cut off in order to induce more branching, more growth from lateral buds, and hence more compactness. Always consider the location of buds, which are the source of new growth.

Autumn in Kentucky

The pageantry of autumn coloration never loses its appeal. Different deciduous trees and shrubs turn red or yellow at different times in the season, thus prolonging the array. Some localities have their peak of coloration at a different time from others, depending on which trees predominate.

In autumn coloration the major factors of heredity and environment are both involved. The walnut and hackberry, for example, do not have in their hereditary make-up what is required to produce a red pigment. The red maple and sweet gum have that hereditary ability, but how much they produce depends on environmental and seasonal factors. When autumn coloration occurs, physiological activities gradually slow down before the leaves die. In a rich soil the leaves stay green and active longer than in a poorer soil, possibly until a freeze kills them, and then there is no chance for coloration. Also in a wet season the leaves may remain green until they fall off. In a drought they dry up and die before changing color.

Every green leaf always contains yellow pigments in addition to the green. With a slowing down of physiological activities the green may break down before the yellow; then we say the leaf "turns" yellow. If a leaf goes from green to brown, the yellow is breaking down with the green. If a leaf becomes red or purple, that pigment is manufactured at the time it appears, usually simultaneously with the breakdown of green. Favoring the production of red in those species which can make it are cool nights and sunny days, much sugar and little nitrogen in the leaves, and ample moisture.

The reasons why there is less brilliant autumn coloration in the rich Bluegrass section than in the hilly sections of the state should begin to be evident. The common Bluegrass trees listed under "Forest Types" contain only a few that can be colorful. And often other colorful species occurring in the Bluegrass are less brilliant than the same species in a poorer and more acid soil.

AUTUMN IN KENTUCKY

Sugar maple (*Acer saccharum*)

Sassafras *(Sassafras albidum)*

Red maple
(*Acer rubrum*)

Winged sumac *(Rhus copallina)*

Hercules'-club *(Aralia spinosa)*

Sweet gum (*Liquidambar styraciflua*)

REPRESENTATIVE FOREST COMMUNITIES

A cypress swamp at Murphey's Pond in Hickman County in the Jackson Purchase region.

A tributary of the Kentucky River in the Inner Bluegrass. Forest communities in this region are now restricted to the gorges of the river and its tributaries.

A hemlock glen at Yahoo Falls in Daniel Boone National Forest in southeastern Kentucky.

Lilly Cornett Woods in Letcher County in the
Cumberland Plateau. Owned by the Commonwealth, this
nearly virgin forest contains many large old-growth trees,
especially oaks of several species and walnuts.

A resistant conglomerate capping the ridge crests of the Red River Gorge, cut in the Pottsville Escarpment at the western edge of the Cumberland Plateau. Here dry pine and oak woods occur on the uplands and mesophytic forest communities in the ravines, coves, and valleys.

The Cumberland Plateau, viewed from Breaks Interstate Park in Pike County. The slopes are covered by second-growth woodland, predominantly oak-hickory.

Part II.

Plates &

Descriptions

Arrangement of Plates for Identification

(*Continued on next page*)

DECIDUOUS TREES

* It should be noted that the stated height of a tree or shrub is the maximum and is seldom seen today. Also a tree growing in a forest is taller and narrower than the same species growing in the open.

Series One: Flowers

Trees, Shrubs, and Woody Vines Grouped According to Colorful or Otherwise Conspicuous Flowers or Inflorescences

(Continued on next page)

Group 3. Flowers minute, without corolla (some with neither calyx nor corolla), staminate and pistillate flowers in separate inflorescences, the staminate always in catkins or pendulous heads
    Staminate flowers always in pendulous catkins 3.1–3.8
    Staminate flowers in pendulous spherical heads or in catkins that are not pendulous 3.9–3.11

Group 4. Flowers without corolla but never borne in catkins, very small individually but often collectively conspicuous 4.1–4.11

Group 5. Pollen-bearing cones of pine 5.1

Flowering dates are for an average season in Kentucky.

The Genera *Liriodendron* and *Magnolia*

Flowers of these genera have numerous pistils on a cone-shaped receptacle and numerous stamens.

1.1 *Liriodendron tulipifera* L.
TULIP TREE,
TULIP POPLAR,
YELLOW POPLAR
Petals 1⅝–2 inches long. May.
Tall tree.
Pp. 482-84, 522-23

1.2a *Magnolia acuminata* L.
CUCUMBER-TREE,
CUCUMBER MAGNOLIA
Petals 2–3 inches long. May.
Large tree.
Pp. 114, 356-57, 523

1.2b *Magnolia fraseri* Walt.
  FRASER'S MAGNOLIA, MOUNTAIN MAGNOLIA
Flowers fragrant, with petals 3–4 inches long.
June. Understory tree.
Pp. 116, 358, 523

1.2c *Magnolia tripetala* L.
  UMBRELLA MAGNOLIA
Flowers unpleasantly odorous, with
slender petals 3¼–4¾ inches long.
May. Understory tree.
Pp. 115, 360, 524

1.2d *Magnolia macrophylla*
  Michx.
  LARGE-LEAF MAGNOLIA
Flowers strongly scented, with
petals 5½–7¼ inches long. June.
Tall slender understory tree.
Pp. 115, 359, 524

1.3 *Calycanthus fertilis* Walt.
CALYCANTHUS,
SWEET SHRUB,
CAROLINA ALLSPICE

Flowers 1–1½ inches wide.
Sepals and petals numerous,
undifferentiated, and inserted at
the summit of the receptacle
as are stamens; pistils within the
receptacle. May. Aromatic
shrub.
Pp. 209, 524

1.4 *Asimina triloba* (L.) Dunal.
PAPAW

Flowers 1–1½ inches across, borne
on branchlets of the preceding year.
April. Small tree or large shrub.
Pp. 120, 255, 361, 524-25

1.5 *Philadelphus hirsutus* Nutt.
MOCK-ORANGE

Flowers ¾–⅞ inch across,
solitary or in clusters of 3; ovary
below the attachment of other
flower parts; fruit a capsule.
Leaves softly hairy on the lower
surface. Shrub.
Pp. 220, 526

P. inodorus L. differs in having
flowers 1⅜–1¾ inches across and
leaves glabrous or nearly so beneath.
Pp. 220, 526

1.6 *Hamamelis
virginiana* L.
WITCH-HAZEL
Petals yellow, ½–¾
inch long, slender and
twisted. October-
November. Shrub.
Pp. 275, 527

1.7 *Amelanchier
arborea*
(Michx. f.) Fernald
SERVICEBERRY,
SARVIS
Flowers opening before
or with the young
leaves. Flower stalks
usually silky; petals
slender and about ½
inch long. April.
Understory tree.
Pp. 134, 398-99, 528-29

In *A. laevis* Wieg. leaves
are half-grown and purple
or bronzy at flowering
time. Pp. 398, 529

The Genus *Prunus* (in part), the PLUMS, CHERRIES, and PEACH

Flowers with a cup-shaped receptacle bearing 5 sepals, 5 petals, and numerous stamens on the rim, and a single pistil, containing 1 ovule, within the cup.

1.8a *Prunus americana* Marsh.

WILD PLUM

Flowers opening before the leaves. Petals nearly ½ inch long. Early April. Small tree, often forming thickets.
Pp. 121, 408, 531

1.8b *Prunus munsoniana* Wight & Hedrick

WILD GOOSE PLUM

Flowers opening before or with the young leaves. Petals ¼–⅜ inch long; sepals bearing glands on the margin. Early April. Small tree, often forming thickets.
Pp. 121, 409, 531

Similar species are: *P. hortulana* Bailey, the hortulan plum, with flowers borne chiefly on prolonged slender branches instead of short lateral branches and opening when the leaves are half-grown. Small tree. Pp. 409, 531

P. angustifolia Marsh., the Chickasaw plum, with flowers less than ½ inch wide. Small tree or large shrub, often forming thickets. Pp. 121, 279, 407, 531

1.8c *Prunus mahaleb* L.

PERFUMED CHERRY

Flowers about ½ inch across, in short racemes or corymbs produced on branchlets of the preceding year, and appearing after the leaves. April. Small tree (occasionally a shrub).

Pp. 411, 531

Other species of wild cherries, having flowers less than ½ inch across, are illustrated on pp. 71–72.

1.8d *Prunus persica* (L.) Batsch

PEACH

Flowers 1–1¼ inches wide, appearing before the leaves. Early April. Small tree.

Pp. 410, 532

The Genus *Pyrus*, the APPLES and PEAR

Flowers differing from those of *Prunus* in having petals abruptly narrowed at the base, a compound pistil with 5 styles, and the ovary concealed within the "cup," which is grown to the ovary wall.

1.9a *Pyrus communis* L.
   PEAR
Flowers white and 1–1¼ inches wide. Early April.
Tree with height greater than spread.
Pp. 402-03, 533

1.9b *Pyrus malus* L.
   APPLE
Flowers tinged with pink,
1–1¼ inches wide. New
growth whitish- or grayish-
woolly. April. Large
spreading tree.
Pp. 400-401, 533

1.9c *Pyrus coronaria* L.
WILD CRAB
Flowers pink or pinkish,
fragrant, and about 1¼
inches across. Early May.
Small tree or large shrub,
usually with some spine-like
branchlets.
Pp. 404-05, 479, 533

1.9d *Pyrus angustifolia* Ait.
WILD CRAB,
NARROW-LEAF
CRAB-APPLE
Differs from *P. coronaria*
principally in leaf shape.
Pp. 406, 533

P. ioensis (Wood) Bailey differs
from our other species of wild
crab-apple in having calyx,
pedicels, and lower surface of
leaves hairy. Pp. 406, 533

The Genus *Crataegus*, the HAWTHORNS

Flowers in corymbs. The 5 sepals, 5 petals, 5–20 stamens, and 1–5 styles all above the ovary which is concealed within the cuplike receptacle grown to the ovary wall. Chiefly small trees (occasionally shrubs), usually bearing stout thorns.

The genus *Crataegus* is easily recognized but many species are difficult to separate. Only a few examples are given here to illustrate the genus.

1.10a *Crataegus crus-galli* L.
COCKSPUR THORN

Flowers about ½ inch wide in many-flowered corymbs. Leaves unlobed, wedge-shaped at the base. Thorns long, straight, and rigid. Late May. Small tree.
Pp. 131, 415, 530

1.10b *Crataegus phaenopyrum* (L. f.) Medic.
WASHINGTON THORN

Flowers usually ½ inch across but often less, in many-flowered compound corymbs. Leaves often 3-lobed, and usually heart-shaped at the base. Thorns slightly curved. May-June. Small tree.
Pp. 131, 479, 530

1.10c *Crataegus mollis*
(T. & G.) Scheele
RED HAW

Flowers ¾–⅞ inch across,
borne in woolly, many-
flowered compound corymbs.
Leaves, and especially
petioles, densely woolly at
flowering time, becoming less
so at maturity. Sparingly
thorny or thornless. April.
Tree.
Pp. 132, 478, 530

The Genus *Rubus*, the RASPBERRIES, BLACKBERRIES, and DEWBERRIES

Stamens and pistils numerous, the latter inserted on a conic
receptacle. Erect, arching, or prostrate shrubs.

1.11a *Rubus enslenii* Tratt.
SOUTHERN
DEWBERRY

Representative of a group of
species which are difficult
to separate. Flowers about 1
inch across, 1–5 on short
upright branches. May.
Prickly prostrate shrubs.
Pp. 185, 535

1.11b *Rubus hispidus* L. (and related species)
SWAMP DEWBERRY
Representative of a small group of species. Flowers about ⅝ inch wide, several in a raceme. Stems slender, bearing bristles instead of prickles. May–June. Prostrate shrubs. Pp. 185, 535

1.11c *Rubus allegheniensis* Porter (and related species)
BLACKBERRY
An example of a large group of species which are usually left to a specialist to separate. Flowers about 1 inch across, in racemes. May. Prickly shrubs.
Pp. 119, 242, 535

1.11d *Rubus occidentalis* L.
BLACK RASPBERRY
Flowers usually ½ inch across (occasionally ⅜ inch); petals shorter than the reflexed sepals. Stems purplish and glaucous. Early May. Prickly shrub.
Pp. 119, 241, 534-35

1.11e *Rubus odoratus* L.
FLOWERING
RASPBERRY
Flowers 1½ inches wide; each sepal with a long taillike tip. June. Erect shrub without prickles.
Pp. 292-93, 535

The Genus *Rosa*, the ROSES

Flowers with prolonged sepals, 5 large petals, numerous stamens, ovaries enclosed within the receptacle, and short styles.

1.12a *Rosa setigera* Michx.
CLIMBING ROSE, PRAIRIE ROSE
Flowers borne in corymbs. Petals about 1 inch long; styles united into a column. Leaflets usually 3. June. Climbing vine or sprawling shrub.
Pp. 130, 184, 534

1.12b *Rosa carolina* L.
CAROLINA ROSE, PASTURE ROSE

Flowers solitary or 2 or 3 together. Petals 1–1¼ inches long; styles separate and short. Leaves usually with 5–7 leaflets. June. Low shrub.
Pp. 130, 239, 533

R. *palustris* Marsh., the swamp rose, also has flowers in corymbs. Petals are pale pink, ¾–1 inch long; styles are very short but not united. Leaflets are usually 7. June–July. Erect shrub. Pp. 130, 240, 534

1.12c *Rosa multiflora* Thunb.
MULTIFLORA ROSE

Racemes many-flowered. Petals about ½ inch long; styles united into a column. Leaves with 7–9 leaflets. Late May. Large arching shrub.
Pp. 130, 238, 533-34

1.13 *Decodon verticillatus* (L.) Ell.
SWAMP LOOSESTRIFE, WATER-WILLOW

Flowers axillary. Petals 5, each about ½ inch long and narrowed at the base; stamens 10. August. Shrub, woody at the base, with long, arching, herbaceous stems.
Pp. 214, 551

1.14 *Stewartia ovata* (Cav.) Weatherby
MOUNTAIN CAMELLIA
Flowers 2½–3½ inches wide. Petals 5 or 6; stamens
numerous, with either purple or white filaments.
Late June. Large shrub or small tree.
Pp. 286, 419, 550

1.15 *Hypericum
spathulatum*
(Spach) Steud.
SHRUBBY ST.
JOHN'S-WORT
Flowers ¾–1 inch in
diameter, with numerous
stamens and 1 pistil with
3–5 styles. July. Shrub.
Pp. 213, 550

H. frondosum Michx., golden
St. John's-wort, has flowers
1–1¾ inches across. Pp. 214,
550
    H. densiflorum Pursh, bushy
St. John's-wort, has flowers ½
inch across, numerous in a
compound inflorescence. Pp.
213, 550

1.16 *Epigaea repens* L.
TRAILING ARBUTUS
Flowers pink or white, fragrant, and ½–¾ inch long, clustered in short spikes. Corolla tube flaring into 5 lobes. Late March and April. Small prostrate shrub with evergreen leaves.
Pp. 174, 554

1.17 *Kalmia latifolia* L.
MOUNTAIN LAUREL
Flowers pink or white, ¾–1 inch wide; buds fluted. Stamens 10, the anthers fitting into pockets in the corolla. Late May and early June. Large shrub with evergreen leaves.
Pp. 173, 554-55

1.18 *Halesia carolina* L.
SILVERBELL
Corolla bell-shaped, 4-lobed,
and ⅝–¾ inch long;
stamens 8. April–May. Small
tree or large shrub.
Pp. 289, 416-17, 559

1.19 *Styrax americana* Lam.
SNOWBELL
Corolla bell-shaped, about ½
inch long, and 5-lobed, the lobes
longer than the tube; stamens
10. Late May. Shrub.
Pp. 289, 560

S. grandifolia Ait., the large-leaf
snowbell, has flowers in elongated
racemes. Pp. 289, 560

1.20 *Chionanthus*
  virginicus L.
  FRINGE-TREE
Corolla ¾–1 inch
long, divided nearly to
the base into 4 linear
lobes; stamens 2. May.
Large shrub or small
tree.
Pp. 140, 210, 560

1.21 *Lonicera*
  sempervirens L.
  TRUMPET
  HONEYSUCKLE
Flowers 1¼–2 inches long,
red or yellow outside and
yellow inside, with 5 nearly
equal lobes at the apex of a
slender corolla tube. June.
Vine.
Pp. 182, 564

1.22 *Cladrastis lutea*
  (Michx. f.) K. Koch
  YELLOW-WOOD
Flowers in panicles.
Corolla 1¼–1½
inches long and pea-
shaped; petals 5,
abruptly narrowed at
the base; stamens 10.
May. Tree.
Pp. 330-31, 536

1.23a *Robinia pseudo-acacia* L.
BLACK LOCUST

Flowers fragrant, borne in racemes. Corolla ⅝–¾ inch long and pea-shaped; 9 stamens united by filaments and 1 separate. May. Tree. Pp. 332-33, 537-38

1.23b *Robinia hispida* L.
ROSE-ACACIA, BRISTLY LOCUST

Flowers about 1 inch long, similar in structure to those of the preceding species but not fragrant. May. Shrub with bristly stems. Pp. 243, 537

1.24 *Cercis canadensis* L.
REDBUD

Clusters of slender-pediceled flowers borne on branchlets of the previous year and opening before the leaves. Corolla about ½ inch long and somewhat pea-shaped; petals 5; stamens 10. April. Small tree. Pp. 374-75, 536

1.25 *Wisteria macrostachya* Nutt.

WISTERIA

Flowers borne in compact racemes. Corolla light bluish purple, ⅝–¾ inch long, and pea-shaped; 9 stamens united by filaments and 1 separate. May. Vine.
Pp. 190, 538

The Genus *Aesculus*, the BUCKEYES

Flowers in panicles. Petals 4 (in our species), some or all abruptly narrowed at the base; stamens usually 7. Trees with opposite, palmately compound leaves.

1.26a *Aesculus glabra* Willd.

OHIO BUCKEYE

Petals greenish yellow and about ¾ inch long, the upper pair tapering to the base and only slightly exceeding the lateral petals, which are abruptly narrowed at the base; all petals shorter than the stamens. April. Medium-sized tree.
Pp. 298-99, 545-46

1.26b *Aesculus octandra* Marsh.

YELLOW BUCKEYE, SWEET BUCKEYE

Petals yellow and ¾–1 inch long, all abruptly narrowed at the base, the upper pair decidedly longer than the lateral ones and equalling or exceeding the stamens. April –early May. Tall tree. Pp. 300-301, 546

1.26c *Aesculus pavia* L.

RED BUCKEYE

Both calyx and corolla red. Petals ¾–1⅛ inches long, the upper pair longer than the lateral ones and as long as or longer than the stamens. April–May. Small tree. Pp. 297, 546

A. discolor Pursh differs from *A. pavia* in having flowers red, red and yellow, or yellow, and leaves woolly beneath. P. 545

The Genus *Rhododendron*, the RHODODENDRONS and AZALEAS

Flowers large and showy. Corolla 5-lobed, funnel-shaped, and almost radially symmetrical; filaments and style elongated and curved. Leaves evergreen in some species, deciduous in others.

1.27a *Rhododendron maximum* L.
GREAT LAUREL, GREAT RHODODENDRON
Corolla about 1½ inches wide; white or pinkish or tinged with rose, and greenish in the throat with yellow spots on the upper lobe. Late June. Large evergreen shrub.
Pp. 172, 556

1.27b *Rhododendron catawbiense* Michx.
PURPLE RHODODENDRON, MOUNTAIN ROSEBAY
Flowers rose-purple or lilac-purple and 2–2¼ inches wide. May–June. Evergreen shrub.
Pp. 171, 556

1.27c *Rhododendron nudiflorum* (L.) Torr.
PINXTER-FLOWER, PINK AZALEA
Flowers pale or deep pink and scarcely fragrant, usually
opening before or with the young leaves. Stamens triple
the length of the corolla tube; style 1¾–2¾ inches long.
Late April. Shrub.
Pp. 258, 557

1.27d *Rhododendron
roseum*
(Loisel.) Rehder
ROSE AZALEA

Flowers bright or pale
pink and fragrant,
opening with the young
leaves. Stamens twice
the length of the
corolla tube; style
1½–2 inches long.
Early May. Shrub.
Pp. 257, 557

1.27e *Rhododendron calendulaceum* (Michx.) Torr.
FLAME AZALEA
Flowering after the leaves appear but before they are full
grown. Corolla varying from yellow to orange to almost
scarlet, 1½–2 inches across, the upper lobe only slightly
wider than the others. Latter half of May. Shrub.
Pp. 260, 556-57

1.27f *Rhododendron cumberlandense* E. L. Braun
RED AZALEA

Flowering after the leaves are full grown. Corolla varying from red to orange-yellow, about 1½ inches across, the upper lobe much wider than the others and bearing an orange or yellow spot. Late June–early July. Shrub.
Pp. 259, 557

1.28a *Lonicera flavida* Cockerell
WILD
HONEYSUCKLE
Flowers yellow, ¾–1 inch long, and hairy within the corolla tube, subtended by a pair of united leaves. May. Small shrubby vine.
Pp. 127, 182, 563

L. prolifera (Kirchn.) Rehd., also with yellow flowers, has the pair of united leaves round, blunt, and whitened above and below. Pp. 182, 564
    L. dioica L., has flowers yellow, red, or purple, and leaves whitened beneath, the united pair pointed. Pp. 127, 182, 563

1.28b *Lonicera japonica* Thunb.
JAPANESE HONEYSUCKLE
Flowers 1¼–1¾ inches long, white becoming cream-colored with age, and very fragrant, in axillary pairs.
May–July. Vine.
Pp. 169, 181, 564

1.29 *Paulownia tomentosa* (Thunb.) Steud.
ROYAL PAULOWNIA, PRINCESS-TREE

Flowers pale violet with yellow stripes inside, 1½–2 inches long, borne in panicles, opening before or with the young leaves. April–May. Tree.
Pp. 320-21, 563

1.30 *Catalpa speciosa* Warder
CATALPA, NORTHERN CATALPA

Crinkly-edged flowers borne in panicles. Corolla 1¾–2 inches wide and sparsely spotted; stamens 2. Early June. Tree.
Pp. 318-19, 563

C. bignonioides Walt., southern catalpa, differs in having flowers 1–1¼ inches across, densely spotted with purple. Pp. 317, 562

1.31 *Campsis radicans*
(L.) Seem.
TRUMPET-VINE,
TRUMPET-CREEPER

Flowers 2¼–3 inches long.
Calyx and corolla tube thick
and leathery, the tube
flaring into 5 lobes; stamens
4. July. Vine with pinnate
leaves.
Pp. 178-79, 562

1.32 *Bignonia
capreolata* L.
CROSS-VINE

Flowers about 2 inches
long. Corolla tube
constricted at the base
and flaring into 5 lobes
at the apex; stamens 4.
May. Vine with
bifoliate leaves.
Pp. 167, 180, 562

1.33 *Aristolochia durior* Hill
DUTCHMAN'S-PIPE
Calyx 1½–1⅝ inches long, dark red-purple, bent like a pipe, and 3-lobed at the apex. Climbing vine.
Pp. 191, 521

A. *tomentosa* Sims, pipe-vine, differs in being hairy. Pp. 191, 521

The Genus *Smilax*, the GREENBRIERS and CATBRIERS

Flowers in simple umbels. Perianth composed of 6 greenish white segments (3 sepals and 3 petals alike); stamens 6; the functional stamens and the pistil in separate flowers. May–June. Green-stemmed, tendril-bearing vines, prickly in 3 of our 4 woody species. Species separated primarily by vegetative characters.

2.1a *Smilax glauca* Walt.
SAWBRIER, CATBRIER
Pp. 136, 163, 192, 500

2.1b *Smilax hispida* Muhl.   HISPID GREENBRIER
Pp. 137, 164, 192, 500

2.2 *Aralia spinosa* L.
HERCULES'-
CLUB, DEVIL'S-
WALKINGSTICK
Umbels numerous in a
large panicle about 3
feet long. Petals and
stamens each 5; styles
usually 5; ovary beneath
the attachment of
other parts. July. Large
spiny shrub with
bipinnate leaves.
Pp. 28, 133, 236, 552

2.3 *Bumelia lycioides* (L.) Gaertn. f.
BUCKTHORN BUMELIA, SOUTHERN BUCKTHORN

Flowers small, borne on pedicels ¼–½ inch long, numerous in axillary umbels. Corolla lobes 5, with a lateral appendage on each side; functional stamens and sterile petal-like stamens each 5. July. Shrub or small tree.
Pp. 255, 371, 559

2.4 *Cephalanthus occidentalis* L.
BUTTONBUSH

Flowers in spherical heads about 1 inch in diameter. Corolla ¼–⅜ inch long, narrowly funnel-shaped with 4 short lobes; style about twice as long as the corolla. July. Shrub.
Pp. 117, 215, 563

2.5 *Physocarpus
opulifolius*
(L.) Maxim.
NINEBARK
Flowers, about ⅜ inch
wide, densely crowded
in short racemes.
Sepals and petals each
5; stamens numerous;
pistils 3–5. June.
Shrub.
Pp. 295, 530-31

The Genus *Prunus* (in part),
the CHERRIES and PLUM

In all members of the genus *Prunus* (including those illustrated on pp. 45-46), flowers have a cup-shaped receptacle
bearing 5 sepals, 5 petals, and numerous stamens on the rim,
and a single pistil within the cup.

For *P. angustifolia* Marsh., the Chickasaw plum, see page 45.

2.6a Prunus serotina Ehrh.
WILD BLACK CHERRY
Flowers about ⅜ inch wide, in
elongate racemes produced on new
branchlets. Petals roundish. May.
Large tree.
Pp. 135, 412-13, 532

2.6b *Prunus virginiana* L.
CHOKE CHERRY

Flowers similar to those of *P. serotina* but in shorter, broader, and denser racemes. The two species differ also in fruit, leaves, twigs, and size. May. Small tree or large shrub.

Pp. 129, 280, 414, 532

2.7 *Itea virginica* L.
VIRGINIA-WILLOW

Flowers in spike-like racemes 2–6 inches long. Petals 5, narrow, and about ¼ inch long; stamens 5; ovary and fruit 2-parted. May–June. Shrub.

Pp. 276, 526

2.8 *Amorpha
fruticosa* L.
INDIGO BUSH,
FALSE INDIGO
Flowers very dark
purple-blue, borne in
spike-like racemes.
Corolla reduced to 1
petal; stamens 10.
Late May. Shrub.
Pp. 244, 536

2.9 *Celastrus scandens* L.
BITTERSWEET
Flowers less than ¼ inch wide with 5 petals; staminate
flowers with 5 stamens and a rudimentary pistil; pistillate
flowers with 1 compound pistil and rudimentary stamens.
Late May–June. Vine.
Pp. 125, 204, 542

2.10 *Staphylea
trifolia* L.

BLADDERNUT

Flowers in drooping
racemes. Sepals,
petals, and stamens
each 5; ovary 3-lobed.
Flowering before leaves
are full grown. Late
April. Shrub with
trifoliate leaves.
Pp. 208, 543

2.11 *Acer spicatum*
Lam.

MOUNTAIN
MAPLE

Flowers in clusters in a
narrow panicle. Petals
slender, greenish, and
about ⅛ inch long;
stamens usually 8.
Late May–June. Small
tree or large shrub.
Pp. 230, 545

A. *pensylvanicum* L., the
striped maple, has yellow
flowers about ¼ inch
long, in slender racemes.
May–June. Pp. 316, 544

2.12 *Ceanothus americanus* L.

NEW JERSEY TEA

Flowers about ⅛ inch across in dense inflorescences on long axillary stalks. Petals 5, abruptly narrowed at the base. June. Small shrub.

Pp. 283, 546

2.13 *Clethra acuminata* Michx.

MOUNTAIN PEPPERBUSH

Racemes hoary (the axis, flower stalks, and sepals all white-woolly). Sepals and petals each 5, shorter than the 10 stamens and the style; petals about ¼ inch long. July–August. Shrub.

Pp. 287, 554

2.14a *Gaylussacia
brachycera*
(Michx.) Gray
BOX-
HUCKLEBERRY

Racemes axillary, dense,
and few-flowered.
Corolla tubular and
about ¼ inch long.
May. Dwarf shrub
with evergreen leaves.
Pp. 141, 175, 554

2.14b *Gaylussacia
baccata*
(Wang.) K. Koch
HUCKLEBERRY

Racemes lateral on
the stem. Corolla
tubular, about ¼ inch
long. May. Shrub
with resin-dotted
leaves.
Pp. 141, 261, 554

2.15a *Vaccinium stamineum* L.
DEERBERRY, SQUAWBERRY
Racemes borne on specialized branches with leafy bracts
resembling small foliage leaves. Corolla open even in bud,
but small and green; at maturity nearly ¼ inch long,
white, and bell-shaped with 5 spreading lobes, shorter than
the stamens. May. Shrub.
Pp. 261, 558

2.15b *Vaccinium
arboreum* Marsh.
FARKLEBERRY
Flowers in racemes.
Corolla less than ¼
inch long, urn-shaped
with very shallow
lobes, and longer than
the stamens. June.
Tall shrub with firm
but not evergreen
leaves.
Pp. 262-63, 558

2.15c *Vaccinium*
  vacillans Torr.
2.15d *Vaccinium*
  pallidum Ait.
LOWBUSH
BLUEBERRIES
Corolla tubular, white
or tinged with red or
pink, and about ¼
inch long. May. Both
species small shrubs
separated largely on
the basis of leaf
characters.
Pp. 142, 263, 264, 558

2.15e *Vaccinium simulatum* Small

2.15f *Vaccinium constablaei* Gray

HIGHBUSH BLUEBERRIES

Corolla between tubular and bell-shaped, white often tinged with pink, ¼ inch long in V. *simulatum* and ¼–⅜ inch long in V. *constablaei*. May–June. Both species large shrubs separated chiefly by leaf and fruit characters.
Pp. 143, 265-66, 558

For V. *alto-montanum* Ashe, the mountain dryland blueberry, a bush of medium size, see p. 79.

2.16 *Oxydendrum arboreum* (L.) DC.

SOURWOOD, SORREL TREE

Flowers borne only on one side of each branch of the inflorescence. Corolla constricted at the throat, velvety, and about ¼ inch long. July. Understory tree.
Pp. 420-21, 555

2.17 *Menispermum canadense* L.
MOONSEED

Flowers borne in small axillary panicles. Sepals longer than petals; stamens numerous in staminate flowers, pistils 2–4 in pistillate flowers. Late June–July. Twining vine.
Pp. 136, 196, 522

For the related *Cocculus carolinus* and *Calycocarpum lyoni* see pp. 195 and 197.

2.18 *Trachelospermum difforme* (Walt.) Gray
CLIMBING DOGBANE

Flower clusters (compound cymes) long-stalked. Corolla pale yellow, 5-lobed at the apex, the tube about ¼ inch long. Leaves varying from lance-shaped to broad. July–August. Twining or trailing vine, only half woody.
Pp. 183, 562

Sepals and petals each 5, stamens numerous, and pistils usually 5.

2.19a *Spiraea tomentosa* L.
STEEPLEBUSH,
HARDHACK
Flowers ⅛ inch wide in a panicle 2–6 inches long. July. Small shrub.
Pp. 290, 536

2.19b *Spiraea japonica* L. f.
JAPANESE SPIRAEA
Flowers nearly ¼ inch wide in an inflorescence 2–6 inches across. June. Small shrub.
Pp. 291, 535-36

2.19c *Spiraea alba*
DuRoi
MEADOWSWEET
Flowers about ¼ inch
wide in a panicle 2–4
inches long. July–
August. Shrub.
Pp. 290, 535

2.20 *Aronia melanocarpa*
(Michx.) Ell.
BLACK CHOKEBERRY
Flowers usually ⅜ inch wide
but occasionally ½ inch;
petals abruptly narrowed at
the base; the 5 sepals, 5
petals, numerous stamens,
and 5 styles all borne above
the ovary, which is in a cup-
shaped receptacle grown to
the ovary wall. May. Shrub.
Pp. 134, 277, 529

A. *prunifolia* (Marsh.) Rehder,
purple chokeberry, and A.
arbutifolia (L.) Ell., red chokeberry, differ from this species
chiefly in fruit and leaf
characters. Pp. 132, 278, 529

2.21a *Ligustrum* spp.
(representing several
species)
PRIVET
Corolla funnel-shaped with
4 spreading lobes; species
differing in the relative
length of corolla tube and
lobes; stamens 2. Several
species with panicles 1½–4
inches long are commonly
cultivated and some escape.
June. Shrubs.
Pp. 139, 174, 211, 562

2.21b *Ligustrum ibota* Sieb.
IBOTA PRIVET
Distinct from other privets
in having panicles only 1–1½
inches long, numerous on
the sides of branches. June.
Shrub.
P. 562

2.22 *Tilia americana* L.
BASSWOOD, AMERICAN LINDEN

Clusters of flowers borne on a stalk attached to a strap-shaped bract. Sepals and petals each 5, stamens numerous (a few sterile and resembling small petals), and style 1; petals ¼–½ inch long. June. Large tree.
Pp. 386-87, 549

Other species of *Tilia* have similar flowers and differ in vegetative characters.

2.23 *Lyonia ligustrina* (L.) DC.
PRIVET-ANDROMEDA, MALE-BERRY

Flower clusters in the leaf axils or on a leafless branchlet terminal on the previous year's growth, thus forming either a leafy or a naked panicle. Corolla about ⅛ inch long, ovoid or nearly globose with 5 minute lobes. June. Shrub.
Pp. 288, 555

The Genus *Rhus*, the SUMACS

Calyx 5-lobed, petals 5, stamens 5, and pistil 1. Shrubs or vines with alternate compound leaves.

2.24a *Rhus aromatica* Ait.
FRAGRANT SUMAC
Flowers appearing before the leaves, sessile or nearly so on short spike-like branches of a small panicle. April. Shrub.
Pp. 128, 248, 539

2.24b *Rhus copallina* L.
WINGED
SUMAC,
SHINING
SUMAC
Panicles up to 6 inches long. Leaf rachis winged between leaflets. July. Shrub.
Pp. 28, 128, 246, 539

2.24c *Rhus glabra* L.
SMOOTH
SUMAC
Panicles dense and up
to 8 inches long.
Stems and leaves
glabrous. June–July.
Large shrub.
Pp. 128, 245, 539

2.24d *Rhus typhina* L.
STAGHORN
SUMAC

Panicles up to 10
inches long. Branches
and leaf stalks densely
hairy. June. Large
shrub (occasionally a
small tree).
Pp. 129, 247, 541

2.24e *Rhus radicans* L.
POISON IVY

Panicles axillary and up to 4 inches long. June. High-climbing or trailing vine or erect shrub with trifoliate leaves.
Pp. 186-87, 540

Flowers of R. *toxicodendron* L., poison oak, a shrub, are similar. Pp. 249, 541.

2.25 *Ailanthus altissima*
  (Mill.) Swingle
TREE-OF-HEAVEN,
  AILANTHUS

Flowers in panicles, the staminate and pistillate on separate trees. Staminate flowers strongly ill-scented. June. Tree.
Pp. 117, 334-35, 539

2.26 *Ptelea trifoliata* L.
HOP-TREE,
WAFER-ASH

Compact compound cymes 2–3 inches across. Flowers ⅜–½ inch wide. Leaves trifoliate. Late May–early June. Shrub.
Pp. 250, 538

2.27 *Hydrangea arborescens* L.
WILD HYDRANGEA

Flowers crowded in compound cymes, forming a flattened or convex inflorescence. Sterile flowers ½–⅝ inch across, consisting only of 3 or 4 large sepals; fertile flowers with a minute calyx, 4 or 5 short petals, 8–10 stamens, and 1 pistil with 2 styles. June. Shrub.
Pp. 231, 526

2.27a *Sambucus canadensis* L.

COMMON ELDER, ELDERBERRY

Inflorescence flat or slightly convex, 5-rayed from the base, and
composed of compound cymes. Corolla about ⅛ inch wide,
deeply lobed (usually 5-lobed) with an equal number of stamens
attached, and with the ovary beneath other flower parts.
June. Shrub.
Pp. 133, 207, 564

2.27b *Sambucus pubens* Michx.
RED-BERRIED ELDER

Inflorescence pyra-
midal, the axis bearing
2 or more pairs of
opposite branches.
Flowers as in the
preceding species.
May. Shrub.
Pp. 133, 206, 564

The Genus *Viburnum*

Flowers in compound cymes. Corolla 5-lobed, ⅛–⅜ inch wide, with 5 stamens attached; style absent, ovary beneath corolla. Species separated largely by characters other than flowers.

2.28a *Viburnum acerifolium* L.
MAPLE-LEAF VIBURNUM
Shrub with 3-lobed leaves. May.
Pp. 137, 229, 564-65

2.28b *Viburnum rufidulum* Raf.
SOUTHERN BLACK-HAW
Tall shrub or small tree with lustrous, finely toothed leaves, obtuse or barely acute. May.
Pp. 138, 224-25, 566

2.28c *Viburnum
prunifolium* L.
BLACK-HAW
Tall shrub or small tree
with acute, finely
toothed leaves. April.
Pp. 138, 223, 565

2.28d *Viburnum lentago* L.
NANNYBERRY
Tall shrub or small tree with leaves long-pointed and finely
toothed. May. Similar to V. *prunifolium*, from which
it is distinguished by leaf and bud characters.
Pp. 138, 222, 565

V. *cassinoides* L., withe-rod, also with finely toothed leaves,
differs from the 3 preceding species in having a stalk between the
branches of the inflorescence and the uppermost pair of leaves.
Flowers are ill-scented. Pp. 222, 565
   V. *nudum* L., possum-haw, with narrower and often smooth-
margined leaves, also has the branched inflorescence borne on
a stalk. Pp. 221, 565

2.28e *Viburnum dentatum* L.
ARROW-WOOD
Shrub with coarsely toothed, long-petioled leaves, not heart-shaped at the base. May.
Pp. 138, 226, 565

2.28f *Viburnum rafinesquianum* Schult.
ARROW-WOOD
Shrub with coarsely toothed, nearly sessile, often heart-shaped leaves. May.
Pp. 138, 227, 565

V. *molle* Michx., Kentucky viburnum, has coarsely toothed, long-petioled, mostly heart-shaped leaves. Pp. 139, 228, 565

The Genus *Cornus*, the DOGWOODS

Flowers about ⅜ inch wide (smaller in *C. florida*), with 4 petals arising above the ovary. Shrubs or small trees with opposite smooth-margined leaves, except 2.29a, which has alternate leaves.

2.29a *Cornus
alternifolia* L. f.
ALTERNATE-
LEAF
DOGWOOD
Leaves alternate,
crowded toward ends
of branchlets. Early
May. Large shrub or
small tree.
Pp. 144, 256, 553

2.29b *Cornus
drummondi* Meyer
ROUGH-LEAF
DOGWOOD
Leaves rough on the
upper surface. June.
Large shrub.
Pp. 144, 216, 553

2.29c *Cornus racemosa* Lam.
GRAY DOGWOOD
Inflorescence strongly convex, in contrast to the flattish or only slightly convex inflorescences in other species of *Cornus*. June. Shrub.
Pp. 145, 217, 553

2.29d *Cornus amomum* Mill.
2.29e *Cornus obliqua* Raf.
SILKY DOGWOOD, PALE DOGWOOD
The two silky dogwoods have similar flowers and inflorescences and are separated by leaf differences. June. Shrubs.
Pp. 144, 218, 219, 553

2.29f *Cornus florida* L.
FLOWERING DOGWOOD
Flower clusters subtended by 4 large white bracts (each 1–1½ inches long at maturity). Flowers greenish yellow in contrast to the white flowers of the shrubby species of dogwood. Late April. Understory tree.
Pp. 123, 322-23, 552

2.30 *Ribes cynosbati* L.
PRICKLY
GOOSEBERRY
Flowers solitary or 2–3 together. Calyx tube ⅛ inch to nearly ¼ inch long; petals 5, shorter than the reflexed calyx lobes; stamens 5; ovary below other flower parts. May. Small prickly shrub.
Pp. 294, 526

The Genus *Ilex*, the HOLLIES

Flowers about ¼ inch wide, borne in axillary clusters. Petals 4–8, with stamens of the same number; pistil 1. Fertile flowers bearing a pistil and stamens with small anthers; staminate flowers (more numerous and on different plants) bearing stamens and a rudimentary pistil.

2.31a *Ilex opaca* Ait.
AMERICAN HOLLY
Slow-growing tree with leathery, evergreen, spiny-edged leaves. Early May.
Pp. 124, 170, 541-42

2.31b *Ilex decidua* Walt.
SWAMP HOLLY,
POSSUM-HAW
Deciduous shrub or small
tree with narrow leaves
tapered at the base. May.
Pp. 124, 281, 541

2.31c *Ilex verticillata* (L.) Gray
WINTERBERRY (*above*)

2.31d *Ilex montana* T. & G.
MOUNTAIN
WINTERBERRY (*left*)
Two very similar species. Petals of
the pistillate flowers usually 4 or 5
(rarely 6) in *I. montana* and 6–8
in *I. verticillata*. In *I. montana*
both petals and sepals ciliate
(having minute marginal hairs);
only sepals ciliate in *I. verticillata*.
June. Deciduous shrubs.
Pp. 125, 282, 541, 542

The Genera *Euonymus* and *Pachistima*

Flowers in these genera have a prominent disk in the center which conceals the ovary.

2.32a *Euonymus atropurpureus* Jacq.
WAHOO, BURNING BUSH
Flowers ¼–⅜ inch wide, borne on long slender stalks in axillary cymes. The 4 brownish purple petals widely spreading and flat. Late May–June. Tall shrub.
Pp. 126, 233, 542

2.32b *Euonymus americanus* L.
STRAWBERRY-BUSH,
HEARTS-A-BURSTING-
WITH-LOVE

Flowers axillary, either solitary or 2–3 together, and ⅜ inch wide; the 5 greenish petals widely spreading. May. Shrub.
Pp. 126, 168, 232, 542

2.32c *Euonymus obovatus* Nutt.
RUNNING STRAWBERRY-BUSH,
RUNNING EUONYMUS
Flowers axillary, ¼–⅜ inch wide, flat, and greenish. May.
Small prostrate shrub or trailing vine.
Pp. 126, 181, 543

2.33 *Pachistima canbyi* Gray
PACHISTIMA,
MOUNTAIN-LOVER
Flowers ¼ inch wide or less, axillary, on slender stalks. Sepals, petals, and stamens each 4. June. Dwarf evergreen shrub.
Pp. 176, 543

2.34 *Acer rubrum* L.
RED MAPLE
Flowers red or reddish, appearing long before the leaves, in crowded clusters growing from lateral buds separate from the leaf buds. Petals less than ⅛ inch (2 mm.) long, sepals shorter and broader; styles 2. Staminate and pistillate flowers borne in different clusters, often on different trees. March. Large tree.
Pp. 27, 117, 314-15, 544

2.35 *Rhamnus
caroliniana* Walt.

CAROLINA
BUCKTHORN

Flowers nearly ¼ inch
wide, in axillary
clusters. Calyx lobes,
petals, and stamens
each 5; pistil 1. June.
Large shrub or small
tree.
Pp. 127, 284, 418, 544

R. *lanceolata* Pursh, lance-
leaf buckthorn, has flower
parts in 4s. Shrub. Pp.
135, 285, 547

2.36 *Diospyros virginiana* L.

PERSIMMON

Calyx and corolla each 4-lobed. Staminate flowers ⅜ inch long,
with 16 long anthers; pistillate flowers ¾ inch long, usually with
8 sterile anthers; the two on separate trees. Early June. Tree.
Pp. 122, 372-73, 559

3.1 *Juglans cinerea* L.
BUTTERNUT, WHITE WALNUT

Staminate catkins 3–5 inches long when mature; pistillate flowers inconspicuous, terminating the young branchlets. May. Large tree.
Pp. 336-37, 507

Catkins of *J. nigra* L., black walnut, are similar.
Pp. 238-39, 506-07

3.2 *Carya ovata* (Mill.) K. Koch
SHAGBARK HICKORY, SHELLBARK HICKORY

Staminate catkins 4–5 inches long, 3 together on a single stalk; pistillate flowers as in *Juglans*, above. May. Tree.
Pp. 346-47, 505

Catkins of other species of *Carya* are similar.

3.3 *Carpinus caroliniana* Walt.
AMERICAN HORNBEAM, BLUE BEECH, IRONWOOD

Staminate catkins 1½ inches long when full grown in early spring; pistillate flowers also in catkins, these smaller and more sparsely flowered. Understory tree.
Pp. 436-37, 508

Ostrya virginiana (Mill) K. Koch, the hop hornbeam, has similar catkins but is vegetatively very different. Pp. 438-39, 509

The Genus *Betula*, the BIRCHES

Staminate catkins appearing in the fall (measuring ¾–1 inch long in winter) but not drooping until they elongate in early spring.

3.4a *Betula lutea* Michx. f.
YELLOW BIRCH
Staminate catkins (illustrated) 3–3½ inches long in spring; pistillate catkins erect and ⅝ inch long. May. Tree.
Pp. 434-35, 508

3.4b *Betula nigra* L.
RIVER BIRCH
Staminate catkins (illustrated) 2–3 inches long in spring; pistillate catkins erect and ⅜ inch long. April. Tree.
Pp. 430-31, 508

3.5 *Alnus serrulata* (Ait.) Willd.
COMMON ALDER

Staminate catkins elongate, pistillate ones short and ellipsoid; both formed in autumn but not fully developed until early spring when the flowers open. Large shrub.
Pp. 273, 507

3.6 *Corylus americana* Walt.
AMERICAN HAZELNUT

Staminate catkins appearing in autumn and maturing with open flowers in March before the leaves develop. Pistillate catkins small, resembling leaf buds, the scales concealing all except the protruding red-purple stigmas. Shrub.
Pp. 274, 508-09

3.7 *Morus rubra* L.
RED MULBERRY

Staminate flowers borne in slender catkins about 2 inches long; pistillate flowers in oblong, densely flowered catkins or spikes about 1 inch long, appearing as the leaves unfold. April–May. Tree.
Pp. 118, 382-83, 520

M. alba L., white mulberry, has similar catkins. Pp. 118, 485, 520

3.8 *Quercus borealis* Michx. f. var. *maxima* (Marsh.) Ashe
RED OAK

Staminate catkins elongated, sparsely flowered, and without bracts; pistillate flowers solitary or in small inconspicuous clusters. May. Large tree.
Pp. 464-65, 512-13

Other species of *Quercus* have similar flowers.

3.9 *Fagus grandifolia* Ehrh. AMERICAN BEECH
Staminate flowers borne in spherical heads on pendent stalks;
pistillate flowers in pairs, inconspicuous. April. Large tree.
Pp. 440-41, 510

3.10a *Castanea dentata*
(Marsh.) Borkh.
AMERICAN
CHESTNUT

Staminate catkins 6–7 inches
long when mature, axillary,
with flowers in clusters along
the axis. Pistillate flowers
in separate smaller catkins.
June. Formerly a large tree.
Pp. 114, 442-43, 509-10

3.10b *Castanea pumila* (L.) Mill.
CHINQUAPIN,
DWARF CHESTNUT

Staminate catkins similar to
C. dentata but 3–6 inches long
when mature, and thinner.
June. Small tree.
Pp. 114, 444-45, 510

The Genus *Salix*, the WILLOWS

Pistillate catkins as large and conspicuous as the staminate.

3.11a *Salix nigra* Marsh.   BLACK WILLOW
Catkins 1–2¾ inches long, appearing with the leaves. (Both staminate and pistillate illustrated.)   April.   Tree.
Pp. 396-97, 503

3.11b *Salix interior* Rowlee
SANDBAR WILLOW
Catkins, 1¼–2¾ inches long, developing after the leaves have appeared. (Pistillate illustrated.)   May. Shrub.
Pp. 270, 502

3.11c *Salix sericea* Marsh.
SILKY WILLOW
Catkins, ½–1¾ inches long,
appearing before the leaves.
(Staminate illustrated.)
April. Large shrub or small
tree.
Pp. 267, 503

3.11d *Salix discolor* Muhl.
PUSSY WILLOW
Catkins appearing before the
leaves, 1¾–2½ inches long when
mature, the pistillate longer than
the staminate. (Staminate
illustrated.) March–April. Small
tree or large shrub.
Pp. 268-69, 373, 502

3.11e *Salix humilis* Marsh.
UPLAND WILLOW,
PRAIRIE WILLOW
Catkins, ⅝–1¼ inches long,
produced before the leaves.
(Staminate illustrated.) Early
April. Small shrub.
Pp. 271, 502

For species of *Salix* not illustrated
here, see pp. 272 and 395.

4.1 *Xanthorhiza simplicissima* Marsh.

SHRUB YELLOWROOT

Racemes or panicles crowded at the ends of erect stems. Flowers ¼ inch wide, with 5 brownish or purplish green sepals (no petals), 5–10 stamens, and 5–10 pistils. April. Small shrub. Pp. 116, 251, 522

4.2 *Pyrularia pubera* Michx.

BUFFALO-NUT, OILNUT

Staminate spikes (illustrated) 1¼–2 inches long; fertile spikes (containing both stamens and pistils) shorter. Stamens borne on a lobed disk. May. Shrub. Pp. 252, 520-21

4.3 *Brunnichia cirrhosa* Gaertn.

BUCKWHEAT VINE, LADIES'-EARDROPS

Flowers about ⅛ inch long, clustered in a spike. The lower spikes axillary, the upper ones forming a loose panicle. July–August. Vine. Pp. 194, 521

4.4 *Sassafras albidum*
(Nutt.) Nees
SASSAFRAS

Few-flowered racemes appearing before the leaves. Sepals 6, stamens 9, and pistil 1; staminate and pistillate flowers usually on different trees. April. Aromatic tree.
Pp. 26, 140, 480-81, 525-26

4.5 *Lindera benzoin*
(L.) Blume
SPICEBUSH

Flowers in dense clusters ¼–⅜ inch thick, appearing before the leaves. Flower structure as in the preceding species; staminate and pistillate flowers usually on different plants. March. Aromatic shrub.
Pp. 133, 253, 525

4.6 *Dirca palustris* L.
LEATHERWOOD

Flowers ¼–⅜ inch long, in clusters of 3 enclosed in bud scales, appearing before the leaves. Calyx funnel-shaped and above the ovary. Late March. Shrub with tough, jointed stems.
Pp. 254, 551

4.7a *Ulmus americana* L.
AMERICAN ELM,
WHITE ELM
Flowers borne on pedicels
¾–1 inch long, and
clustered. February–
March. Tree.
Pp. 424-25, 518-19

4.7b *Ulmus rubra* Muhl.
SLIPPERY ELM,
RED ELM
Pedicels shorter than
those of the preceding
species. Early March.
Tree.
Pp. 426-27, 519

Other elms have similar early
flowers except *U. serotina*
Sarg., September elm, which
flowers in September. Pp.
423, 519

4.8 *Vitis aestivalis* Michx.
SUMMER GRAPE
Panicles 3–6 inches long.
Calyx minute or lacking;
petals soon falling; some
flowers staminate, some
with both stamens and a
pistil. June. Vine.
Pp. 202, 548

Other species of grape have
similar flowers and inflorescences.

4.9a *Acer saccharum*
Marsh.
SUGAR MAPLE

Flowers in umbels
(staminate and pistillate separate),
pendulous on slender
stalks 2–3 inches long,
appearing as the leaf
buds open. April.
Large tree.
Pp. 25, 310-11, 545

4.9b *Acer negundo* L.
BOX ELDER

Flowers appearing as
the leaves unfold, the
staminate flowers in
umbel-like clusters and
the pistillate (illustrated) in drooping
racemes. April. Tree.
Pp. 308-09, 543

4.10 *Fraxinus quadrangulata* Michx.
BLUE ASH

Flowers in racemes or panicles from axils of the previous year's leaves; containing both stamens and pistils in this species but unisexual in other species of *Fraxinus*. Large tree.

Pp. 304-05, 561

4.11 *Forestiera ligustrina* (Michx.) Poir.
UPLAND FORESTIERA

Flowers small and crowded in the axils of opposite leaves. August. Large shrub.

Pp. 139, 234, 560

F. acuminata (Michx.) Poir., the swamp privet, has flowers similar but preceding the leaves. April. Shrub. Pp. 139, 234, 560

5.1 *Pinus rigida* Mill.

PITCH PINE

Staminate cones, each about ¾ inch long,
present only in spring (usually early May),
when they are numerous and conspicuous,
producing great quantities of pollen. (At the
time of pollination the fertile cones are small
and very inconspicuous, enlarging and
remaining on the tree almost two years before
shedding seed.) Evergreen tree. Staminate
cones of other pines are similar.
Pp. 152-53, 496

Series Two: Fruits

Trees, Shrubs, and Woody Vines
Grouped According to Colorful Fruits

The term fruit has no reference to edibility. The fruit is the structure which develops from the ovary of the flower, sometimes with accessory parts, and which contains the seed. It should be noted that many so-called "berries" are not berries in a botanical sense.

"Colorful" here generally refers to a color other than green or brown. Most fruits are illustrated in Series Three through Nine.

ARRANGEMENT OF PLATES

Group 1. Nonfleshy fruits   1.1–1.6

Group 2. Fleshy fruits

      Multiple and aggregate fruits (1 fruit formed from several pistils or even from several flowers)   2.1–2.2

      Simple fruits (such as true berries, drupes, and pomes) formed from 1 pistil, and fruits in which the aggregate origin is not evident

            Fruits ¾ inch or more in diameter or length   2.3–2.5

            Fruits less than ¾ inch in diameter or length
               Red or orange   2.6–2.21a
               Purple, black, blue, or white   2.21b–2.41

1.1 *Castanea pumila*
(L.) Mill.
CHINQUAPIN,
DWARF CHESTNUT

Nut about ½ inch long,
solitary within a spiny bur
which splits open.
September–early October.
Small tree.
Pp. 104, 444-45, 510

The now rare C. *dentata*
(Marsh.) Borkh., American
chestnut, has larger nuts, 2 or 3
to a bur. Pp. 104, 442-43,
509-10

The Genus *Magnolia*

Fruits large, cone-shaped, and formed from many separate
pistils on an enlarged conical receptacle, each one splitting at
maturity, exposing 2 red seeds hanging on threads. Illustrations are of immature fruits (late summer and early fall);
mature fruits redder and darker.

1.2a *Magnolia acuminata* L.
CUCUMBER TREE,
CUCUMBER MAGNOLIA

Fruits resembling cucumbers when
young and green; at maturity,
dark red and 2–3 inches long.
Large tree.
Pp. 41, 356-57, 523

1.2b *Magnolia tripetala* L.
UMBRELLA
MAGNOLIA
Fruits 2½–4 inches long,
bright rose-colored when
mature. Understory tree.
Pp. 43, 360, 524

1.2c *Magnolia macrophylla*
Michx.
LARGE-LEAF
MAGNOLIA
Fruit 3–3½ inches long and
2–3 inches wide, bright rose-
colored when mature. Tall
slender understory tree.
Pp. 42, 359, 524

1.2d *Magnolia fraseri* Walt.
FRASER'S MAGNOLIA,
MOUNTAIN MAGNOLIA
Fruits 4–5 inches long, 1½–2
inches wide, and bright rose-red
when mature; the ovaries with
needle-like tips. Understory
tree.
Pp. 42, 358, 523

1.3 *Xanthorhiza
simplicissima* Marsh.
SHRUB YELLOWROOT
Several small pods produced by
each flower, in racemes and
panicles. September. Small
shrub.
Pp. 107, 251, 522

1.4 *Ailanthus altissima* (Mill.) Swingle
TREE-OF-HEAVEN, AILANTHUS
Fruits single-seeded and winged, 1–2 inches long, in large panicles. Early autumn. Tree.
Pp. 87, 334-35, 539

1.5 *Acer rubrum* L.
RED MAPLE
Fruits key-shaped and winged, as in all maples, but more showy by being red; ½–1 inch long, maturing in spring. Large tree.
Pp. 27, 98, 314-15, 544

1.6 *Cephalanthus occidentalis* L.
BUTTONBUSH
Fruiting heads about ¾ inch in diameter, composed of numerous angular nutlets. October. Shrub.
Pp. 70, 215, 563

2.1a *Morus alba* L.　WHITE MULBERRY
2.1b *Morus rubra* L.　RED MULBERRY
Fruits about 1 inch long, dark purple when mature, formed
from many individual flowers in a catkin, the style still
protruding from each. Summer. Trees.
Pp. 103, 118, 382-83, 485, 520

The Genus *Rubus*, the RASPBERRIES, BLACKBERRIES, and DEWBERRIES

Each fruit a cluster of drupelets (each drupelet formed from a separate pistil) inserted on a convex or conical receptacle. Not true berries.

2.2a *Rubus occidentalis* L.
BLACK RASPBERRY
Fruits ⅜–⅝ inch thick, slipping from the hard receptacle which remains on the stalk. Late June–early July. Shrub.
Pp. 51, 241, 534-35

2.2b *Rubus allegheniensis* Porter, and related species
BLACKBERRY
Fruits ½–1 inch long, separating from the stalk with the fleshy receptacle included in the "berry." July. Prickly shrubs.
Pp. 51, 242, 535

2.2c *Rubus flagellaris* Willd., and related species
NORTHERN DEWBERRY
Fruits resembling blackberries in structure but shorter,
sometimes nearly hemispheric, ½–⅝ inch long. Late
June–July. Prickly prostrate shrub.
Pp. 185, 535

2.3 *Asimina triloba* (L.) Dunal.
PAPAW
Fruits 3–5 inches long and 1¼–1¾ inches
thick, ripening in late September. Small tree
or large shrub.
Pp. 43, 255, 361, 524-25

The Genus *Prunus* (in part), the PLUMS

Fruits drupes, about ⅞ inch thick, each with a slightly flattened 2-edged stone.

2.4a *Prunus americana* Marsh.
WILD PLUM
Fruits red or purple-red. August. Small tree, often forming thickets.
Pp. 45, 408, 531

2.4b *Prunus munsoniana* Wight & Hedrick
WILD GOOSE PLUM
Fruits red or orange-red. July. Small tree, often forming thickets.
Pp. 45, 409, 531

P. angustifolia Marsh., the Chickasaw plum, is similar but has smaller fruits, ½–⅝ inch thick. Pp. 279, 407, 531

2.5 *Diospyros virginiana* L.
PERSIMMON
Fruits about 1 inch thick, containing 1–4 seeds. October. Tree.
Pp. 99, 372-73, 559

2.6 *Taxus canadensis* Marsh.
CANADIAN YEW, AMERICAN YEW
Fleshy covering of the seed cup-shaped, about
¼ inch thick. September. Evergreen shrub.
Pp. 160, 495

2.7 *Cocculus
carolinus* (L.) DC.
CAROLINA
SNAILSEED
Drupes about ¼ inch
long and slightly
flattened. Stone
flattened and thick-
ened at the margin
for ¾ of the
circumference.
September–October.
Vine.
Pp. 195, 522

2.8 *Lindera benzoin*
(L.) Blume
SPICEBUSH
Drupes ¼–½ inch
long, axillary, and
spicy-aromatic.
September–October.
Shrub.
Pp. 108, 253, 525

2.9 *Cornus florida* L.
FLOWERING
DOGWOOD
Drupes ⅜–⅝ inch long in
terminal clusters. September–
October. Understory tree.
Pp. 93, 322-23, 552

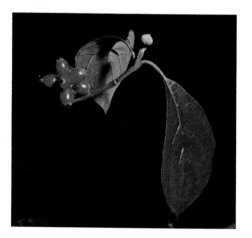

The Genus *Ilex*, the HOLLIES

"Berries" (actually drupes) in axillary clusters, each containing several nutlets.

2.10a *Ilex opaca* Ait.   AMERICAN HOLLY
Fruits about ⅜ inch thick. November–February. Evergreen tree.
Pp. 95, 170, 541-42

2.10b *Ilex decidua* Walt.
  SWAMP HOLLY, POSSUM-HAW
Fruits ¼–⅜ inch thick, maturing in September to
October and persisting after leaf fall. Large deciduous
shrub or small tree.
Pp. 96, 281, 541

2.10c *Ilex verticillata* (L.) Gray
WINTERBERRY
Fruits ¼–⅜ inch thick, maturing in autumn and persisting into winter
after leaf fall. Nutlets smooth on the back though ribbed on the sides,
in contrast to *I. montana* (below). Deciduous shrub.
Pp. 96, 282, 542

2.10d *Ilex montana* T. & G.
MOUNTAIN
WINTERBERRY
Fruits about ¼ inch thick.
Nutlets grooved on the back
as well as the sides, in
contrast to *I. verticillata*
(above). Large deciduous
shrub.
Pp. 96, 282, 541

2.11 *Celastrus
scandens* L.
BITTERSWEET
Fruits yellow-orange
and ⅜–½ inch thick;
maturing in autumn,
each splitting into 3
valves and exposing the
seeds covered with
red pulp. Vine.
Pp. 73, 204, 542

The Genus *Euonymus*

Fruits lobed and ¾ inch thick, splitting at maturity and exposing seeds with scarlet covering.

2.12a *Euonymus americanus* L.
STRAWBERRY-BUSH, HEARTS-A-BURSTING-WITH-LOVE
Fruits knobby and 3- to 5-lobed. September–October. Shrub.
Pp. 97, 168, 232, 542

2.12b *Euonymus obovatus* Nutt.
RUNNING STRAWBERRY-BUSH, RUNNING EUONYMUS
Fruits knobby and 3-lobed. September. Small prostrate shrub or trailing vine.
Pp. 98, 181, 543

2.12c *Euonymus atropurpureus* Jacq.
WAHOO, BURNING BUSH
Fruits rose-colored, smooth, and 4-lobed. October. Tall shrub.
Pp. 97, 233, 542

2.13 *Rhamnus caroliniana* Walt.
CAROLINA BUCKTHORN

"Berries" (actually 3-stoned drupes) axillary, ¼–⅜ inch thick, most conspicuous in September when ruby-red and immature; black when mature in late autumn. Large shrub or small tree.
Pp. 99, 284, 418, 547

2.14 *Symphoricarpos orbiculatus* Moench
BUCKBERRY, CORALBERRY

Berries purplish red, ⅛–¼ inch thick, in close axillary clusters, from early fall through winter. Shrub.
Pp. 212, 564

2.15 *Lonicera dioica* L.
WILD HONEYSUCKLE

Berries ¼–⅜ inch in diameter, subtended by a pair of united leaves. July. Vine or sprawling shrub.
Pp. 65, 182, 563

Fruits of *L. flavida* Small and *L. prolifera* (Kirchn.) Rehd. are similar to those of *L. dioica*, the species differing chiefly in characters of the joined leaves.
Pp. 65, 182, 563, 564

2.16a *Rhus aromatica* Ait.
FRAGRANT SUMAC
Bright red, densely hairy berries, each about ¼ inch thick.
June–early July. Shrub.
Pp. 85, 248, 539

2.16b *Rhus glabra* L.
SMOOTH SUMAC
Panicled fruits bright red in full
sunlight, covered with minute
sticky hairs, ripening in September
and persisting into winter. Large
shrub.
Pp. 86, 245, 539

Fruits of *R. copallina* L., winged
sumac, are similar but less red. Pp. 28,
85, 246, 539

2.16c *Rhus typhina* L.
STAGHORN SUMAC
Panicled fruits, each about ¼ inch thick and covered with long hairs, pink in August and September, red from October into winter. Large shrub, occasionally a small tree.
Pp. 86, 247, 541

2.17 *Prunus
virginiana* L.
CHOKE CHERRY
Fruits ⅜–½ inch thick, borne in racemes, astringent, and dark red when mature. July–August. (Compare with *P. serotina*, p. 135.) Small tree or large shrub.
Pp. 72, 280, 414, 532

2.18a *Rosa carolina* L.
CAROLINA ROSE,
PASTURE ROSE
"Fruits" about ½ inch in
diameter, maturing in
autumn and persisting into
winter, formed, as in all roses,
from the receptacle and
containing hard achenes
which are the true fruits. .
Small shrub.
Pp. 53, 239, 533

Other species of roses have
similar fruits except R. *multiflora*.

2.18b *Rosa multiflora*
Thunb.
MULTIFLORA ROSE
Fruits each about ¼ inch
thick and numerous in a
pyramidal inflorescence.
October through winter.
Large arching shrub.
Pp. 53, 238, 533-34

The Genus *Crataegus*, the HAWTHORNS

Fruits pomes, resembling miniature apples. Trees usually with thorns.

2.19a *Crataegus phaenopyrum* (L. f.) Medic.
WASHINGTON THORN
Fruits less than ¼ inch thick, ripening in October and persisting through winter. Small tree.
Pp. 49, 479, 530

2.19b *Crataegus crus-galli* L.
COCKSPUR THORN
Fruits about ½ inch thick. October. Small tree.
Pp. 49, 415, 530

2.19c *Crataegus mollis*
(T. & G.) Scheele
RED HAW
Fruits about ½ inch in
diameter, usually ripening in
September. Tree.
Pp. 50, 478, 530

Fruits of other hawthorns are
generally similar, ripening from
August to October.

2.20 *Aronia arbutifolia*
(L.) Ell.
RED CHOKEBERRY
Small red pomes nearly ¼
inch in diameter, in clusters
terminal on the stem and
on short axillary branches.
September-October. Shrub.
Pp. 82, 278, 529

2.21a *Sambucus pubens* Michx.
RED-BERRIED ELDER
Red berries borne in compound
cymes in a pyramidal inflorescence,
ripening in June (immature in
the illustration). Shrub.
Pp. 89, 206, 564

2.21b *Sambucus canadensis* L.
COMMON ELDER, ELDERBERRY
Black berries (with red juice) less than ¼ inch thick, borne in compound cymes in a convex inflorescence. September. Shrub.
Pp. 89, 207, 564

2.22 *Aralia spinosa* L.
HERCULES'-CLUB, DEVIL'S-WALKINGSTICK
Berries black, ¼ inch thick, in numerous umbels forming a very large panicle with rose-red branches. September–October. Large spiny shrub.
Pp. 28, 69, 236, 552

2.23 *Amelanchier arborea*
(Michx. f.) Fernald
SERVICEBERRY,
SARVIS
Small pomes resembling
miniature apples, dark red-
purple when mature (im-
mature in the illustration),
few in each raceme. June.
Understory tree.
Pp. 44, 398-99, 528-29

2.24 *Aronia melanocarpa* (Michx.) Ell.
BLACK CHOKEBERRY
Black pomes about ¼ inch in diameter, few together
in clusters terminal on the stem and on short
axillary branches. September. Shrub.
Pp. 82, 277, 529

2.25 *Prunus serotina* Ehrh.
WILD BLACK
CHERRY

Drupes reddish when
immature and dark purple or
nearly black when mature,
about ⅜ inch thick. Late
July–August. Large tree.
Pp. 71, 412-13, 532

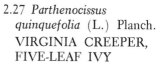

2.26 *Rhamnus lanceolata* Pursh
LANCE-LEAF
BUCKTHORN

"Berries" black and about ¼
inch thick, borne in axils of
the lowest leaves on a
branchlet. August. Shrub.
Pp. 99, 285, 547

Fruits of R. *caroliniana* Walt.,
the Carolina buckthorn (p. 127),
are black at maturity in October.

2.27 *Parthenocissus quinquefolia* (L.) Planch.
VIRGINIA CREEPER,
FIVE-LEAF IVY

Berries dark blue and about
¼ inch thick; pedicels often
red when growing in full
sunlight. September. Vine.
Pp. 188-89, 547

2.28 *Vitis vulpina* L.
FROST GRAPE
Berries black, ¼–⅜ inch in
diameter, with 4 or fewer
seeds. September-October.
Vine climbing by tendrils.
Pp. 200, 549

For other species of grape, see
pp. 199–203.

2.29 *Menispermum
    canadense* L.
MOONSEED
Fruits resembling the frost
grape, above, but poisonous;
drupes spherical (but
developing inequilaterally, as
shown by the stigma-scar on
1 side); the seed crescent-
shaped. Ripening in late
September and persisting
into winter. Twining vine.
Pp. 80, 196, 522

2.30a *Smilax glauca*
    Walt.
SAWBRIER,
CATBRIER
Berries very glaucous,
¼–⅜ inch thick, borne
in umbels. Fall and
winter. Prickly vine.
Pp. 68, 163, 192, 500

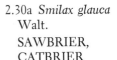

2.30b *Smilax rotundifolia* L. GREENBRIER
Berries black, about ¼ inch thick, borne in umbels.
Fall and winter. Prickly vine.
Pp. 166, 193, 500

S. hispida Muhl. and *S. bona-nox.* L. also have black
berries in umbels. Pp. 69, 164, 165, 192, 193, 500

The Genus *Viburnum*

Fruits 1-seeded drupes, borne in compound cymes, blue-black
in our species when mature, varicolored when immature.
Stones flattened except in V. *dentatum.*

For description of *Viburnum* fruits not shown here, see pp. 221-22.

2.31a *Viburnum acerifolium* L.
MAPLE-LEAF VIBURNUM
Fruits ellipsoid or nearly spherical, and ¼–⅜ inch
long. August–September. Shrub.
Pp. 90, 229, 564-65

2.31b *Viburnum rufidulum* Raf.
SOUTHERN BLACK-HAW
Fruits ellipsoid, about ½ inch long. September–October. Tall shrub (sometimes a small tree).
Pp. 90, 224-25, 566

V. *prunifolium* L., black-haw, and V. *lentago* L., nannyberry, have similar fruits and inflorescences, all 3 species having an inflorescence branching immediately above the terminal pair of leaves without an intervening stalk. Pp. 92, 227, 565

2.31c *Viburnum rafinesquianum* Schult.
ARROW-WOOD
Fruits flat, ellipsoid, and about ¼ inch long. August–September. Shrub.
Pp. 92, 226, 565

2.31d *Viburnum dentatum* L.
ARROW-WOOD
Fruits nearly spherical, ¼–⅜ inch thick; stones plump and ellipsoid. September–October. Shrub.
Pp. 92, 228, 565

2.31e *Viburnum molle*
Michx.
KENTUCKY
VIBURNUM
Drupes blue-black, flat-
ellipsoid, and ⅜ inch long.
September–October. Shrub.
Pp. 92, 228, 565

2.32 *Forestiera ligustrina*
(Michx.) Poir.
UPLAND
FORESTIERA
Drupes black, about ⅜ inch
long. Autumn. Large shrub.
Pp. 111, 234, 560

F. acuminata (Michx.) Poir.,
the swamp privet, has drupes
½–¾ inch long and slender-
ellipsoid. Summer. Pp. 111,
234, 560

2.33 *Ligustrum* spp. (representing several species)
PRIVET
"Berries" dark blue or nearly
black, drupaceous, ⅜ inch
in diameter, and in small
panicles, terminal in some
species, lateral in others.
Autumn. Shrubs.
Pp. 83, 174, 211, 562

2.34 *Chionanthus
virginicus* L.
FRINGE-TREE
Drupes dark blue, ½–¾
inch long, and 1- to 3-seeded.
September. Large shrub
(occasionally a small tree).
Pp. 57, 210, 560

2.35 *Nyssa sylvatica*
Marsh.
SOUR GUM,
BLACK GUM,
BLACK TUPELO
Drupes dark blue,
about ½ inch long,
single-seeded, and
borne 2 or more per
stalk. September. Tree.
Pp. 364-65, 551

2.36 *Sassafras albidum*
(Nutt.) Nees
SASSAFRAS
Pedicel red and expanded at
the apex, forming a cup at
the base of the purplish-blue,
⅜-inch-long fruit. September. Aromatic tree.
Pp. 26, 108, 480-81, 525-26

2.37a *Gaylussacia baccata* (Wang.) K. Koch
   HUCKLEBERRY

Berries black, ¼ inch in diameter, and 10-celled with 10
seeds, the seeds larger than those of *Vaccinium*, the
blueberries (pp. 142-43). August. Shrub with resin-dotted
leaves.
Pp. 76, 261, 554

2.37b *Gaylussacia brachycera* (Michx.) Gray
   BOX-HUCKLEBERRY

Purple berries ripening in August. Dwarf shrub with
evergreen leaves.
Pp. 76, 175, 554

The Genus *Vaccinium*, the BLUEBERRIES

Berries blue or dark purple, glaucous in some species and not in others, containing numerous small seeds, and borne in racemes. The species are highly variable due to polyploidy and hybridization, both past and present.

2.38a *Vaccinium pallidum* Ait.
2.38b *Vaccinium vacillans* Torr.
LOWBUSH BLUEBERRIES
Berries about ¼ inch in diameter, ripening in July. Berries that are blue and glaucous when mature are pink when immature; those that are dark purple at maturity are orange-red when immature. Small shrubs.
Pp. 78, 263, 264, 558

2.38c *Vaccinium alto-montanum* Ashe
MOUNTAIN DRYLAND BLUEBERRY
Berries about ⅜ inch in diameter, usually glaucous. Late July. Medium high shrub.
Pp. 264, 557-58

2.38d *Vaccinium simulatum* Small, and *Vaccinium constablaei* Gray
HIGHBUSH BLUEBERRIES
Berries ⅜–½ inch in diameter, dark purple and sometimes glaucous (orange-red when immature) or blue and glaucous (pink when immature). August. Tall shrubs.
Pp. 79, 265-66, 558

2.39a *Cornus alternifolia* L. f.
ALTERNATE-LEAF DOGWOOD
Drupes ⅜ inch in diameter, and dark blue.
July– August. Large shrub or small tree.
Pp. 93, 256, 553

2.39b *Cornus amomum* Mill.
SILKY DOGWOOD
Drupes blue, about ¼ inch
in diameter. September–
October. Shrub.
Pp. 94, 218, 553

C. obliqua Raf., with blue fruits
maturing in August–September,
differs from *C. amomum* chiefly
in leaf characters. Pp. 94, 219,
553

2.39c *Cornus drummondi*
Meyer
ROUGH-LEAF
DOGWOOD
Drupes ¼ inch thick or less,
white on red pedicels.
September. Large shrub.
Pp. 93, 216, 553

2.39d *Cornus racemosa*
Lam.

GRAY DOGWOOD

Drupes about ¼ inch thick;
cymes somewhat panicled
and more nearly pyramidal
than the inflorescences of
other dogwoods. Shrub.
Pp. 94, 217, 553

2.40 *Juniperus virginiana* L.

RED CEDAR

"Berries" blue and glaucous, about ¼ inch thick. October–
December. Evergreen tree.
Pp. 148-49, 499

2.41 *Phoradendron flavescens*
(Pursh) Nutt.
MISTLETOE
Berries gelatinous and sticky, ⅛
inch or more thick, ripe from
November through January.
Evergreen parasite on branches of
trees.
Pp. 162, 521

Series Three: Evergreens

Evergreen Trees, Shrubs, and Woody Vines Grouped According to Vegetative Characters

ARRANGEMENT OF PLATES

Group 1. With needle-like or scale-like leaves
Leaves opposite, principally scale-like and appressed or sharp and spreading 1.1
Leaves in bundles, long and needle-like 1.2
Leaves alternate, linear and flat 1.3–1.4 ·

Group 2. With linear and parallel-veined leaves 2.1

Group 3. With leaves broader than linear and chiefly net-veined
Parasite on branches of trees 3.1
Vines 3.2–3.6
Trees and shrubs 3.7–3.13

1.1 *Juniperus virginiana* L.
RED CEDAR

Tree up to 50 feet in height, rarely taller. Leaves principally scale-like, 1/16 inch long; leaves on young plants and fast-growing branchlets linear, stiff, and sharp-pointed, ½–¾ inch long. Bark light brown and thin, peeling in long, narrow, fibrous strips.
Pp. 145, 499

The Genus *Pinus*, the PINES

Needles in bundles of 2, 3, or 5. Pollen-bearing cones appearing briefly in spring (see p. 112); seed-bearing cones becoming woody and maturing usually in autumn of their second year, and often persisting after shedding seed.

1.2a *Pinus strobus* L.
WHITE PINE

Tall tree up to 100 feet in height.
Needles in bundles of 5, slender, soft,
blue-green, 3–5 inches long, and
whitened along 1 surface. Cones 4–6
inches long. Bark thin and smooth
on branches and young trees,
becoming dark gray-brown and
fissured on old trunks.
Pp. 496-97

1.2b *Pinus rigida* Mill.

PITCH PINE

Medium-sized tree, 40–50 feet in height, rarely up to 70 feet. Needles in bundles of 3, stiff, dark yellow-green, and 2½–5 inches long. Cones 1½–3 inches long, with stout sharp prickles on the scales. Bark brown, deeply furrowed, and broken into rough irregular plates.

Pp. 112, 496

1.2c *Pinus echinata* Mill.

YELLOW PINE, SHORTLEAF PINE

Tree up to 80–100 feet in height. Leaves in bundles of 2 or 3 (predominantly 2), dark green, slender, and flexible, 2½–5 inches long. Cones 1½–2 inches long (rarely 2½ inches), the smallest cones of any of our pines. Prickles on cone scales weak and usually deciduous. Bark with dark furrows between smooth plates.

Pp. 495–96

1.2d *Pinus virginiana* Mill.

SCRUB PINE, VIRGINIA PINE

Tree usually not over 30 or 40 feet in height (rarely up to 70 feet). Leaves 2 per bundle, 1½–3 inches long, light green, and usually twisted. Cones numerous, 1½–2½ inches long, with persistent prickles. Bark dark brown and scaly, with shallow fissures.
P. 497

1.3 *Tsuga canadensis* (L.) Carr.
EASTERN HEMLOCK, CANADA HEMLOCK

Tall tree up to 75–100 feet in height. Foliage in flattened sprays, somewhat drooping on the branches. Leaves ⅜–⅝ inch long, flat, blunt, and petioled, with 2 white lines on the lower surface. Twigs roughened by petiole bases which persist after leaf fall. Cones ½–1 inch long. Bark brown, divided into scaly ridges.
Pp. 497–98

1.4 *Taxus canadensis* Marsh.
CANADIAN YEW,
AMERICAN YEW
Straggling shrub with stems
rarely over 4 feet in Kentucky. Foliage in flattened
sprays; leaves ½–1 inch long,
flat, acute, and yellow-green
beneath. Leaf bases lying
against the stem.
Pp. 122, 495

2.1 *Arundinaria gigantea*
(Walt.) Chapm. CANE

A woody member of the grass
family with stems 6–10 feet high
and ½–¾ inch in diameter.
Stems hollow except at the
nodes. Leaves parallel-veined,
4–10 inches long.
Pp. 499–500

3.1 *Phoradendron flavescens* (Pursh) Nutt.   MISTLETOE
Shrub 12–24 inches across, parasitic on the branches of various deciduous trees, causing a stunting of each branch beyond the attachment of the parasite. Stems green. Leaves thick, dull green, and
¾–1½ inches long.
Pp. 146, 521

3.2a *Smilax glauca* Walt.   SAWBRIER, CATBRIER

Vine with tough wiry stems bearing stout prickles. Leaves usually reddish above in winter, whitish beneath.
Pp. 68, 136, 192, 500

3.2b *Smilax hispida* Muhl.   HISPID GREENBRIER

High-climbing vine with main stems green and bearing blackish bristles.
Leaves evergreen in mild winters.

Pp. 69, 137, 192, 500

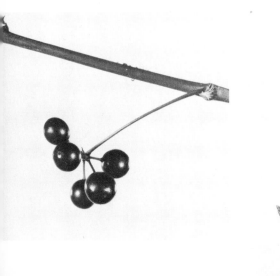

3.2c *Smilax bona-nox* L.
BRISTLY GREENBRIER

High-climbing vine with stems green, scaly at the base, and armed with stout prickles. Leaves evergreen in mild winters.
Pp. 137, 193, 500

3.2d *Smilax rotundifolia* L.   GREENBRIER

Vine with tough, green, usually angled stems bearing stout prickles.
Leaves evergreen in mild winters.
Pp. 137, 193, 500

3.3 *Bignonia capreolata* L.
CROSS-VINE

High-climbing vine with slender stems. Leaves opposite and compound, each composed of a pair of leaflets, 2½–5 inches long, and a tendril; usually bronzy in winter. Pp. 67, 180, 562

3.4a *Euonymus fortunei* (Turez.) Hand-Mazz. WINTERCREEPER

Trailing vine or bushy climber supported by aerial roots, frequently escaping from cultivation. Stems green. Leaves ½–2 inches long, dark green with pale veins.
Pp. 542–43

3.4b *Euonymus americanus* L. STRAWBERRY-BUSH, HEARTS-A-BURSTING-WITH-LOVE

Shrub 3–6 feet tall. Leaves 1–3½ inches long, glabrous and semievergreen. Twigs green and 4-sided.
Pp. 97, 126, 232, 542

3.5 *Hedera helix* L.
ENGLISH IVY

Vine trailing or climbing by aerial roots, occasionally escaping from cultivation. Leaves 2–4 inches wide, dark green with pale veins.
P. 552

3.6 *Lonicera japonica* Thunb.
JAPANESE HONEY-SUCKLE

Twining vine forming a dense tangle. Leaves 1½–2½ inches long, with hairs on veins and petioles, semi-evergreen in mild winters.
Pp. 65, 181, 564

3.7 *Ilex opaca* Ait.   AMERICAN HOLLY

Tree up to 40–50 feet in height, rarely more. Leaves thick and leathery, 2–4 inches long, dark green above, light yellow-green beneath. Bark smooth and light greenish gray, slightly warty on old trees.   Pp. 95, 124, 541–42

3.8a   *Rhododendron catawbiense* Michx.

PURPLE RHODODENDRON, MOUNTAIN ROSEBAY

Shrub usually under 9 feet tall in Kentucky, taller farther south.
Leaves thick and leathery, smooth on both sides, 2½–6 inches long.
Pp. 61, 556

3.8b *Rhododendron maximum* L.

GREAT LAUREL, GREAT RHODODENDRON

Tall shrub (or rarely a straggling tree up to 25 feet in height) with crooked stems and irregular branches. Leaves thick and leathery, 4–8 inches long, rolling lengthwise in drought or cold; upper surface dark green and smooth, lower surface and petioles pale and scaly or closely hairy. Mature capsules brown, ½–⅝ inch long, persisting through winter. Fertile bud in winter illustrated; leaf buds smaller. Pp. 61, 556

3.9 *Kalmia latifolia* L.
MOUNTAIN LAUREL

Shrub much branched, gnarled with age, and up to 12 feet tall. Leaves 2–4 inches long, leathery, smooth on both surfaces, dark green and somewhat glossy above, pale beneath. Capsules brown and nearly spherical, persisting through winter. Pp. 55, 554–55

3.10 *Epigaea repens* L.
TRAILING ARBUTUS

Prostrate shrub, creeping and rooting at intervals, with branches rarely rising more than 4 inches above the ground. Leaves 1–2¾ inches long, leathery and somewhat rough, bearing rusty hairs.
Pp. 55, 554

3.11 *Ligustrum* spp. (representing several species)
PRIVET

Introduced shrubs, a few of the several species escaping and becoming naturalized. Leaves dark green, smooth, and semievergreen. Branchlets slender and gray, minutely hairy in several species.
Pp. 83, 139, 211, 562

3.12 *Gaylussacia brachycera*
(Michx.) Gray
BOX-HUCKLEBERRY
Small shrub 8–15 inches tall, form-
ing colonies. Leaves leathery,
glossy, ½–⅞ inch long, and finely
toothed.
Pp. 76, 141, 554

3.13 *Pachistima canbyi* Gray
PACHISTIMA, MOUNTAIN-LOVER, CLIFF-GREEN
Small shrub 4–12 inches tall, forming colonies. Leaves leathery, glossy, and ½–¾ inch long.
Pp. 98, 543

Series Four: Deciduous Vines

With Climbing, Trailing, or Sprawling Stems, Grouped According to Vegetative Characters

ARRANGEMENT OF PLATES

Group 1. With opposite leaves,* leaf scars, and buds
   Leaves compound 1.1–1.2
   Leaves simple 1.3–1.5
Group 2. With alternate leaves,* leaf scars, and buds
   Leaves compound 2.1–2.6
   Leaves simple
    Leaves smooth-margined 2.7–2.11
    Leaves coarsely toothed or lobed 2.12–2.15
    Leaves finely toothed 2.16

---

* See diagrams on pages 569, 570, and 573.

In woody plants with either simple or compound leaves, buds can usually be seen in the leaf axils except when leaves are immature.

Note that in woody plants with compound leaves the lateral buds are on the stem and not in the axils of leaflets on the rachis.

Note also that alternate compound leaves may have opposite leaflets.

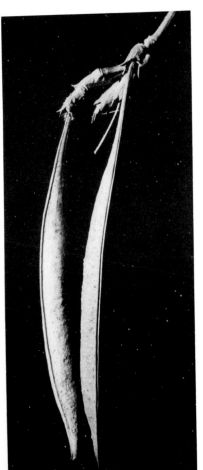

1.1 *Campsis radicans* (L.) Seem.
  TRUMPET-VINE,
  TRUMPET-CREEPER

Large vine, up to 100 feet high,
with straw-colored bark and
branchlets, twining as well as
climbing by aerial roots. Leaves
pinnate; leaflets 1½–3 inches long,
either long-pointed or acute. Capsules 4–6 inches long, containing
winged seed.
Pp. 67, 562

1.2 *Bignonia capreolata* L.
CROSS-VINE
High-climbing vine with slender
stems. Each leaf composed of a
pair of leaflets, 2½–5 inches long,
and a tendril; rarely a few leaves
simple. Capsules 6–8 inches long,
bearing winged seed.
Pp. 67, 167, 562

1.3 *Euonymus obovatus* Nutt.   RUNNING STRAWBERRY-
  BUSH, RUNNING EUONYMUS

Stems trailing, and with erect or reclining branches 8–16 inches high.
Leaves 1¼–2½ inches long, margin with minute blunt teeth.
Pp. 96, 126, 543

1.4a *Lonicera japonica* Thunb.   JAPANESE HONEYSUCKLE

Twining or trailing vine with stems 6–20 feet long, forming a dense
tangle. Leaves 1¼–2½ inches long, dark green, usually with smooth
margins but occasionally lobed. Berries black, subtended by leaflike
bracts, ripening in September.
Pp. 65, 169, 564

1.4b *Lonicera flavida* Cockerell   WILD HONEYSUCKLE

Stems straggling, often reclining but not climbing. Leaves pale beneath, the uppermost pair joined. Berries red.
Pp. 65, 127, 563

L. dioica L. and *L. prolifera* (Kirchn.) Rehd, also have the uppermost pair of leaves grown together. *L. dioica* has leaves whitened beneath; *L. prolifera* has the leaf-disk round and whitened above. Pp. 65, 127, 563, 564

    L. sempervirens L., trumpet honeysuckle, also with the uppermost pair of leaves usually joined, is an introduced twining vine which occasionally escapes from cultivation. Pp. 57, 564

1.5 *Trachelospermum
difforme* (Walt.) Gray
CLIMBING DOGBANE

Semiwoody twining or trailing vine, sometimes woody
only at the base. Leaves 2–4
inches long, of 2 shapes:
lanceolate and broadly oval
or ovate. Fruit a slender cylindric pod 6–8 inches long.
Pp. 80, 562

2.1 *Rosa setigera* Michx.

CLIMBING ROSE, PRAIRIE ROSE

Stems climbing, leaning, or sprawling, 4–14 feet long. Leaflets predominantly 3, sometimes 5 on new stems; terminal leaflet 1½–3 inches long. Stipules with glandular hairs on the margin.

Pp. 52, 130, 534

2.2a Rubus flagellaris Willd. (including *R. enslenii* Tratt. and related species)
DEWBERRIES
Stems prostrate, armed with recurved prickles and bearing short erect branches. Leaflets 3–5.
Pp. 50, 120, 535

2.2b Rubus hispidus L. (and related species)
SWAMP DEWBERRY
Stems trailing or low-arching, very slender and bristly, bearing numerous erect flowering stems. Leaflets ¾–2 inches long, usually firm and glossy, persisting through winter. Fruit small and seedy.
Pp. 51, 535

2.3 *Rhus radicans* L. POISON IVY

Entire plant poisonous to the touch. Large
vine high-climbing by aerial roots, or trailing
or bushy. Leaflets either with smooth margins
or with few teeth. Berries whitish, in axillary
panicles, ripening in early fall. Winter buds
hairy, the terminal bud slender.

To distinguish poison ivy from other plants
that superficially resemble it, note the alternate
trifoliate leaves with long-stalked terminal
leaflets.

Pp. 87, 540

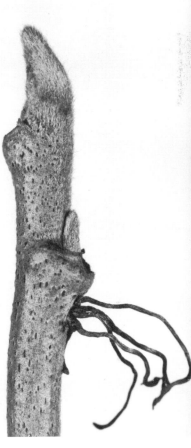

2.4 *Parthenocissus quinquefolia* (L.) Planch.
VIRGINIA CREEPER, FIVE-LEAF IVY
High-climbing vine, held to the support by adhesive disks
on the ends of branched tendrils. Leaves palmate with
5 sharply toothed leaflets, each 2½–5 inches long.
Pp. 135, 547

2.5 *Wisteria macrostachya* Nutt.   WISTERIA

High-climbing twining vine with stout stems. Leaves pinnate; leaflets averaging 2 inches in length. Pods 2–4 inches long. Winter buds silky; leaf scar bearing a small hornlike protuberance on each side.

Pp. 59, 538

2.6 *Ampelopsis arborea* (L.) Koehne
PEPPER-VINE

High-climbing or bushy vine bearing few tendrils. Leaves bipinnate, 4–8 inches long (leaflets 1–2 inches), thin and dark green. Flowers small, in compact clusters arranged in panicles shorter than the leaves. Fruit a blackish berry, ripening in early autumn.
P. 547

2.7 *Aristolochia tomentosa* Sims
PIPE-VINE

High-climbing twining vine. Leaves 4–8 inches long, hairy beneath; petioles hairy. Flower curved, resembling a pipe, 1½–1⅝ inches long. Fruit cylindric, about 3 inches long.
Pp. 68, 521

A. durior Hill, dutchman's-pipe, differs principally in being smooth and not hairy. Pp. 68, 521

2.8a *Smilax glauca* Walt.
SAWBRIER,
CATBRIER

Vine often forming tangles
in thickets. Stems tough and
wiry. Leaves whitened be-
neath, having a leathery texture though not thick.
Leaves 2–4 inches long,
varying from broadly lanceolate to ovate, rarely contracted in the middle.
Pp. 68, 136, 163, 500

2.8b *Smilax hispida* Muhl.
HISPID GREENBRIER

High-climbing vine with
main stems green, bearing
blackish bristle-like prickles;
small branches without
prickles. Leaves usually
ovate, 2½–5 inches long.
Pp. 69, 137, 164, 500

2.8c *Smilax bona-nox* L.   BRISTLY GREENBRIER

High-climbing vine with stems green, scaly at the base, and armed
with stout prickles. Leaves often mottled above, 2–5 inches long,
ovate or more frequently with sides contracted, and with
thickened margins.
Pp. 137, 165, 500

2.8d *Smilax rotundifolia* L.
GREENBRIER

Vine with tough, green, usually
angled stems bearing stout prickles.
Leaves 1¾–4 inches long, usually
ovate (varying from roundish to
nearly lanceolate, sometimes contracted below the middle), and
with the margin not strongly
thickened.
Pp. 137, 166, 500

2.9 *Brunnichia cirrhosa* Gaertn.
BUCKWHEAT VINE, LADIES'-EARDROPS

Vine high-climbing by tendrils. Stems with a narrow hairy ring at each node. Leaves smooth-margined, up to 4 inches long. Fruiting calyx brown, about 1 inch long, containing an achene.
Pp. 107, 521

2.10 *Berchemia scandens* (Hill) K. Koch
SUPPLE-JACK

High-climbing vine with tough, flexible, twining stems. Leaves 1¼–2¼ inches long, usually wavy-margined; lateral veins straight. Flowers small, greenish white, in terminal and axillary panicles. Fruit a bluish drupe ¼–⅜ inch long.
P. 546

2.11 *Cocculus carolinus* (L.) DC.
CAROLINA SNAILSEED

Semiwoody twining vine. Leaves 2–6
inches long, heart-shaped, ovate, or
triangular, or sometimes 3-lobed.
Flowers minute, white, and unisexual;
sepals, petals, and stamens each 6;
pistils 3 or 6. Fruit a red drupe ¼–⅜
inch in diameter. Stone flattened,
thickened at the margin for ¾ of the
circumference.
Pp. 123, 522

2.12 *Menispermum canadense* L.
MOONSEED

Semiwoody twining vine. Leaves usually lobed, 4–5 inches long and about as broad; petiole attached to the blade ⅛–¼ inch inside the margin. Stone flattened and crescent-shaped, about ¼ inch wide. Pp. 80, 136, 522

2.13 *Calycocarpum lyoni* (Pursh) Nutt.   CUPSEED
High-climbing vine. Leaves 3- to 7-lobed, 3–6 inches
long, wider than long. Flowers small and numerous in
panicles, unisexual, with 6 sepals but no petals. Fruit a
black drupe, ¾ inch to nearly 1 inch long.
P. 521

2.14 *Ampelopsis cordata* Michx.
HEART-LEAF AMPELOPSIS

High-climbing vine; tendrils few, borne chiefly on the main branches. Leaves 2½–4 inches long, smooth, with hairs only at the summit of the petiole. Flower and fruit clusters broader than long, in contrast to those of grapes. Fruit bluish, ¼–⅜ inch thick. Bark tight, not shredded as in all grapes save one.
P. 547

The Genus *Vitis*, the GRAPES

Woody vines high-climbing by tendrils. Leaves toothed and palmately veined, more or less lobed in most species, and more deeply lobed on fast-growing vegetative shoots. Flowers small, greenish, and fragrant, growing in panicles (see p. 109), and followed by berries (see p. 136). Bark shreddy and the pith interrupted by diaphragms at the nodes in all species except V. *rotundifolia*, the muscadine (p. 203). Most species usually flowering in June and fruiting in autumn.

2.15a *Vitis vulpina* L.   FROST GRAPE

Leaves 3½–5½ inches long, either unlobed or obscurely lobed with the lobes pointing outward rather than forward; sides of teeth convex; hairs on mature leaves mostly restricted to veins and vein-axils beneath.
Pp. 136, 549

2.15b *Vitis riparia* Michx.   RIVERBANK GRAPE

Similar to the more common *V. vulpina*. Leaves usually lobed, the lobes pointing forward; teeth sharply pointed, usually with one side convex and one concave. Fruit ⅜–½ inch in diameter, black and glaucous.
P. 548

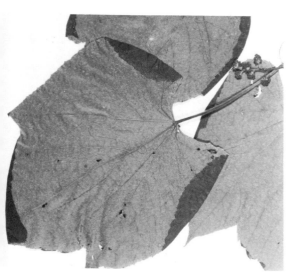

2.15c *Vitis cinerea* Engelm.
GRAYBARK GRAPE,
SWEET WINTER
GRAPE

Branchlets angled, bearing dense gray hairs. Leaves dull dark green, 3–6 inches long, unlobed or shallowly lobed, with dense, short, grayish hairs beneath; marginal teeth short. Fruit ¼–⅜ inch in diameter, usually not glaucous.
P. 548

2.15d *Vitis palmata* Vahl   CATBIRD GRAPE
Branchlets bright red, becoming reddish brown with age. Petioles bright red; leaf blades bright green, 2–4½ inches long, longer than broad; leaf lobes long-pointed, the lobing deep on vigorous shoots, shallow on old stems. Fruit black, ⅜ inch in diameter.
P. 548

2.15e *Vitis aestivalis* Michx.
SUMMER GRAPE

Leaves 3–6 inches long, deeply lobed on vigorous shoots, more shallowly lobed on old stems. Leaves whitened beneath and bearing some cobwebby hairs in var. *argentifolia* (illustrated), not strongly whitened but densely cobwebby beneath in var. *aestivalis*. Fruit glaucous, averaging ⅜ inch in diameter.
Pp. 109, 548

2.15f *Vitis labrusca* L.
FOX GRAPE

Leaves covered beneath with rusty or grayish "felt." Fruit ½–¾ inch in diameter. (Fruit in all other wild grapes less than ½ inch, except V. *rotundifolia*.)
P. 548

2.15g *Vitis rotundifolia* Michx.
MUSCADINE
Leaves firm and glossy, 2½–4
inches long. Panicles short. Fruit
averaging ½ inch in diameter,
few together in roundish clusters.
Bark tight, with abundant lenticels, in contrast to the shredding
bark of all other grapes.
P. 549

2.16 *Celastrus scandens* L.   BITTERSWEET

High-climbing twining vine. Leaves 2–3 inches long and finely toothed. Winter buds small and roundish; bud scales pointed. Pith large and white.
Pp. 73, 125, 542

Series Five: Deciduous Shrubs (1)

With Opposite Leaves, Leaf Scars, and Buds, Grouped According to Vegetative Characters

* See diagrams on pages 569, 570, and 573.

In woody plants with either simple or compound leaves, buds can usually be seen in the leaf axils except when leaves are immature.

Note that in woody plants with compound leaves the lateral buds are on the stem and not in the axils of leaflets on the rachis.

Note also that alternate compound leaves may have opposite leaflets.

1.1a *Sambucus pubens* Michx.
RED-BERRIED ELDER

Shrub 8–12 feet tall. Leaflets
usually 7 (5–7), each 2½–4½
inches long. Buds globular, red,
and stalked, with 2–3 pairs of bud
scales. Pith large and brown.
Pp. 89, 133, 564

1.1b *Sambucus canadensis* L.
COMMON ELDER, ELDERBERRY

Shrub up to 8 feet tall, spreading by runners and often making a large colony; individual stems with few branches. Leaflets usually 9 (5–11), each 3–5 inches long, the lowest often divided into 3 sub-leaflets. Buds conical, light brown or green, with 4–5 pairs of bud scales. Pith large and white.
Pp. 89, 133, 564

1.2 *Staphylea trifolia* L.   BLADDERNUT

Shrub 3–10 feet tall with upright stems. Leaflets
2–3 inches long at maturity. Fruit an inflated
capsule, 3-lobed at the apex, conspicuous all
summer, and about 2 inches long at maturity in
September. Pair of buds at the stem tip causing a
forking in stem growth.
Pp. 74, 543

2.1 *Calycanthus fertilis* Walt.
CALYCANTHUS, SWEET SHRUB

Aromatic shrub 3–9 feet tall. Leaves essentially without hairs beneath, in contrast to those of *C. floridus*, which is more generally planted. Aggregate fruit 2–2½ inches long, containing hard ovoid achenes, which are the actual fruits. Pp. 43, 524

2.2 *Chionanthus virginicus* L. FRINGE-TREE

Large shrub or small tree 6–20 feet tall. Leaves 3–6 inches long. Branchlets slightly 4-angled and hairy; leaf scars crescentic or half round, and raised.
Pp. 57, 140, 560

2.3 *Ligustrum* spp. (representing several species)
PRIVET

Much-branched semievergreen shrubs up to 12 feet
tall. Leaves dark green and
1–2 inches long.
Pp. 83, 139, 174, 562

2.4 *Symphoricarpos orbiculatus*
Moench
BUCKBERRY, CORALBERRY
Shrub 1½–4½ feet tall; stems with
shreddy bark. Leaves about 1 inch
long, hairy beneath. Flowers greenish,
about ⅛ inch long, in tight clusters
in the leaf axils.
Pp. 127, 564

2.5a *Hypericum spathulatum*
   (Spach) Steud.
   SHRUBBY ST. JOHN'S-WORT
Shrub 2½–5 feet tall. Leaves 1¼–2¼
inches long, ¼–½ inch wide; minute
glandular dots visible on the upper
surface. Capsule about ½ inch long,
illustrated in winter after splitting.
Young stems sharply 2-edged.
Pp. 54, 550

H. densiflorum Pursh, of the same height,
has leaves 1–1⅝ inches long and about
¼ inch wide, and numerous small flowers.
Pp. 54, 550

2.5b *Hypericum frondosum*
Michx.
GOLDEN ST. JOHN'S-
WORT
Small shrub 20–40 inches
tall, with angled stems.
Leaves 1¼–2¼ inches long,
½–¾ inch wide; minute
glandular dots visible on the
upper surface. Capsule about
½ inch long; sepals unequal,
the larger ones ¾–1¼ inches
long.
Pp. 54, 550

2.6 *Decodon verticillatus* (L.) Ell.
SWAMP LOOSESTRIFE, WATER-WILLOW

Shrub with slender arching stems 3–9 feet long, woody only at the
base. Leaves 3–6 inches long, usually in whorls of 3 or 4. Capsule
nearly spherical and less than ¼ inch in diameter, with sepals and
appendages attached above.
Pp. 53, 551

2.7 *Cephalanthus occidentalis* L.   BUTTONBUSH

Shrub 5–8 feet tall. Leaves 2½–5 inches long, opposite or sometimes in whorls of 3; margin often wavy but without teeth. Twigs reddish and glossy; terminal bud lacking; each lateral bud small and conical, in a depression above the roundish raised leaf scar; stipule scars connecting the leaf scars.
Pp. 70, 117, 563

The Genus *Cornus*, the DOGWOODS (shrub species)

Lateral veins curving forward toward the apex of the leaf; a pair of leaf scars meeting around the stem. Leaves opposite in all species except *C. alternifolia* (p. 256).

2.8a *Cornus drummondi* Meyer
ROUGH-LEAF DOGWOOD
Large shrub up to 18 feet tall. Leaves rough above, whitish and hairy beneath, 2–3½ inches long. Twigs reddish brown.
Pp. 93, 144, 553

2.8b *Cornus racemosa* Lam.
GRAY DOGWOOD
Shrub 3½–7½ feet tall. Leaves
1½–3 inches long, glaucous or
mealy below with very short
hairs. Twigs gray, without hairs.
Pp. 94, 145, 553

2.8c *Cornus amomum* Mill.

SILKY DOGWOOD

Shrub 5–9 feet tall. Leaves 2½–4 inches long, at least half as wide as long, rounded at the base, with short abrupt tips at the apex, and with 4–6 veins on each side; the undersurface with both appressed and spreading hairs. Twigs reddish, bearing silky hairs.
Pp. 94, 144, 553

2.8d *Cornus obliqua* Raf.
SILKY DOGWOOD,
PALE DOGWOOD

Shrub similar to *C. amomum*,
with which it hybridizes,
but differing in having
leaves 1¼–3½ inches long,
less than half as wide as long,
and tapering at base and
apex, with 3–5 veins on each
side; the undersurface with
appressed hairs only.
Pp. 94, 144, 553

Species of shrub dogwoods rare
in Kentucky and not illustrated
are *C. stolonifera* Michx., red
osier, and *C. foemina* Mill., stiff
dogwood. *C. stolonifera* has twigs
bright red and shining, leaves
ovate or oval, whitened and hairy
beneath, and fruit white. *C.
foemina* has twigs gray or reddish
brown, leaves lanceolate or ovate-
lanceolate, green beneath and
without hairs, and fruit white
turning blue. Both have white
pith in 1- to 2-year-old twigs in
contrast to brownish or drab
pith in our other species. P. 553

2.9a *Philadelphus inodorus* L.
SCENTLESS MOCK-ORANGE

Shrub 6–8 feet tall. Leaves 1½–3 inches long, with widely spaced teeth or smooth-margined, glabrous or nearly so. Flowers and capsules usually in 3s. Twigs glabrous, second-year bark shreddy. Leaf scar crescentic, covering the bud until it bursts; terminal bud lacking.
Pp. 43, 526

2.9b *Philadelphus hirsutus* Nutt.
HAIRY MOCK-ORANGE

Shrub 3–6 feet tall. Leaves 1–2¼ inches long, finely toothed, and hairy beneath. Flowers and capsules solitary or in 3s or 4s. Twigs hairy, second-year bark shreddy. Leaf scar crescentic; lateral buds fully exposed; terminal bud lacking.
Pp. 43, 526

The Genus *Viburnum*

An important genus of shrubs or small trees with opposite simple leaves. Flowers white or whitish, in compound terminal clusters. Fruit a drupe, usually blue-black or black in autumn when mature. Winter buds in our species with only 1 or 2 pairs of scales.

2.10a *Viburnum nudum* L.
POSSUM-HAW,
SWAMP-HAW

Shrub up to 18 feet in height. Leaves 2½–5 inches long, minutely blunt-toothed or smooth-margined, lustrous above, and somewhat thick. Fruits nearly spherical. Twigs glossy; winter buds brown.
Pp. 91, 565

2.10b *Viburnum cassinoides* L.
WITHE-ROD

Shrub 3–9 feet tall. Leaves somewhat thick, dull, 1–5 inches long;
margin with rounded teeth or sometimes nearly smooth-edged. Young
leaves and young branchlets somewhat scurfy. Inflorescence on a
stalk ½–2 inches long, above the
uppermost pair of leaves and below
the branches of the cluster. Fruit
oblong or nearly spherical. Winter
buds yellow-scurfy with a single
pair of scales; terminal flower bud
⅝–1 inch long, swollen at the
base; lateral buds slender and
curved.
Pp. 91, 565

2.10c *Viburnum lentago* L.
NANNYBERRY

Large shrub 6–10 feet tall, or bushy
tree up to 18 feet. Leaves 1¾–3
inches long, variable in width,
abruptly long-pointed, and usually
glabrous; petioles with wavy margins. Buds brownish to lead-
colored, terminal buds ¾–1 inch
long, flower buds (not illustrated)
swollen near the base.
Pp. 91, 138, 565

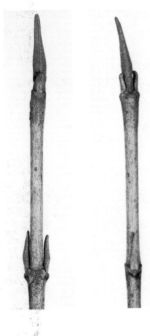

2.10d *Viburnum prunifolium* L.
BLACK-HAW

Large shrub or small tree up to
20 feet tall. Leaves ovate or
elliptic, either narrowly or
broadly so, 2–3½ inches long,
and acute or obtuse at the apex
but never long-pointed; petioles
slender and usually glabrous.
Small twigs somewhat stiffly
spreading. Buds ashy-brown;
terminal flower bud short-
pointed, swollen toward the
middle, and about ½ inch long.
Pp. 91, 138, 565

2.10e *Viburnum rufidulum* Raf.
SOUTHERN BLACK-HAW

Shrub or small tree up to 30 feet in height. Leaves thick and lustrous, variable in size and shape but usually obtuse, the principal ones usually 2–3 inches long; petioles wide-margined. Dark rusty-red scurf on buds, petioles, and lower surface of leaves near base. Bark on large specimens deeply cut in squarish blocks. Pp. 90, 138, 566

2.10f Viburnum dentatum L. (and related species in the "dentatum complex")
ARROW-WOOD

Shrubs 4–15 feet tall. Leaves tapering or rounded at the base, not heart-shaped; blades 1½–3½ inches long on petioles ½–1 inch long. Hairiness, or lack of it, on blades, petioles, and twigs varying within the complex. Buds without a "collar." Bark tight.
Pp. 92, 138, 565

2.10g *Viburnum rafinesquianum* Schult.   ARROW-WOOD
Shrub up to 5 feet in height. Leaves 1¼–2¾ inches long, sessile or
on short petioles, sometimes slightly heart-shaped at the base, either
hairy beneath or nearly glabrous. Buds with a "collar" at the base.
Pp. 92, 138, 565

2.10h *Viburnum molle* Michx.
KENTUCKY VIBURNUM
Shrub 3–9 feet tall. Leaves 2–3½ inches
long, heart-shaped at the base, slightly hairy
on the veins beneath, and borne on petioles
½–2 inches long; the 3 lowest pairs of veins
originating at the same point, thus suggesting palmate venation. Buds without a
"collar." Bark exfoliating in thin flakes.
Pp. 92, 139, 565

2.10i *Viburnum acerifolium* L.
MAPLE-LEAF VIBURNUM
Shrub 2–6 feet tall with slender erect stems.
Leaves 2–5 inches long, downy and with dark
dots beneath. Petioles and branchlets usually
hairy.
Pp. 90, 137, 564–65

2.11 *Acer spicatum* Lam.   MOUNTAIN MAPLE

Tall shrub or small bushy tree up to 25 feet in height. Leaves 4–5 inches long, thin, downy beneath. Winged fruits in slender panicles maturing in midsummer.
Pp. 74, 545

2.12 *Hydrangea arborescens* L.   WILD HYDRANGEA

Shrub 3–5 feet tall with somewhat straggling stems. Leaf blades
2–5 inches long on petioles ½–4 inches long. Capsules tipped with
2 persistent styles and splitting between them. Leaf scars
crescentic, with a connecting line. Bark shreddy when old.
Pp. 88, 526

2.13a *Euonymus americanus* L.
STRAWBERRY-BUSH,
HEARTS-A-BURSTING-WITH-LOVE

Shrub 3–6 feet tall. Leaves thickish, bright green, 1–3½ inches long, and glabrous or nearly so. Twigs green and somewhat 4-sided.   Pp. 97, 126, 168, 54?

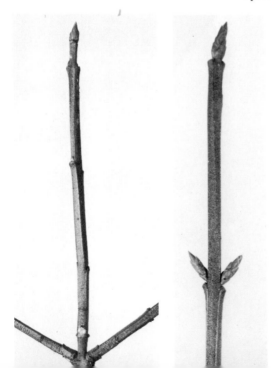

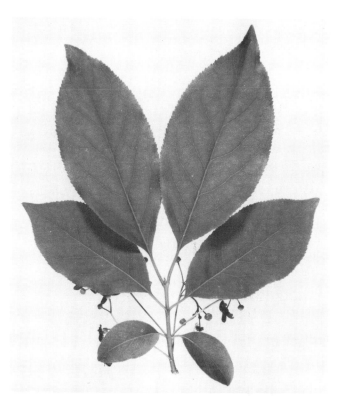

2.13b *Euonymus atropurpureus* Jacq.
  WAHOO, BURNING BUSH
Tree-like shrub with upright stems 6–20
feet tall. Leaves 1½–5 inches long, hairy
beneath.
Pp. 97, 126, 542

2.14 *Forestiera acuminata* (Michx.) Poir.
SWAMP PRIVET

Large shrub or small tree up to 12 feet tall. Leaves 2–3 inches long, tapering at both ends; margin with a few fine teeth or nearly smooth. Drupes slender-ellipsoid, black or dark purple, ½–¾ inch long when mature, pointed and curved when young (immature illustrated). Bark smooth and gray.
Pp. 111, 139, 560

F. ligustrina (Michx.) Poir., the upland forestiera, has leaves elliptic, ½–1¾ inches long, obtuse or acute but not long-pointed. Pp. 111, 139, 560

Series Six: Deciduous Shrubs (2)

With Alternate Leaves, Leaf Scars, and Buds, Grouped According to Vegetative Characters

* See diagrams on pages 569, 570, and 573.

In woody plants with either simple or compound leaves, buds can usually be seen in the leaf axils except when leaves are immature.

Note that in woody plants with compound leaves the lateral buds are on the stem and not in the axils of leaflets on the rachis.

Note also that alternate compound leaves may have opposite leaflets.

1.1 *Aralia spinosa* L.
HERCULES'-CLUB,
DEVIL'S-WALKINGSTICK

Shrub up to 18 feet tall with erect, stout, spiny stems
and few branches. Leaves twice pinnate, the whole
leaf about 3 feet long; leaflets 1¼–3 inches long.
Pp. 28, 69, 133, 552

1.2 *Xanthoxylum americanum* Mill.
PRICKLY ASH

Shrub 5–10 feet tall. Leaves aromatic, bearing minute translucent dots; leaflets 1¼–3½ inches long, hairy beneath, oblique at the base. Flowers greenish white, about ⅛ inch across, unisexual, in clusters appearing before the leaves. Fruit dry, reddish, and less than ¼ inch long, maturing in August and September. Twigs resembling those of black locust (pp. 332–33) in having prickles beside a leaf scar, but differing in having rusty-red woolly buds.   P. 538

1.3a *Rosa multiflora* Thunb.
  MULTIFLORA ROSE
Shrub with arching stems 6–10 feet
long. Leaves with fringe-toothed stip-
ules.
Pp. 53, 130, 533–34

1.3b *Rosa carolina* L.
CAROLINA ROSE, PASTURE ROSE

Shrub 1–3 feet tall. Leaflets usually 5 (3–7). Stems bearing slender straight prickles in contrast to the curved prickles in our other species of roses.
Pp. 53, 130, 533

R. *palustris* and R. *carolina* occasionally hybridize.

R. *canina* L., dog-rose, and R. *eglanteria* L., sweetbrier, species which have been introduced from Europe, may sometimes be found as escapes. P. 533

1.3c *Rosa palustris* Marsh.
SWAMP ROSE

Shrub 3–8 feet tall. Leaflets usually 7,
finely toothed. Fruit red in autumn;
calyx lobes about 1 inch long, bearing
stalked glands, eventually deciduous.
Pp. 53, 130, 534

The Genus *Rubus*, the RASPBERRIES
and BLACKBERRIES

Stems biennial, the leaves differing on the first- and second-year canes or stems, only the second-year canes bearing flowers and fruit.

1.4a *Rubus occidentalis* L.
BLACK RASPBERRY
Shrub with stems 3–6 feet long, often rooting at the tip, young ones whitened, old ones purple and glaucous. Leaves whitened beneath.
Pp. 51, 119, 534–35

1.4b *Rubus allegheniensis*
   Porter (and related species)
   BLACKBERRY

Shrubs with stems 3–7 feet long,
somewhat angled, and either
red, brown, or greenish. Leaves
green on both sides; leaflets usually 5 per leaf on a first-year cane
and 3 on a second-year cane.
Pp. 51, 119, 535

1.5 *Robinia hispida* L.
  ROSE-ACACIA, BRISTLY
  LOCUST
Shrub 3–9 feet tall. Leaflets 1¼–
2¼ inches long. Stems covered
with stiff bristles and usually
bearing a pair of spines at each
node.
Pp. 58, 537

1.6 *Amorpha fruticosa* L.
INDIGO BUSH, FALSE INDIGO

Shrub 6–13 feet tall, with twigs angled below the nodes. Leaflets ⅝–1½ inches long. Pods ¼–⅜ inch long, warty, and crowded in spikes.
Pp. 73, 536

1.7a *Rhus glabra* L.
SMOOTH SUMAC
Shrub 5–10 feet tall. Leaflets 2–4 inches
long, glaucous beneath. Leaves and branchlets without hairs or nearly so; branchlets
keeled below the buds.
Pp. 86, 128, 539

1.7b *Rhus copallina* L.
WINGED SUMAC,
SHINING SUMAC

Shrub 4–8 feet tall. Rachis of leaves
wing-margined; leaflets 2–4 inches
long, lustrous above. Branchlets usually with short hairs.
Pp. 28, 85, 128, 539

1.7c *Rhus typhina* L.
STAGHORN SUMAC

Large shrub or small tree up
to 25 feet in height. Leaflets
2–4 inches long. Branches,
petioles, and fruit densely
covered with soft hairs.
Pp. 86, 129, 541

1.7d *Rhus aromatica* Ait.
FRAGRANT SUMAC
Shrub 3–8 feet tall. Terminal leaflet 1½–3 inches long, not stalked.
(Contrast with *R. radicans*, poison
ivy.) Twigs slender, with a strong
odor when broken. Terminal bud
absent, lateral vegetative buds hid-
den, flower buds conspicuous in
winter.
Pp. 85, 128, 539

1.7e *Rhus radicans* L.

POISON IVY

Erect shrub, or trailing or high-climbing vine. Leaflets either smooth-margined or with a few large teeth; terminal leaflet stalked. Fully described and illustrated on pp. 186–87. Pp. 87, 540

R. toxicodendron L., poison oak, is an erect shrub up to 3½ feet tall. Stems are usually unbranched, bearing leaves crowded near the summit. Leaflets are obtuse, hairy above and velvety beneath, usually with a slightly lobed margin. Pp. 87, 541

1.8 *Ptelea trifoliata* L.

HOP-TREE, WAFER-ASH

Shrub 5–15 feet tall. Leaves somewhat glossy, bearing minute translucent dots; leaflets 2–6 inches long. Flat, winged fruit ½–1 inch across. Leaf scar surrounding the small, flat, silky bud; terminal bud absent. Pp. 88, 538

1.9 *Xanthorhiza simplicissima* Marsh.
SHRUB YELLOWROOT

Low shrub 12–20 inches tall and only slightly branched. Pinnate leaves and drooping racemes crowded, growing from a large terminal bud. Leaf scars more than half encircling the stem. Wood and roots bright yellow.   Pp. 107, 116, 522

2.1 *Pyrularia pubera* Michx.

BUFFALO-NUT, OILNUT

Shrub 4–12 fet tall. Leaves 2–6 inches long. Fruit about 1 inch long, containing a large stone. Terminal bud absent; lateral buds with short basal scales and elongated, green upper scales.
Pp. 107, 520–21

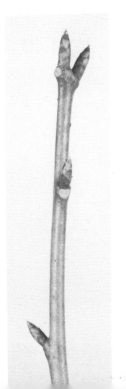

2.2 *Lindera benzoin* (L.) Blume
SPICEBUSH
Spicy-aromatic shrub 6–12 feet tall. Leaves 2–5
inches long. Twigs in winter bearing clustered
flower buds and singly arranged leaf buds.
Pp. 108, 133, 525

2.3 *Dirca palustris* L.

LEATHERWOOD

Shrub 3–7 feet tall. Leaves 2–3½ inches long. Fruit a drupe, ⅜ inch long, greenish or reddish, maturing in May and falling soon. Twigs jointed, covered by tough bark which will not break.
Pp. 108, 551

2.4 *Asimina triloba* (L.) Dunal.

PAPAW

Small tree 10–35 feet tall, sometimes shrubby, described on p. 361.
Pp. 43, 120, 524–25

2.5 *Bumelia lycioides* (L.) Gaertn. f.

BUCKTHORN BUMELIA, SOUTHERN BUCKTHORN

Shrub or small tree 9–25 feet tall. Leaves alternate on new branchlets, clustered on spurs on old wood, 2½–5 inches long, with the margin slightly rolled under. Fruit nearly black, about ½ inch long, in axillary clusters, maturing in October.
Pp. 70, 371, 559

2.6 *Cornus alternifolia* L. f.
ALTERNATE-LEAF DOGWOOD
Large shrub, sometimes treelike and up to
18 feet tall, with a horizontal arrangement
of branches. Leaves 2–4 inches long, crowded
toward the tips of branchlets, differing from
all other dogwoods in being alternate;
petioles up to 2 inches long. Pith white.
Pp. 93, 144, 553

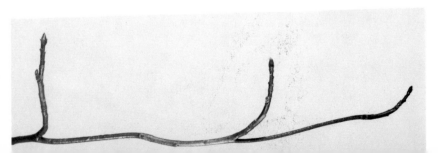

The Genus *Rhododendron* (in part), the AZALEAS

Leaves and buds close together near the ends of branchlets, which often radiate from the ends of older twigs. Leaves hairy along the margin. Capsules 5-celled, persisting through most of the winter. Flower buds much larger than leaf buds. Leaf scar containing a single vascular bundle.

For evergreen species of *Rhododendron*, see pp. 171–72.

2.7a *Rhododendron roseum* (Loisel.) Rehder
ROSE AZALEA

Shrub up to 12 feet in height. Leaves grayish-hairy beneath and slightly hairy above, 2–4 inches long. Capsules and pedicels bearing gland-tipped bristles. Branchlets and buds gray-hairy.

Pp. 62, 557

2.7b *Rhododendron nudiflorum* (L.) Torr.
PINXTER-FLOWER, PINK AZALEA

Shrub up to 8 feet in height. Leaves 2–3½ inches long, acute or (as illustrated) somewhat obtuse, and glabrous except on the margin and the midrib beneath. Capsules with stiff hairs (no glandular hairs). Branchlets slightly hairy or nearly glabrous. Buds red-brown and nearly glabrous.
Pp. 62, 557

2.7c *Rhododendron cumberlandense*
E. L. Braun

RED AZALEA

Shrub up to 10 feet in height. Leaves 1½–2½
inches long, glabrous except on the margin and
the midrib beneath. Branchlets slightly hairy
or nearly glabrous. Buds glabrous, the outer
scales of the flower buds bristle-tipped.
Pp. 64, 557

2.7d *Rhododendron calendulaceum*
   (Michx.) Torr.
   FLAME AZALEA

Shrub up to 12 feet in height. Leaves
2–4 inches long, closely short-hairy
beneath. Capsules and pedicels bearing both fine and stiff hairs. Branchlets with stiff hairs; buds brown, glabrous except for marginal hairs on the
scales.
Pp. 63, 556–57

2.8 *Gaylussacia baccata* (Wang.) K. Koch
HUCKLEBERRY

Much-branched shrub 1–3 feet tall, with slender twigs. Leaves 1–2 inches long, bearing small yellowish, resinous globules on the lower surface.
Pp. 76, 141, 554

2.9a *Vaccinium stamineum* L.
DEERBERRY, SQUAWBERRY

Shrub 2–5 feet tall. Principal leaves 1½–3 inches long, usually pale beneath; leaflike bracts on flowering and fruiting branchlets much smaller than leaves on vegetative branches. Berries greenish, yellowish, or pale purple, usually glaucous, ⅜–½ inch in diameter, and inedible, ripening in July to August.
Pp. 77, 558

2.9b *Vaccinium arboreum* Marsh.
FARKLEBERRY

Shrub, often treelike, up to 18 feet in height. Leaves 1–2 inches long, lustrous and firm but not evergreen in Kentucky. Berries shiny black at maturity (October), about ¼ inch in diameter, dry and inedible.
Pp. 77, 558

The BLUEBERRIES, a subgenus of *Vaccinium*, often growing in colonies, are shrubs with slender greenish or reddish,
granular-surfaced twigs. Flowers are urn-shaped, and the berry
is many-seeded, blue or dark purple, either with or without
a frosty coating. As in the other subgenera of *Vaccinium*
(which include *V. arboreum* and *V. stamineum*) and in
Gaylussacia, all buds are small, leaf buds being slender and
flower buds plump, and there is one bundle scar per leaf
scar.

Of the following five species of blueberries, the two lowbush species (2.9c and d) can easily be separated from the
two highbush species (2.9f), and usually from the medium-
high species (2.9e). However, all species are variable and precise identification is often difficult. Hybridization can occur
within each group, and crossing long ago has resulted in intermediates of varying degrees in regard to different characters; one may even sometimes find both leaves and berries
characteristic of two species on the same bush.

For more detailed study, consult the standard manuals (see
page 568) and W. H. Camp, "The North American Blueberries, with notes on other groups of Vacciniaceae," *Brittonia*
5 (1945): 203–75.

2.9c *Vaccinium vacillans*
Torr.

LOWBUSH
BLUEBERRY

Stems 8–20 inches tall. Leaves
¾–1⅝ inches long, variable
in shape but at least a few
obtuse, usually glabrous but
occasionally hairy, usually
smooth-margined but occa-
sionally slightly fine-toothed.
Pp. 78, 142, 558

2.9d *Vaccinium pallidum* Ait.
LOWBUSH BLUEBERRY
Stems 1–3 feet tall. Leaves 1–2
inches long, usually acute, usually very finely toothed, completely glabrous or hairy along
the veins.
Pp. 78, 142, 558

2.9e *Vaccinium alto-montanum* Ashe
MOUNTAIN DRYLAND BLUEBERRY
Stems 2–4 feet tall. Leaves narrowly elliptic, 1⅜–2 inches long,
glaucous or pale green, smooth-margined, and glabrous (rarely
slightly hairy beneath).
Pp. 143, 557–58

2.9f *Vaccinium simulatum* Small
Vaccinium constablaei Gray
HIGHBUSH BLUEBERRIES

The two species vegetatively similar. V. *simulatum* up to 10 feet tall, V. *constablaei* up to 15 feet. Leaves in V. *simulatum* up to 1¼ inches wide (averaging 1 inch), in V. *constablaei* up to 1½ inches wide (averaging 1¼). Leaves in both 2–2¾ inches long, smooth-margined or finely toothed, completely glabrous or hairy on the midvein beneath.
Pp. 79, 143, 558

(Continued)

V. *simulatum* and V. *constablaei*
(*continued*)

The Genus *Salix*, the WILLOWS

Alternate-leaved trees or shrubs. Flowers lacking a perianth and borne in catkins, the staminate and pistillate borne on different plants. Fruit a small capsule; each seed bearing a tuft of long hairs. Each bud covered by a single scale. The arborescent species of willow, though sometimes suggesting shrubs when young, are illustrated on pp. 395–97.

2.10a *Salix sericea* Marsh.
SILKY WILLOW
Shrub 4–15 feet tall. Leaves 2–4 inches long, dark green and glabrous or nearly so above, silvery-silky beneath with appressed glistening hairs; stipules conspicuous on vigorous shoots, soon deciduous. Pistillate catkins ¾–1¼ inches long when seeds mature (as illustrated); mature capsules silky, ⅛–¼ inch long.
Pp. 106, 503

2.10b *Salix discolor* Muhl.
PUSSY WILLOW

Large shrub or small tree 6–18 feet
tall. Leaves wavy-margined and
veiny, 2–3½ inches long, glaucous
beneath, glabrous or nearly so
above; stipules roundish and conspicuous. Buds of 2 sizes, the larger
ones producing catkins before the
growth of leaves from the smaller
buds. Pistillate catkins (illustrated)
becoming 1–3 inches long in fruit;
the woolly capsules about ⅜ inch
long.
Pp. 106, 373, 502

2.10c *Salix interior* Rowlee
SANDBAR WILLOW

Shrub with numerous upright stems, 4–12 feet tall, forming large colonies. Leaves 2–5 inches long, glabrous when mature but silky-hairy when young; teeth widely spaced and somewhat outwardly pointing; stipules absent. Catkins 1–3 inches long, borne on lateral leafy branchlets, appearing after the leaves have grown (pistillate illustrated). Bark gray; branchlets reddish brown. Pp. 105, 502

2.10d *Salix humilis* Marsh. UPLAND WILLOW, PRAIRIE WILLOW
Shrub 3–7 feet tall with many stems. Leaves 2–4 inches long, varying
from linear-oblanceolate (as illustrated) to nearly obovate, either pale
and glaucous (without hairs) or white-woolly beneath; margin often wavy,
usually slightly rolled under. Catkins averaging nearly 1 inch in length
(shedding seed in illustration).
Pp. 106, 502

S. tristis Ait., dwarf upland willow, is a similar species but smaller in every respect. Stems are 2–3 feet tall, with leaves 1¼–2 inches long and narrowly
oblanceolate, and with catkins about ½ inch long. P. 503

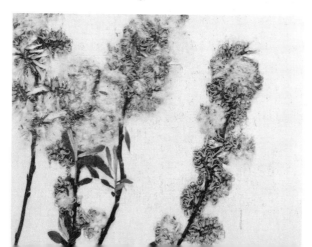

2.10e *Salix rigida* Muhl.
HEART-LEAF WILLOW
Shrub 6–12 feet tall. Leaves 3–5
inches long, finely toothed, and
rounded at the base; stipules roundish and conspicuous. Catkins 1–2
inches long; capsules smooth,
about ¼ inch long at maturity
(shedding seed in the illustration).
P. 503

2.10f *Salix caroliniana* Michx.
CAROLINA WILLOW
Shrub 4–10 feet tall or rarely a tree
up to 25 feet in height. Leaves 3–5
inches long, glaucous beneath;
stipules roundish, glaucous beneath, often as much as ½ inch
long. Catkins slender, 1½–4 inches
long and ⅜–½ inch wide, developing with the leaves and flowering
in May.
P. 502

2.11 *Alnus serrulata* (Ait.) Willd.

COMMON ALDER

Shrub with smooth fluted trunks up to 18 feet tall. Leaves finely toothed, 2–4 inches long. Staminate catkins originating in summer, becoming conspicuous in winter, the flowers maturing in early spring before leaves appear. Fruit woody and cone-like, the fruiting bracts persisting after the nuts escape. Leaf buds stalked, with few scales. Pp. 102, 507

2.12 *Corylus americana* Walt.
AMERICAN HAZELNUT

Shrub 4–10 feet tall. Leaves 2-ranked, hairy beneath, and usually 3–4 inches long. Staminate catkins about 2 inches long, conspicuous all winter, maturing in late February or early March. Nuts, maturing in October, enclosed in a leafy cup of 2 bracts. Branchlets usually hairy; buds 2-ranked.

Pp. 102, 508–09

2.13 *Hamamelis virginiana* L.

WITCH-HAZEL

Large shrub 6–18 feet tall, with spreading
branches bearing flattened sprays of leaves.
Leaves 2–4 inches long, and oblique at
the base. Capsules woody, not splitting until a
year after flowering. Bark smooth and gray;
buds stalked, without scales, and 2-ranked.
Pp. 44, 527

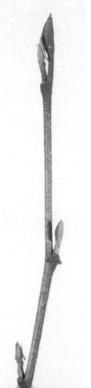

2.14 *Itea virginica* L.
VIRGINIA-WILLOW

Shrub up to 9 feet in height. Leaves 2½–3½ inches long. Capsules about ⅜ inch long, grooved and 2-parted. Lateral buds small and round, terminal bud conical; leaf scars small, half-round, and not raised. Pith white, with diaphragms.
Pp. 72, 526

2.15a *Aronia melanocarpa* (Michx.) Ell.
BLACK CHOKEBERRY
Slender shrub 2–3 feet tall. Leaves 2–3 inches long,
finely toothed, bearing minute glands along the midrib on the upper surface. Leaf scars shallowly U-shaped;
buds oblong and pressed against the stem.
Pp. 82, 134, 529

2.15b *Aronia arbutifolia* (L.) Ell.
RED CHOKEBERRY
Shrub 3–10 feet tall. Young branchlets and lower surface of leaves densely
and softly white-woolly; leaves 1–3
inches long. Winter buds hairy; otherwise buds and leaf scars as in A.
melanocarpa.
Pp. 82, 132, 529

A. *prunifolia* (Marsh.) Rehder, the purple chokeberry, is similar to A. *arbutifolia*
but is less hairy and has purple fruit.
Pp. 82, 529

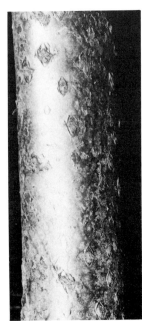

2.16a *Prunus angustifolia* Marsh.   CHICKASAW PLUM
Large shrub up to 13 feet in height, often forming thickets;
branches numerous and crooked, some short ones resembling
thorns, branchlets reddish and glabrous.   Leaves 1–3 inches long,
lanceolate, and usually folded; petioles red.
Pp. 45, 121, 407, 531

2.16b *Prunus virginiana* L.
  CHOKE CHERRY
Large shrub or small tree up to 20 feet in
height. Leaves oblong, 2–4 inches long. Twigs
with rank odor (not aromatic or almond-like as
in *P. serotina*, pp. 412–13). Buds ¼–⅜ inch
long, dull brown, the scales appearing dotted
and sometimes with light margins.
Pp. 72, 129, 414, 532

2.17a *Ilex decidua* Walt.

SWAMP HOLLY, POSSUM-HAW

Tall shrub or small tree up to 25 feet in height, with light gray bark. Leaves 1½–3 inches long, usually in bundles on short branchlets or alternate on vigorous shoots.
Pp. 96, 124, 541

2.17b *Ilex montana* T. & G.
  MOUNTAIN WINTERBERRY
Shrub or small tree up to 20 feet in height. Leaves
2½–5 inches long, thin, and usually long-pointed.
Pp. 96, 125, 541

2.17c *Ilex verticillata* (L.) Gray
  WINTERBERRY
Shrub 6–15 feet tall. Leaves dull, either thick or
thin, usually veiny, and 1½–4 inches long.
Pp. 96, 125, 542

2.18 *Ceanothus americanus* L.   NEW JERSEY TEA

Shrub 2–3½ feet tall. Leaves usually 2–3 inches long, velvety-hairy beneath, with 3 main veins from the base. Fruit 3-lobed, falling away and leaving a cup-shaped base which persists through winter, facilitating recognition. Pp. 75, 546

2.19a *Rhamnus caroliniana*
 Walt.

CAROLINA BUCKTHORN

Tall shrub or small tree up
to 25 feet in height. Leaves
lustrous, 2½–5 inches long;
margin obscurely fine-
toothed, the lateral veins
curving before reaching the
margin. Buds without scales,
the terminal bud ⅜ to nearly
½ inch long. Bark gray.
Pp. 99, 127, 418, 547

2.19b *Rhamnus lanceolata* Pursh
LANCE-LEAF BUCKTHORN
Shrub 4–6 feet tall. Leaves 1½–3½ inches
long, the lateral veins curving before reaching
the margin. Buds with overlapping scales.
Pp. 99, 135, 547

2.20 *Stewartia ovata* (Cav.)
Weatherby
MOUNTAIN CAMELLIA
Shrub or small tree up to 16
feet in height. Leaves 3–6 inches
long, hairy beneath, and finely
or obscurely toothed. Capsule
about 1 inch long, 5-angled, and
hairy. Buds hairy; leaf scar containing a single bundle trace.
Pp. 54, 419, 550

2.21 *Clethra acuminata* Michx.　MOUNTAIN PEPPERBUSH

Shrub 5–15 feet tall having hairy branchlets with leaves and leaf scars clustered toward the tips. Leaves usually 3–5 inches long on soft-hairy petioles ½–1 inch long. Capsules and axis of raceme hairy; capsules about ⅛ inch wide, splitting in 3 parts, the old raceme hanging on through winter. Leaf scar triangular with a single bundle scar slightly protruding. Lateral buds small and obscure, the terminal bud ovoid with loosely spreading scales. Bark red-brown with light streaks.
Pp. 75, 554

2.22 *Lyonia ligustrina* (L.) DC.
PRIVET-ANDROMEDA,
MALE-BERRY

Shrub up to 10 feet in height.
Leaves 1¼–2¾ inches long, and
very finely toothed. Flowers (June)
borne in clusters in the leaf axils
or on a leafless branchlet that is
terminal on a stem of the previous
year, thus forming either a leafy or
a naked panicle. Corolla roundish,
about ⅛ inch across; capsule
spherical, slightly more than ⅛
inch in diameter.
Pp. 84, 555

2.23 *Halesia carolina* L.
SILVERBELL
A small tree fully described
on pp. 416–17. Leaves 3–4
inches long, finely toothed,
and thinly hairy beneath.
Fruit oblong, longitudinally
winged, about 1½ inches
long.
Pp. 56, 416–17, 559

2.24 *Styrax americana* Lam.   SNOWBELL
Erect slender shrub 5–9 feet tall; branchlets zigzag with leaves and buds 2-ranked. Leaves 1–4 inches long; principal lateral veins prolonged beyond the margin, producing a few shallow teeth. Fruit a dry hairy drupe about ⅜ inch in diameter, maturing in September.
Pp. 56, 560

S. grandifolia Ait., the large-leaf snowbell, has branchlets densely hairy; leaves are 3½–6 inches long, densely gray-woolly beneath; lateral veins are curving and do not end in teeth. Pp. 56, 560

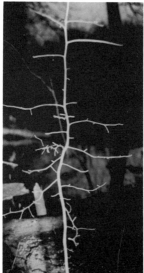

2.25a *Spiraea tomentosa* L.
STEEPLEBUSH, HARDHACK

Shrub 2–4 feet tall with slender erect stems, papery bark, and woolly branchlets. Leaves 1½–2¾ inches long, either acute or blunt at the apex, the lower surface covered with light tawny wool. Panicles of dry split fruits persisting through winter, thus facilitating recognition; usually 5 small "pods" produced per flower, each less than ⅛ inch long. Leaf scars raised; buds small and hairy.
Pp. 81, 536

2.25b *Spiraea alba* DuRoi
MEADOWSWEET

Shrub 2½–4½ feet tall with slender erect stems, papery bark, and slightly hairy branchlets. Leaves 1½–2¾ inches long, either acute or blunt at the apex, and glabrous or sparingly hairy. Fruit over ⅛ inch in length, otherwise as in *S. tomentosa*.
Pp. 82, 535

2.25c *Spiraea japonica* L. f.
JAPANESE SPIRAEA

Slender-stemmed shrub 3–5 feet tall. Leaves
2½–4 inches long, pale beneath. Flat-topped
clusters of old split "pods" (5 produced per
flower) persisting through winter, each about
⅛ inch long.
Pp. 81, 535–36

2.26 *Rubus odoratus* L.
FLOWERING RASPBERRY
Shrub 1½–4 feet tall; stems without prickles. Young stems, petioles,
pedicels, and calyx bearing bristly glandular hairs. Leaves 4–6
inches long, and hairy. Fruit red,
somewhat dry and inedible. Bark
light tan, and shredding.
Pp. 52, 535

2.27 *Comptonia peregrina* (L.) Coult.

SWEET-FERN

Shrub up to 3 feet in height with much-branched stems. Leaves slender, 3–5 inches long, deeply lobed, resinous-dotted, and fragrant. Flowers in catkins, the staminate cylindric and the pistillate roundish, becoming burlike in fruit. P. 503

2.28 *Ribes cynosbati* L.
PRICKLY GOOSE-
BERRY
Spreading shrub 2–4 feet tall.
Leaves 1–2¾ inches across,
in bundles on short lateral
branchlets and alternate on
fast-growing twigs. Stems
usually bearing 1–3 spines
at a node, young stems often
prickly along internodes.
Fruit about ½ inch in di-
ameter, maturing in August.
Pp. 95, 526

R. missouriense Nutt., the Missouri gooseberry, has smooth
fruit. P. 526

2.29 *Physocarpus opulifolius* (L.) Maxim. NINEBARK
Shrub up to 9 feet in height. Leaves 1½–3 inches long, 3-
lobed on vegetative branches but often unlobed on fertile
branches. Pods reddish or purplish brown, usually 3 produced
per flower, each splitting along 2 lines, averaging about ⅜
inch in length, persisting in winter. Twigs with lines extending down from the nodes; leaf scars raised. Bark shredding
in thin brown strips.
Pp. 71, 530–31

Series Seven: Deciduous Trees (1)

With Opposite Leaves,* Leaf Scars, and Buds, Grouped According to Vegetative Characters

ARRANGEMENT OF PLATES

Group 1. With palmately compound leaves   1.1

Group 2. With pinnately compound leaves   2.1–2.2

Group 3. With lobed simple leaves   3.1

Group 4. With toothed or smooth-margined simple leaves   4.1–4.5

---

* See diagrams on pages 569, 570, and 573.

In woody plants with either simple or compound leaves, buds can usually be seen in the leaf axils except when leaves are immature.

Note that in woody plants with compound leaves the lateral buds are on the stem and not in the axils of leaflets on the rachis.

Note also that alternate compound leaves may have opposite leaflets.

The Genus *Aesculus*, the BUCKEYES

Leaves palmately compound, the leaflets 5 in our native species. Twigs, terminal buds, and leaf scars relatively large. Fruit a capsule 1–3 inches long containing 1, 2, or 3 seeds; each seed about 1–1½ inches in diameter, lustrous, and dark brown, with a light spot.

1.1a *Aesculus pavia* L.
RED BUCKEYE
Small tree up to 20 feet tall.
Leaflets 4–7 inches long.
Capsules smooth.
Pp. 60, 546

1.1b *Aesculus glabra* Willd.
OHIO BUCKEYE
Tree up to 50 feet tall. Leaflets
3–6 inches long. Capsule with
weak prickles. Twigs strongly
ill-smelling when cut or broken.
Bark scaly, becoming furrowed
on old trunks.
Pp. 59, 545–46

1.1c *Aesculus octandra* Marsh.
YELLOW BUCKEYE,
SWEET BUCKEYE
Tree up to 90 feet in height.
Leaflets as in A. *glabra*. Capsules without prickles. Twigs
not ill-scented. Bark smooth
when young, furrowed and
broken into irregular plates
when old.
Pp. 60, 546

The Genus *Fraxinus*, the ASHES

Leaves pinnately compound. Fruit 1-seeded and winged, resembling the blade of a canoe paddle; seed thick in all Kentucky species except *F. quadrangulata*. Twigs stout, upturned (see p. 304); buds and leaf scars relatively large, the leaf scars with numerous bundle scars; bud scales with a somewhat granular texture. For flowers, see page 111.

F. americana

2.1a *Fraxinus americana* L. WHITE ASH

Large tree up to 100 feet in height. Leaves 8–12 inches long, usually with 7 (5–9) leaflets, white or whitish beneath, with some variation in shape. Fruit 1¼–2 inches long, the wing not overlapping the seed. Buds brown; leaf scar notched below the bud. Bark dark, with ridges and furrows, the ridges often but not always cut crosswise (as in illustration). P. 560

F. americana var. *biltmoreana* (Beadle) J. Wright, the Biltmore ash, also with leaflets whitened beneath, differs in having branchlets, petioles, and lower leaf surfaces velvety-hairy. P. 561

2.1b *Fraxinus quadrangulata* Michx. BLUE ASH

Tall tree up to 90 feet but with a narrow crown even
when growing in the open. Leaves 8–12 inches long
with 7–11 slender, long-pointed leaflets, characteristically
bent downward from the rachis on a mature tree,
broader and more spreading on a young tree. Wing of
fruit blunt at the apex and nearly surrounding the flat
seed at the base. Twigs either strongly or obscurely
4-angled; buds gray or tawny; leaf scar concave below
the bud. Bark light gray and scaly, developing a pattern of fissures on an old trunk.
Pp. 111, 561

2.1c *Fraxinus pennsylvanica* Marsh. var. *subintegerrima* (Vahl) Fernald
GREEN ASH

Tree up to 60 feet, with spreading branches. Leaves 10–12 inches long
with 7–9 leaflets, lustrous and bright green on both surfaces. Wing of
fruit extending to the middle of the seed. Buds brown; upper margin of
leaf scar straight or convex. (Bark of old tree illustrated.)
P. 561

F. pennsylvanica Marsh. (typical variety), the red ash, has branchlets, buds, petioles,
and leaf rachises hairy. It is easily distinguished from the Biltmore ash, which has
leaflets whitened beneath, and is best distinguished from the pumpkin ash by
leaf scars which are straight or convex on the upper margin, fruit 1–2½ inches
long, and fruiting calyx less than ⅛ inch long. P. 561

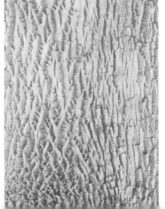

2.1d *Fraxinus tomentosa* Michx. f.
PUMPKIN ASH

Tall tree up to 90 feet in height with short-spreading branches forming a narrow crown. Leaves 9–18 inches long, usually with 7 (5–9) leaflets, thick and firm in texture; leaflets, rachis, and petiole densely velvety-hairy. (Leaflets may be long-pointed and more slender than those illustrated.) Fruit 2–3 inches long at maturity, the wing extending to the middle of the seed or beyond; fruiting calyx more than ⅛ inch long. Branchlets densely velvety-hairy; leaf scars concave at the top; buds hairy. Bark gray with shallow fissures. Compare with the red ash, described at left.
P. 561

The Genus *Acer*, the MAPLES

Leaves simple with palmate lobes and venation in all species except A. *negundo*, which has pinnately compound leaves. Fruit 2-seeded and double-winged. Leaf scars broadly U-shaped.

2.2 *Acer negundo* L.   BOX ELDER

Medium-sized tree up to 60 feet in height, the trunk usually dividing near the base into several stout spreading or erect branches. Leaves with 3–5 leaflets; petioles 2–3 inches long, enlarged at the base. Year-old branchlets bright green. Bark smooth when young, furrowed on old trees.

Pp. 110, 543

3.1a *Acer saccharum* Marsh.
  SUGAR MAPLE

Large tree up to 100 feet in height.
Leaf blades flat, often pale beneath,
and 3–5 inches long; petioles slender, not greatly enlarged at the base.
Fruit ripening in late summer.
Winter buds brown. Bark smooth
and light gray when young, gray-
brown and furrowed between scaly
ridges on old trunks.
Pp. 25, 110, 545

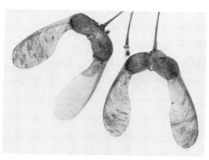

3.1b *Acer nigrum* Michx. f.
BLACK MAPLE,
BLACK SUGAR
MAPLE

Large tree similar to A. *saccharum*, differing as follows: leaf blades 4–6 inches long, curved downward at the sides, dull dark green above, yellow-green beneath; petioles abruptly thickened near the base and enclosing the lateral buds; stipules present. Winter buds dark brown or almost black. Pp. 543–44

3.1c *Acer saccharinum* L.
SILVER MAPLE,
WATER MAPLE

Large tree up to 90 feet in height. Leaves 3–7 inches long, deeply 5-lobed; margin of lobes toothed; blades white beneath. Flowers usually opening in late February; fruit ripening in April or May. Branchlets upturned from spreading branches; rank odor in broken twigs. Flower buds roundish and clustered; leaf buds slender. Bark gray, smooth on young trees and scaly on old trunks.
Pp. 544–45

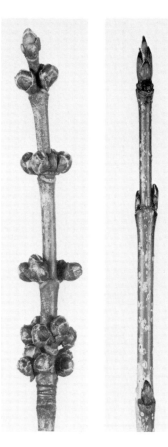

A. *rubrum* (typical)

A. *rubrum* (var.) *trilobum*

3.1d *Acer rubrum* L.   RED MAPLE

Large tree up to 100 feet tall with somewhat upright branches
usually forming a fairly narrow crown. Leaves 2–5 inches long,
3–5 lobed, the lobes with toothed margins; blades white beneath;
petioles usually red. Twigs not upturned at the tips and without
rank odor when broken (in contrast to A. *saccharinum*). Flower
buds illustrated; leaf buds more slender. Bark on young trees
and branches light gray and smooth, becoming shallowly fissured
on old trunks.
Pp. 27, 98, 117, 544

A. *rubrum* var. *trilobum* K.
Koch, has leaves 3-lobed and
rounded at the base. Otherwise it is like the typical
variety. P. 544

3.1e *Acer pensylvanicum* L. STRIPED MAPLE

Slender tree up to only 30 feet in height with small
and somewhat upright branches. Leaves 3-lobed,
finely toothed, 4–6 inches long. Flowers (late May)
and fruit (summer) in long drooping racemes. Buds
bright red, and stalked. Bark of young trunk and
branches striped.
Pp. 74, 544

A. spicatum, more shrubby than arborescent, is illustrated
on p. 230.

4.1a *Catalpa bignonioides* Walt.
SOUTHERN CATALPA, INDIAN BEAN

Tree up to 50 feet in height, irregularly spreading, with a wide crown. Leaves opposite or whorled, 5–8 inches long, with points shorter than those of *C. speciosa*, ill-scented when bruised, and hairy beneath. Capsules 6–16 inches long, ¼–⅜ inch thick in the middle, and thin-walled, each half flat after splitting. Bark thin and scaly.
Pp. 66, 562

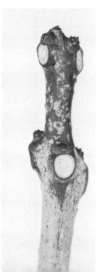

4.1b *Catalpa speciosa* Warder
NORTHERN CATALPA, CIGAR-TREE

Tree up to 90 feet in height, usually taller than broad. Leaves opposite or whorled, 6–12 inches long, not ill-scented when bruised, and hairy beneath. Capsules 8–20 inches long, ½–¾ inch thick in the middle, and thick-walled, each half remaining convex after splitting. Bark thick and furrowed.
Pp. 66, 563

4.2 *Paulownia tomentosa*
(Thunb.) Steud.
ROYAL PAULOWNIA,
PRINCESS-TREE
Tree up to 50 feet in height
with a roundish crown.
Leaves opposite, or occasionally whorled, velvety beneath,
6–13 inches long, and rarely
lobed. Capsules 1¼–1¾
inches across. Bark with an
interlacing pattern.
Pp. 66, 563

4.3 *Cornus florida* L. FLOWERING DOGWOOD

Small tree up to 30 or rarely 40 feet in height with spreading branches and branchlets curving upward at the tip. Leaves 2–5 inches long and opposite, with smooth margins; lateral veins curving toward the apex, following the line of the leaf margin. Flower buds buttonlike; terminal leaf buds pointed, with 1 pair of scales. Bark checkered.
Pp. 93, 123, 552

Other species of dogwoods are shrubby rather than arborescent and are illustrated on pp. 216–19.

4.4 *Forestiera acuminata* (Michx.) Poir. SWAMP PRIVET

Small tree up to 25 feet in height, in Kentucky rarely over 15 feet; often a tree-like shrub. Described and illustrated on page 234. Pp. 111, 139, 560

4.5a *Viburnum pruni-folium* L. BLACK-HAW

4.5b V. *rufidulum* Raf. SOUTHERN BLACK-HAW

Small trees up to 20 or 30 feet in height, or shrubs. Described and illustrated with other species of *Viburnum* on pages 223–25.

Series Eight: Deciduous Trees (2)

With Alternate Compound Leaves*
and Alternate Leaf Scars and Buds,
Grouped According to Vegetative Characters

ARRANGEMENT OF PLATES

Group 1. *With bipinnate leaves (some with pinnate leaves also)*
1.1–1.2

Group 2. *With pinnate leaves only*   2.1–2.5

* See diagrams on pages 569, 570, and 573.

In woody plants with either simple or compound leaves, buds can usually be seen in the leaf axils except when leaves are immature.

Note that in woody plants with compound leaves the lateral buds are on the stem and not in the axils of leaflets on the rachis.

Note also that alternate compound leaves may have opposite leaflets.

1.1 *Gymnocladus dioica* (L.) K. Koch
KENTUCKY COFFEE-TREE

Slender tree up to 75–100 feet in height. Winter silhouette: irregular stout branchlets without small twigs. Summer aspect: lacy
foliage. Leaves twice pinnate, 1–3 feet long; leaflets 1¼–1½ inches
long. Staminate and pistillate flowers on different trees. Pods (borne
only on pistillate trees) 5–8 inches long; seeds separated by dark
sweet pulp. Pith of branchlets salmon-pink. Bark ridges curling out
at the sides.
P. 537

1.2a *Gleditsia triacanthos* L.   HONEY LOCUST
Tree up to 100 feet in height with slender spreading branches, usually somewhat flat-topped. Leaves pinnate and bipinnate; leaflets ½–1½ inches long. Pods 8–15 inches long, often twisted, containing sweet pulp around the seeds. Thorns stout and branched, frequently abundant but occasionally few or absent. Bark with fissures and ridges roughened especially on the edges.
Pp. 536–37

1.2b *Gleditsia aquatica* Marsh.
  WATER LOCUST
Tree up to 50 feet in height,
usually with stout spreading
branches forming a broad
crown. Leaves pinnate and
bipinnate; leaflets ¾–1 inch
long. Pods 1½–2 inches long,
usually containing 1 seed, rarely
more. Thorns 2–4 inches long,
unbranched or with short
branches. Bark smooth when
young; old trunk developing
shallow fissures and small scales.
P. 536

2.1 *Cladrastis lutea*
  (Michx. f.) K. Koch
  YELLOW-WOOD
Tree up to 50 feet in height,
with slender widely-spreading
branches forming a round crown.
Trunk usually divided fairly near
the base. Leaves pinnate; leaflets
alternate, 2–3 inches long. Leaf
bases, and hence leaf scars, surrounding the buds. Pods about
3 inches long when mature.
Bark smooth and gray.
Pp. 57, 536

2.2 *Robinia pseudo-acacia* L.
BLACK LOCUST

Medium-sized tree up to 75 feet in height, with small, somewhat erect branches forming a narrow crown. Leaves pinnate; leaflets 1–2 inches long. Paired spines at many nodes, developing from the stipules in about a year. Pods 2–4 inches long. Bark deeply furrowed.
Pp. 58, 537–38

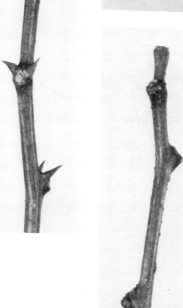

2.3 *Ailanthus altissima* (Mill.) Swingle
TREE-OF-HEAVEN, AILANTHUS

Medium-sized tree with oval crown and stout erect branchlets. Leaves pinnate, 12–24 inches long; leaflets with 1–3 gland-tipped teeth near the base. Bark thin and smooth on young trees, becoming only slightly fissured on old trunks. Pp. 87, 117, 539

The Genus *Juglans*, the WALNUTS

Trees with stout branchlets and aromatic foliage. Leaves pinnate, 1–2 feet long; leaflets 2–3½ inches long. Nut roughly sculptured, the hull not splitting. Pith chambered, with thin cross-plates. Leaf scars large and 3-lobed, with 3 U-shaped clusters of bundle scars.

2.4a *Juglans cinerea* L.
BUTTERNUT,
WHITE WALNUT
Medium-sized tree rarely attaining a height of 75 feet. Leaves clammy, with 11–17 leaflets. Fruit oblong; hull hairy and clammy. Nut pointed, bearing 4 longitudinal ridges. Terminal buds elongate. Leaf scars with a downy pad on the upper margin. Pith brown. Bark with light gray, smooth ridges between the furrows. Pp. 100, 506

2.4b *Juglans nigra* L.   BLACK WALNUT

Large tree up to 100–125 feet in height. Branches
upwardly spreading, forming a round-topped crown.
Leaves with 11–23 leaflets. Nut nearly spherical.
Terminal buds broadly ovoid. Leaf scars without a
downy pad as found in the butternut. Pith light-
colored. Bark dark brown and furrowed; ridges rough.
Pp. 100, 506–07

The Genus *Carya*, the HICKORIES

Foliage aromatic. Leaves usually with fewer leaflets than in the walnuts. Nuts smooth or wrinkled. Pith solid. Leaf scars oval or roundish, usually slightly 3-lobed, with clusters of small bundle scars. For catkins, see page 100.

2.5a *Carya illinoensis* (Wang.) K. Koch   PECAN
Tall tree with slender branchlets. Leaflets 9–17, somewhat curved, and 3–6 inches long. Fruit 1½–2½ inches long. Terminal bud with a pair of scales meeting at the edges. Bark fissured, with narrow scaly ridges.
Pp. 504–05

2.5b *Carya cordiformis* (Wang.) K. Koch
BITTERNUT HICKORY
Tall tree, sometimes nearly 100 feet. Leaflets 7–9, each 3–5
inches long. Fruit ¾–1⅜ inches long; hull thin, splitting
halfway; shell thin; kernel very bitter. Terminal buds bright
yellow and scurfy, with a pair of scales meeting at the edges.
Bark with shallow fissures.
P. 504

2.5c *Carya aquatica*
(Michx. f.) Nutt.
WATER HICKORY

Medium-sized tree occasionally reaching 75 feet in height. Leaflets 7–13, each 3–5 inches long. Fruit about 1½ inches long with a thin hull tardily splitting; shell thin and wrinkled. Bark shaggy with long loose strips.
P. 504

2.5d *Carya tomentosa* Nutt.
MOCKERNUT, WHITE HICKORY

Medium sized tree up to 75 feet in height. Twigs, leaf rachis, and lower surface of leaflets hairy. Leaflets usually 7 (5–9), the largest 4–7 inches long. Fruit 1¼–2 inches long; hull thick, tardily splitting; shell thick. Terminal buds ½–¾ inch long, the outer scales deciduous in autumn, leaving silky inner scales in winter. Bark tight, with a network of shallow fissures.
Pp. 504, 506

2.5e *Carya ovata* (Mill.) K. Koch
SHAGBARK HICKORY, SHELLBARK HICKORY
Tall tree up to a height of 75 or sometimes 100 feet. Leaflets
5, the terminal one 5–7 inches long and larger than the others;
margin with a tuft of hairs on the side of each tooth. Fruit
1¼–2 inches long; hull thick, splitting readily; shell thin.
Terminal buds ½–¾ inch long; tips of the outer scales slightly prolonged. Bark smooth on a young trunk, shaggy when
mature.
Pp. 100, 504, 505

2.5f *Carya laciniosa* (Michx. f.) Loud.
  BIG SHAGBARK HICKORY,
  BIG SHELLBARK HICKORY, KINGNUT
Tall tree up to 100 feet in height. Leaflets usually 7 (5–9),
the largest 4–8 inches long. Fruit 1¾–2½ inches long;
hull thick, splitting readily; shell very thick. Terminal bud
¾–1 inch long; scales with spreading tips. Bark smooth
on a young trunk, shaggy when mature.
Pp. 504, 505

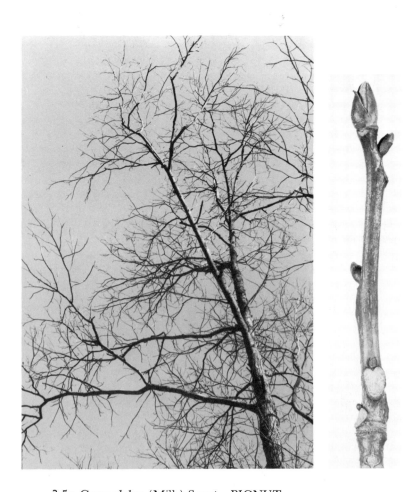

2.5g *Carya glabra* (Mill.) Sweet   PIGNUT

Tree up to 60–70 feet in height with small spreading
branches forming a somewhat narrow crown. Leaflets
usually 5 (5–7). Fruit 1–1½ inches long; hull thin, usually
not splitting; shell thin. Terminal buds less than ½ inch
long. Branchlets slender. Bark tight, fissured on old trunks.
P. 504

C. pallida (Ashe) Engl. & Graebn., the pale hickory, is similar,
differing chiefly in having silvery scales on the lower surfaces of
leaflets and on winter buds. P. 505

2.5h *Carya ovalis* (Wang.) Sarg.

SWEET PIGNUT, SMALL-FRUITED HICKORY

Tree up to 75 feet in height with a narrow crown, similar in appearance to C. *glabra*. Leaflets usually 7 (5–7). Fruit usually about 1 inch long; hull thin and splitting; shell thin; kernel sweeter than that of C. *glabra*. Branchlets slender; terminal buds less than ½ inch long. Bark tight and fissured, or slightly scaly in long narrow strips. P. 505

Series Nine: Deciduous Trees (3)

With Alternate Simple Leaves*
and Alternate Leaf Scars and Buds
Grouped According to Vegetative Characters

ARRANGEMENT OF PLATES

Group 1. With smooth-margined leaves
    Branchlets feathery with soft linear leaves 1.1
    Leaves 6 inches or more in length 1.2–1.3
    Leaves averaging less than 6 inches in length
        Pinnately veined 1.4–1.9
        Palmately veined 1.10–1.11

Group 2. With toothed leaves
    Palmately veined 2.1–2.4c
    Pinnately veined
        Lateral veins curving before reaching
        the margin 2.4d–2.13
        Lateral veins extending straight to the margin
        Teeth more numerous than the main
        lateral veins 2.14–2.18
        Teeth equal in number to the main
        lateral veins (a vein extending to
        each tooth) 2.19–2.21

Group 3. With lobed leaves
    Pinnately lobed 3.1–3.5
    Palmately lobed 3.6–3.10

---

* See diagrams on pages 569, 570, and 573.

In woody plants with either simple or compound leaves, buds can usually be seen in the leaf axils except when leaves are immature.

Note that in woody plants with compound leaves the lateral buds are on the stem and not in the axils of leaflets on the rachis.

Note also that alternate compound leaves may have opposite leaflets.

1.1 *Taxodium distichum* (L.) Richard.

BALD CYPRESS

A deciduous conifer up to 125 feet in height, pyramidal when young, round-topped when old, slender when growing in a forest. Trunk buttressed at the base and roots developing "knees" when growing in standing water. Foliage feathery; leaves ¼–¾ inch long, soft, and light green; branchlets usually deciduous with the leaves. Staminate cones numerous in drooping panicles; seed-bearing cones spherical, about 1 inch in diameter, with closely fitting scales, maturing in autumn. Bark with flat ridges, fibrous and shredding.

Pp. 498-99

The Genus *Magnolia*

Leaves large, smooth-margined, and alternate. Branchlets encircled at each node by a line left as a stipular scar (the stipules functioning as bud scales). Leaf scars containing numerous bundle scars.

1.2a *Magnolia acuminata* L. CUCUMBER-TREE, CUCUMBER MAGNOLIA

Tree up to 75 feet in height. Leaves 6–9 inches long, scattered along the branchlets in contrast to our other magnolias which have leaves clustered near the tip. Winter buds densely covered with long lustrous hairs.

Pp. 41, 114, 523

1.2b *Magnolia fraseri* Walt.

FRASER'S MAGNOLIA, MOUNTAIN MAGNOLIA

Tree up to 40 feet in height with stout branches and branchlets. Leaves 10–15 inches long with ear-like lobes at the base. Buds smooth and purplish. Bark brown, either smooth or warty, slightly scaly on very old trunks. Pp. 42, 116, 523

1.2c *Magnolia macrophylla* Michx.
LARGE-LEAF MAGNOLIA

Tree up to 50 feet in height; branchlets stout and relatively few. Leaves 20–30 inches long, white beneath, with ear-like lobes at the base. Terminal buds large and densely white-woolly. Bark smooth, light gray.

Pp. 42, 115, 524

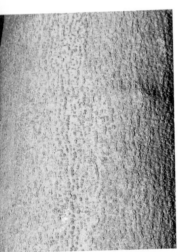

1.2d *Magnolia tripetala* L.
UMBRELLA MAGNOLIA
Tree up to 30 feet in height with
stout branches and branchlets,
sometimes with several stems around
the base of the main trunk. Leaves
12–20 inches long, tapered to an
acute base, clustered around the tip
of the stem. Buds smooth, purplish,
and glaucous. Bark light gray,
either smooth or warty.
Pp. 42, 115, 524

1.3 *Asimina triloba* (L.) Dunal. PAPAW
Small tree or large shrub up to 25 feet in
height (rarely more), often forming clumps or
thickets by suckering. Leaves 6–12 inches
long, 2-ranked, ill-scented when bruised.
Buds silky-hairy, dark brown, the terminal
bud clearly without scales. Bark smooth
except on old trees.
Pp. 43, 120, 255, 524-25

1.4 *Maclura pomifera* (Raf.) Schneid.
OSAGE ORANGE, HEDGE APPLE
Round-topped tree up to 50 feet in
height with a short trunk. Leaves
3–4 inches long, glossy, and long-
pointed. Flowers minute, the staminate
in racemes, the pistillate in spherical
heads each of which develops into a
multiple fruit 4–5 inches in diameter,
light green, and rough on the surface,
maturing in autumn. Twigs zigzag,
usually bearing stiff thorns about ½
inch long. Bark of the trunk brown,
orange within the furrows; that of
the roots a brilliant orange.
P. 520

1.5a *Nyssa sylvatica* Marsh.

SOUR GUM, BLACK GUM, BLACK TUPELO

Usually a medium-sized tree, rarely large and up to 100 feet in height, somewhat narrow and flat-topped in outline. Leaves crowded at the ends of lateral branches, or scattered on vigorous shoots, 2–5 inches long, glossy, either thick and firm or thin, usually broader beyond the middle and abruptly pointed, and rarely with 1 or 2 large teeth. Buds with several overlapping scales. Bark deeply cut and usually checkered, resembling an alligator hide on old trunks.
Pp. 140, 551

1.5b *Nyssa aquatica* L. TUPELO GUM, WATER TUPELO
Tree up to 80 feet in height with a buttressed base and short
branches forming a narrow head. Leaves usually 5–6 (rarely 7)
inches long; margin smooth or with 1 or 2 large teeth. Fruit
about 1 inch long, mature in early autumn. Branchlets stout with
prominent, nearly round leaf scars; terminal bud globose. Bark
with shallow furrows and small scales on the ridges.
P. 551

1.6a *Quercus imbricaria* Michx.   SHINGLE OAK
Usually a medium-sized tree up to 60 feet in height, rarely
80 feet. Leaves 4–6 inches long, narrowly elliptic, thick,
lustrous above and hairy beneath, often with an undulate
margin (rarely with a suggestion of lobes); midrib extending
from the leaf apex as a bristle; some brown leaves usually
hanging on through winter. Acorns about ½ inch long and
equally broad, the nut enclosed for nearly half its length
in the cup; scales of cup thin and hairy. Buds acute,
brown, and hairy, clustered at the stem tip as in all oaks.
P. 513

Q. nigra L., water oak, sometimes with smooth-margined leaves but
more often slightly 3-lobed, is described and illustrated on p. 477.

1.6b *Quercus phellos* L. WILLOW OAK

Tree up to 70 feet in height, conical or round-topped, with numerous small branches and slender branchlets. Leaves 2½–5 inches long, lanceolate with an undulate margin, the midrib extending from the tip as a bristle. Acorns about ½ inch long, the nut enclosed only at the very base in a saucer-shaped cup. Buds clustered at the stem tip as in all oaks, and pointed; bud scales with pale margins. Bark on old trunks with narrow fissures and scaly ridges, on young trees somewhat smooth.

P. 516

For other species of oaks, see pages 446-77.

1.7 *Bumelia lycioides* (L.) Gaertn. f.

BUCKTHORN BUMELIA, SOUTHERN BUCKTHORN

Small tree (or shrub) up to 25 feet in height. Leaves alternate or clustered on spurs. Buds small, hemispherical; leaf scars raised. Twigs often bearing thorns.

Pp. 70, 255, 559

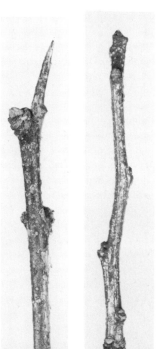

1.8 *Diospyros virginiana* L.
PERSIMMON

A medium-sized, usually round-
topped tree rarely over 50 feet
in height although known to have
attained a height of 100 feet in
favorable forest conditions.
Leaves 4–6 inches long, oval or
elliptic, dark green above and
pale green beneath, exceptionally
smooth or sleek in texture. Twigs
with diaphragmed pith; end bud
false; lateral buds with 2 dark
brown or purplish lustrous scales;
leaf scar with a single bundle scar.
Bark very dark, deeply divided
into squarish blocks.
Pp. 79, 122, 559

1.9 *Salix discolor* Muhl
PUSSY WILLOW
Large shrub or small tree
fully described and illustrated
on pp. 268–69.

1.10 *Cercis canadensis* L.   REDBUD

Usually a small tree but sometimes attaining a
height of 40 feet. Leaves heart-shaped, 3–5 inches
long. Pods 2–4 inches long, mature in summer.
Twigs zigzag with 2-ranked leaf scars and buds. Bark
with narrow ridges and furrows.
Pp. 58, 536

1.11a *Celtis laevigata* Willd.

SUGARBERRY,
SMOOTH HACKBERRY

Tree up to a height of 60 feet with a broad head, spreading branches, and slender branchlets. Leaves 2½–5 inches long, glabrous, smooth-margined (rarely toothed), unsymmetrical at the base, with 3 veins from the base. Fruit a small drupe about ¼ inch in diameter, axillary, orange-red when ripe in September. Lateral buds ovoid, pointed, and in 2 rows; end bud false. Bark light gray and very warty.
P. 517

1.11b *Celtis tenuifolia* Nutt.

DWARF HACKBERRY

Irregularly branching small tree up to a
height of 25 feet, the branches sometimes
contorted. Leaves 1½–2½ inches long with 3
main veins from the base, usually smooth-
margined but occasionally toothed. Fruit
¼–½ inch in diameter, orange in late
summer and becoming dark reddish in
autumn. Lateral buds in 2 rows, the end bud
false. Bark gray, either smooth or warty on
young trees, fissured on old trunks.
P. 518

2.1 *Celtis occidentalis* L. HACKBERRY

Tree up to a height of 80 feet, round-topped with spreading branches and slender branchlets. "Witches' brooms" common in the branchlets. Leaves 3–7 inches long, unsymmetrical at the base, sometimes rough on the surface. Fruit a drupe, about ⅜ inch in diameter, dark red when mature in late autumn. Bark gray with warty ridges. Leaf scars and buds 2-ranked; leaf scars raised; apex of buds closely appressed; end bud false.

A variable species in which several varieties have been named.
Pp. 517-18

2.2 *Morus rubra* L. RED MULBERRY

Tree up to 50 or 60 feet in height with spreading branches making a round-topped crown. Leaves 3–5 inches long, smooth or slightly rough above, hairy beneath, usually unlobed but sometimes with acute palmate lobes on vigorous shoots. Bud scales 3–6; bundle scars numerous, usually forming an ellipse; end bud false.
Pp. 103, 118, 520

Compare *M. alba*, the white mulberry, p. 485, and *Broussonetia papyrifera*, the paper mulberry, p. 486.

The Genus *Tilia*, the BASSWOODS or LINDENS

Leaves 3–6 inches long, more or less unsymmetrical at the base, with marginal gland-tipped teeth. Inflorescence attached to a strap-shaped bract. Fruit nutlike, ¼–⅜ inch in diameter. Buds green or red and glistening, 2-ranked; end bud false. For flowers, see page 84.

Species of *Tilia* are sometimes difficult to separate. The distinctions given here, following Braun's *Woody Plants of Ohio* (1960), can usually be made, although intermediates sometimes occur.

2.3a *Tilia heterophylla* Vent.
WHITE BASSWOOD

Tree 60–70 feet tall with slender branches and usually a narrow pyramidal crown. Lower surface of leaves white, densely hairy, and feltlike. Bracts glabrous on the inflorescence side, hairy on the reverse side.
Pp. 549-50

2.3b *Tilia floridana*
(V. Engler) Small
BASSWOOD, LINDEN

Tree 50–60 feet tall. Lower surface of the leaves velvety to the touch although appearing glabrous, bearing dense invisible hairs; tufts of hairs usually present in the axils of the veins. Bracts often hairy on both surfaces.
P. 549

2.3c *Tilia americana* L.

BASSWOOD, AMERICAN LINDEN

Large tree 70–80 feet in height, rarely up to 100 feet, round-topped with downswept branches. Leaves glabrous and green on both surfaces (sometimes with inconspicuous tufts of hairs in the axils of the veins). Bracts glabrous on both surfaces.   Pp. 84, 549

2.3d *Tilia neglecta* Spach
BASSWOOD, LINDEN
Tree 70–80 feet tall with downswept branches. Leaves with prominent and conspicuous tufts of hairs in the vein axils, otherwise thinly hairy beneath. Bracts glabrous on both surfaces.
P. 550

The Genus *Populus*, the ASPENS, COTTONWOODS, and true POPLARS

Trees unisexual; catkins pendulous. Pods of the fruiting catkins opening in late spring and releasing seed, each bearing a tuft of cottony hairs.

2.4a *Populus grandidentata* Michx.   LARGE-TOOTH ASPEN
Medium-sized tree up to 60 feet in height. Leaves 2½–4 inches long on flattened petioles. Bark pale and smooth when young, becoming furrowed on old trunks.
P. 501

2.4b *Populus heterophylla* L.
SWAMP COTTONWOOD,
DOWNY POPLAR

Tree up to 90 feet in height with a
narrow head. Leaves 4–7 inches long,
usually heart-shaped at the base and
obtuse at the apex; lower surface
hairy, at least on the veins; marginal
teeth blunt. Pith orange. Bud
scales hairy toward the base.
P. 501

2.4c *Populus gileadensis* Rouleau
   BALM-OF-GILEAD
Tree up to 80 feet in height.
Sterile, lacking staminate flowers,
probably of hybrid origin, and
spreading by sprouts. Leaves 2–6
inches long, hairy beneath, at least on
the veins, fragrant when crushed.
Buds sticky and resinous, appearing
varnished.
P. 501

2.4d *Populus deltoides* Marsh. COTTONWOOD

Tree up to nearly 100 feet in height. Leaves 3–5 inches long, usually triangular but occasionally slightly heart-shaped, hanging on flattened petioles; marginal teeth with hard incurved tips. Buds glabrous and slightly resinous. Young bark smooth and greenish yellow; old bark deeply furrowed and gray.
P. 501

(Continued)

P. deltoides
(continued)

2.5a *Salix alba* L.

EUROPEAN WHITE WILLOW

Tree up to 60 feet tall with a spread greater than the height, often with several trunks. Leaves 2½–5 inches long, lanceolate, white and silky beneath. Branchlets yellow. Otherwise resembling the preceding species.
P. 502

S. fragilis L., the crack willow, is a similar introduced species, differing from the white willow in having leaves more coarsely toothed and branchlets less yellow and more brittle at the base. P. 502

 S. amygdaloides Anders., the peach-leaf willow, a tree up to 30 feet in height or sometimes only a large shrub, has somewhat pendulous twigs and broadly lanceolate leaves which are 2½–5 inches long, glabrous and whitish beneath. P. 502

2.5b *Salix nigra* Marsh.

BLACK WILLOW

Tree 30–40 feet tall, rarely up to 70 feet,
often with several trunks and often
bushy in habit of growth. Leaves 2½–5
inches long, green on both sides,
narrowly lanceolate and often scythe-
shaped. Branchlets yellow-brown; buds
with a single scale; end bud false;
leaf scars U-shaped.
Pp. 105, 503

2.6 *Amelanchier arborea* (Michx. f.) Fernald
   SERVICEBERRY, SARVIS
Usually a small tree but sometimes up to 50 feet in height, with
small branches forming a narrow crown. Leaves 1¾–3½
inches long, more or less heart-shaped at the base, densely white-
hairy when young and becoming less so when mature, sometimes
becoming nearly glabrous except on the petioles. Short
spur-branches often present. Buds slender, pinkish or reddish with
about 6 dark-tipped scales.
Pp. 44, 134, 528-29

A. *laevis* Wieg., the smooth serviceberry, is completely glabrous when
mature and nearly so when young. Pp. 44, 529

2.7a *Pyrus malus* L.

APPLE

A spreading, round-topped tree, 20–30 feet
tall, rarely 50 feet. Leaves and young
shoots woolly; leaves 2–4 inches long,
some crowded on short spur branches.
Terminal bud ovoid and generally blunt.
Pp. 47, 533

2.7b *Pyrus communis* L.

PEAR

Tree up to a height of 35 feet or
rarely more, having several strong
upright branches and a narrow crown.
Leaves 2–3 inches long, glabrous,
some on short spur branches.
Terminal bud conical and pointed.
Pp. 47, 533

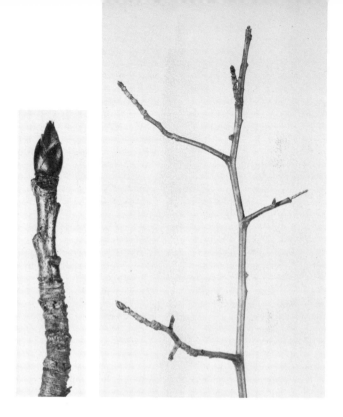

2.7c *Pyrus coronaria* L.   WILD CRAB

Small tree up to 30 feet in height, sometimes forming thickets.
Leaves 1¼–3 inches long, varying in width and amount of
lobing, sharply toothed, pointed at the apex, and rounded at the
base. Fruit yellow-green even at maturity and very acid, 1–2
inches in diameter. Spine-tipped spur branches numerous.
Buds conical and acute.
Pp. 48, 533

2.7d *Pyrus angustifolia* Ait.

WILD CRAB, NARROW-LEAF CRAB

Differing from the preceding species chiefly in having leaves lanceolate, oblong, or narrowly oblong, blunt-toothed, more or less blunt-tipped, and wedge-shaped at the base.
Pp. 48, 533

P. ioensis (Wood) Bailey, the prairie crab, is woolly on the petioles and on the lower surface of leaf blades. Pp. 48, 533

The Genus *Prunus*, the PLUMS, CHERRIES, and PEACH

Branches and branchlets bearing prominent horizontal lenticels. Petioles or the base of the leaf blade bearing a gland or pair of glands in all species except *P. americana*. Leaf scars raised; bundle scars 3. Buds with about 6 scales; true terminal buds absent in plums and present in cherries and peach. Plums usually with some spine-tipped spur branches. Species of plums variable, with intermediates occurring.

2.8a *Prunus angustifolia* Marsh.
CHICKASAW PLUM
Small tree up to 20 feet in height, or a large shrub, thicket-forming. Leaves 1–2 inches long, lanceolate and folded, lustrous on the upper surface, borne on bright red petioles on red branchlets. The raised leaf scar hiding the lower half of each bud.
Pp. 45, 121, 279, 531

2.8b *Prunus americana* Marsh.

WILD PLUM

Small, widely spreading tree up
to 30 feet in height, usually with
crooked branches, often forming
thickets. Leaves 3–4 inches
long; leaf surface somewhat
wrinkled and veiny; margin sharply
toothed; petioles usually without
glands.

Pp. 45, 121, 531

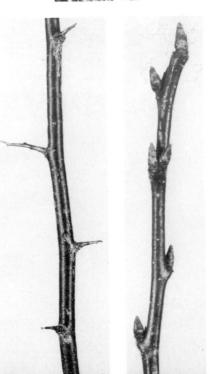

2.8c *Prunus munsoniana*
Wight & Hedrick
WILD GOOSE PLUM

Small tree up to 20 feet in height, often forming thickets. Leaves 2–3½ inches long, usually folded, lustrous on the upper surface at maturity, with minute marginal teeth blunt and gland-tipped; petioles usually red. Pp. 45, 121, 531

P. hortulana Bailey, the hortulan plum, also called wild goose plum, differs in having leaves flat at maturity with larger, triangular teeth. Not producing suckers from the roots as freely as does *P. munsoniana*, it is less thicket-forming. Pp. 45, 531

2.8d *Prunus persica* (L.) Batsch
PEACH

Small spreading tree up to 20 feet in height. Leaves lanceolate, 3–6 inches long. Twigs bright green or red; lenticels small and numerous. Buds densely short-hairy at least toward the tip; collateral buds usually present.
Pp. 46, 532

2.8e *Prunus mahaleb* L.
PERFUMED CHERRY
Small tree up to 25 feet in height.
Leaves 1–2½ inches long. Twigs fragrant
and velvety; older branches silvery and
lustrous. Buds ovoid.
Pp. 46, 531

2.8f *Prunus serotina* Ehrh. WILD BLACK CHERRY

Tall tree sometimes attaining a height of 90–100 feet with slender branches and typically with a narrow oblong head, although sometimes widely spreading when growing in the open. Leaves 2–5 inches long, lanceolate or oblong, and lustrous. Marginal teeth minute and blunt. Twigs with the odor of almond. Buds glossy, acute, with scales keeled on the back. Bark scaly on old trunks, smooth and red-brown on branches.

Pp. 71, 135, 532

2.8g *Prunus virginiana* L.
CHOKE CHERRY
Tall shrub or small tree up to 20
feet in height. Leaves 2–4
inches long, oblong or obovate,
with marginal teeth sharp.
Twigs with rank odor. Bud
scales dull brown, rounded and
often lighter at the tip,
roughened, and appearing
dotted.
Pp. 72, 129, 280, 532

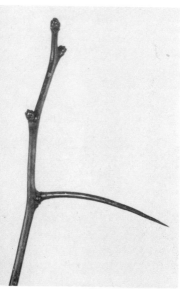

2.9 *Crataegus crus-galli* L.
COCKSPUR THORN

Small tree up to a height of 25 feet. Mature leaves usually thick and glossy, 1–4 inches long. Thorns on branches up to 4 inches long, those on the trunk longer. Buds, as in all hawthorns, nearly spherical. Pp. 49, 131, 530

2.10 *Halesia carolina* L.

SILVERBELL

Small tree up to 30 feet in height.
Leaves 3–4 inches long, finely toothed,
thinly hairy beneath. Fruit 4-winged,
about 1½ inches long. Branchlets
spreading at right angles from the
branches. Bark on young trunks and
branches appearing striped as furrows
begin; old bark furrowed and scaly.
Leaf scars half-round and notched;
bundle scar 1, crescent-shaped; end
bud false.
Pp. 56, 289, 559

2.11 *Rhamnus caroliniana* Walt.

CAROLINA BUCKTHORN

Tall shrub or small tree up to 25 feet in height.
Leaves lustrous, 2½–5 inches long, with obscurely
fine-toothed margins. Buds without scales; bark gray
and smooth.

Pp. 99, 127, 284, 547

2.12 *Stewartia ovata*
(Cav.) Weatherby
MOUNTAIN CAMELLIA
Small tree, or more often a
tree-like shrub, up to a height of
16 feet. Leaves 3–6 inches long,
hairy beneath, finely or
obscurely toothed. Capsule
5-angled, hairy, about 1 inch
long. Buds hairy; leaf scar
containing a single bundle scar.
Pp. 54, 286, 550

2.13 *Oxydendrum arboreum* (L.) DC.

SOURWOOD, SORREL TREE

Tree frequently 30 feet and sometimes 50 feet tall,
usually with a straight trunk, slender spreading branches,
and a narrow oblong crown. Leaves 4–6 inches long,
bright green, glossy, and pointed at the apex; leaf
margins minutely toothed. Capsules, each held erect on
a recurved pedicel, remaining through winter, after
which the whole panicle falls off. Leaf scar containing a
single bundle scar; end bud false.

Pp. 79, 555

2.14 *Planera aquatica* (Walt.) J. F. Gmel.
 WATER ELM

Small tree up to 30 feet in height. Leaves
and buds 2-ranked; leaves 2–3 inches
long, often oblique at the base. Fruit a
drupe ⅜ inch long, covered by elongated
projections, maturing in May. Youngest
branchlets reddish; leaf scars nearly
round, containing a row of bundle scars.
Bark gray or brown, revealing a red-brown
inner bark between the shaggy strips.
P. 518

The Genus *Ulmus*, the ELMS

Leaves and buds 2-ranked; leaves straight-veined, doubly toothed, often oblique at the base. Fruit with a membranous winged margin. Buds with many scales; end bud false; leaf scars with 3 bundle scars. See page 109 for flowers.

2.15a *Ulmus alata* Michx.

WINGED ELM

Small or medium-sized tree rarely up to 50 feet in height, with slender twigs, some of which usually bear 2 corky ridges on opposite sides. Leaves 1½–3½ inches long, smooth above and hairy beneath. Fruit ⅜ inch long, lance-ovate, maturing in spring. Bark with shallow fissures.
P. 518

U. serotina Sarg., the September elm, is similar to the winged elm but has flowers in September and oblong fruit, about ½ inch long, maturing in October and November. Pp. 109, 519

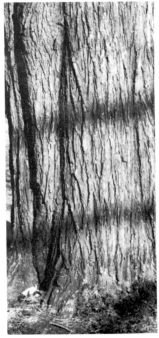

2.15b *Ulmus americana* L.

AMERICAN ELM,
WHITE ELM

Large tree up to 100 feet in height,
vase-shaped when growing in the
open, with the trunk dividing into
several large branches. Leaves 3–5
inches long, smooth or slightly
rough above and usually slightly
hairy beneath. Fruit less than ½
inch long, ripening as the leaves
unfold. Bark deeply fissured.
Pp. 109, 518-19

2.15c *Ulmus rubra* Muhl.
SLIPPERY ELM,
RED ELM

Tree up to 60 feet in height with spreading branches and usually a somewhat flat-topped open head. Leaves 4–6 inches long, sandpapery above and hairy beneath. Fruits ½–¾ inch long, ripening before or with the unfolding of leaves. Twigs rough and hairy; buds rusty-hairy. Bark with shallow fissures.

Pp. 109, 519

2.15d *Ulmus thomasi* Sarg.   ROCK ELM, CORK ELM

Tree up to 80 feet in height, with a single trunk, stout spreading branches, and slender branchlets. Branches and branchlets often with 3–4 irregular corky ridges. Leaves 3–6 inches long, smooth or slightly rough above, hairy beneath. Fruit about ⅝ inch long, maturing when the leaves are half grown. Twigs and buds more or less hairy; bud scales notched and fringed with hairs. Bark gray and fissured as in *U. americana*.
P. 519

The Genus *Betula*, the BIRCHES

Trees with 2-ranked leaves and buds; leaves straight-veined, doubly toothed, often in pairs or clustered on short spur branches. Staminate catkins slender, present all winter and producing pollen in early spring; fruiting catkins, when mature in late summer, cone-like with overlapping scales subtending the nutlets. True terminal buds lacking except on the short spur branches. Bud scales 2 or 3; bundle scars 3. Bark containing horizontal lenticels.

2.16a *Betula nigra* L. RIVER BIRCH
Tree up to 75 feet in height with a trunk often divided into 2 or 3 diverging limbs. Leaves 1¼–3½ inches long, wedge-shaped at the base, with 7–9 pairs of lateral veins. Buds appressed. Bark on young trunks and branches pinkish tan, peeling and curling; bark on old trunks furrowed.
Pp. 101, 508

2.16b *Betula lenta* L.
SWEET BIRCH, CHERRY BIRCH

Tree up to 75 feet in height with slender branches forming a narrow, rounded, and graceful crown. Leaves 2–4½ inches long, with 9–13 pairs of lateral veins, slightly heart-shaped at the base, usually lustrous on the upper surface. Twigs aromatic with with a wintergreen scent. Buds divergent. Bark dark, resembling that of cherry.

P. 507

433

2.16c *Betula lutea* Michx. f.

YELLOW BIRCH

Tall tree, occasionally attaining a height of 100 feet, with slender branches and a round-topped crown. Leaves 2–4½ inches long, with 9–13 pairs of lateral veins, rounded or slightly heart-shaped at the base. Buds appressed. Bark shiny, yellowish or silvery, peeling and curling on old trunks, smooth on young trunks and branches.

Pp. 101, 508

2.17 *Carpinus caroliniana* Walt.

AMERICAN HORNBEAM,
BLUE BEECH, IRONWOOD

Small bushy tree rarely over 30 feet in height; branches spreading into flattened sprays. Leaves and buds 2-ranked; leaves 2–4 inches long, doubly toothed. Staminate catkins in spring slender and pendulous; fruiting catkins, maturing in latè summer, bearing deeply toothed bracts subtending the nutlets, each bract ¾–⅞ inch long. Branchlets very slender and zigzag. Buds angled; end bud false. Bark gray, smooth, and fluted.
Pp. 100, 508

2.18 *Ostrya virginiana* (Mill.) K. Koch
  HOP-HORNBEAM,
  IRONWOOD

Small or medium-sized tree usually
not over 25 feet in height, occasionally
up to 50 feet, with slender branches.
Leaves and buds 2-ranked; leaves
2–4½ inches long, doubly toothed,
hairy on the petioles and the veins
beneath. Staminate catkins in spring
slender and pendulous; fruiting catkins
1½–2 inches long, hop-like, with
nutlets enclosed in overlapping sacs;
seeds ripe in late summer. Twigs
zigzag; end bud false. Bark shreddy
on mature trees.
Pp. 100, 509

2.19 *Fagus grandifolia* Ehrh.

AMERICAN BEECH

Large tree up to a height of 80 feet, rarely more, with branches slightly drooping and spreading in flattened sprays. Leaves and buds 2-ranked; leaves 2½–5 inches long. Fruit a 4-valved, soft-prickly bur ½–¾ inch long, enclosing 2 or 3 triangular nuts. Buds long, sharply pointed, lustrous, and many-scaled. Bark gray and smooth.
Pp. 104, 510

2.20a *Castanea dentata* (Marsh.) Borkh.
AMERICAN CHESTNUT
Originally a tall tree up to a height of 100
feet but now rarely living beyond 15 feet,
usually seen as sprouts from a stump or as
standing skeletons. Leaves and buds
2-ranked except on vigorous erect shoots;
leaves 4–8 inches long. Spiny bur 2–2½
inches across, containing 2 or 3 nuts. Buds
few-scaled; end bud false. Twigs fluted.
Bark smooth on young trunks and branches,
deeply fissured on old ones.
Pp. 104, 114, 509-10

2.20b *Castanea pumila* (L.) Mill.
CHINQUAPIN,
DWARF CHESTNUT

Small bushy tree usually not over 15
feet tall. Leaves and buds 2-ranked
except on vigorous erect shoots;
leaves 3–5 inches long, tawny and
velvety beneath. Spiny bur 1–1½
inches across, containing a single
nut, mature in autumn. Twigs
and buds hairy; twigs fluted; end
bud false.
Pp. 104, 114, 510

The Genus *Quercus*, the OAKS

Fruit an acorn: a nut borne in a cup covered with overlapping scales; maturing in autumn. Buds clustered at the ends of the branchlets, resulting in a distinctive branching pattern; bud scales numerous, and bundle scars numerous in each leaf scar. Leaves variable within a species, those exposed to the sun high on the tree narrower and more deeply lobed than those on the lower branches and in the shade. Hybrids between species sometimes found.

2.21a–d Leaves coarsely toothed
3.1a–d Leaves lobed, without bristle tips ⎱ The "white oaks"
3.1e–l Leaves lobed, with bristle tips   The "red" and "black oaks"

See pages 368-71 for oaks with nontoothed and nonlobed leaves. See page 103 for staminate catkins.

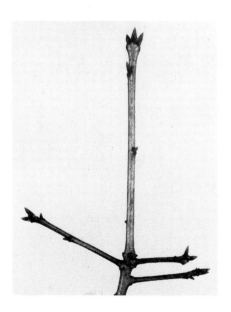

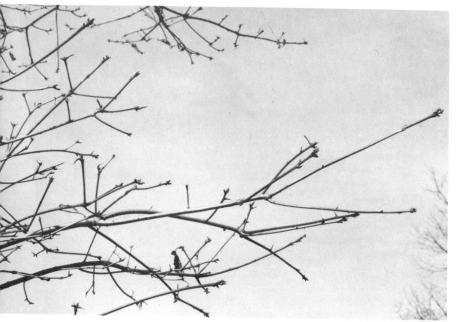

2.21a *Quercus montana* Willd.
CHESTNUT OAK,
MOUNTAIN CHESTNUT OAK
Tree up to a height of 70 feet. Leaves 4–8
inches long, yellow green beneath, with a
blunt apex and rounded teeth. Acorns
1–1½ inches long, and lustrous; the cup
covered with thick knoblike scales.
Branchlets stout; buds conical. Bark dark
and deeply furrowed.
P. 515

2.21b *Quercus muehlenbergii* Engelm.

CHINQUAPIN OAK, YELLOW OAK

Large tree attaining a height of 100 feet. Leaves 4–7 inches long, pale grayish and slightly hairy beneath, sharp at the apex; marginal teeth pointed, each tipped with a gland or callus; leaves high in the crown narrow, thick, and shiny; lower leaves broader, thinner, and duller. Acorns ½–¾ inch long. Branchlets slender; buds ovoid. Bark light gray and scaly.

P. 515

2.21c *Quercus michauxii* Nutt.

SWAMP CHESTNUT OAK, BASKET OAK, COW OAK

Tall tree up to 100 feet in height. Leaves 4–8 inches long, pale grayish and densely velvety-hairy beneath. Acorns 1–1½ inches long. Buds ovoid and acute. Bark light gray and scaly.
P. 515

2.21d *Quercus bicolor* Willd.

SWAMP WHITE OAK

Tree up to a height of 80 feet. Leaves 5–6 inches long with only 4–6 pairs of veins, irregularly toothed and sometimes slightly lobed, densely hairy and whitish beneath. Acorns ¾–1 inch long, on stalks 1¼–2¾ inches long, often 2 per stalk. Buds blunt. Bark light gray and scaly.

P. 512

3.1a *Quercus alba* L.

WHITE OAK

Large tree up to 100 feet, occasionally 150 feet in height, with widely spreading stout limbs when growing in the open, or with a narrow round-topped crown when growing in a forest. Leaves 4–8 inches long, glabrous and pale beneath; depth of lobing varying greatly. Acorns ¾–1 inch long; the cup bowl-shaped, covering ⅜ or less of the nut; scales blunt and knobby. Twigs glabrous; buds obtuse. Bark gray, fissured and scaly.

Pp. 511-12

3.1b *Quercus lyrata* Walt.   OVERCUP OAK

Tree up to 80 feet in height. Leaves 4–8 inches long, smooth on the upper surface and finely hairy beneath; lobes ascending, acute, the 3 terminal ones the largest. Nut nearly spherical, ½–⅞ inch long, always nearly enclosed within the cup (to be distinguished from abnormal and undeveloped nuts in other oaks); scales blunt and knobby near the base, pointed near the rim. Branchlets glabrous or nearly so. Bark light gray and scaly.

P. 514

3.1c *Quercus stellata* Wang. POST OAK

Medium-sized tree up to 60 feet in height with stiff branches forming a broad head. Leaves 4–8 inches long, thick, rough above, hairy beneath, in shape often resembling a cross with the middle lobes larger than the others. Acorns ½–¾ inch long; the cup finely hairy, covering ⅜–½ of the nut. Branchlets stout and hairy; buds hairy and blunt. Bark gray, deeply fissured and broken into plates.

P. 517

3.1d *Quercus macrocarpa* Michx. BUR OAK
Massive tree with large branches, attaining a height
of 170 feet and a spread as great or greater. Leaves
4–10 inches long, glabrous above and hairy beneath,
with a pair of deep indentations dividing the blade
into 2 portions, the terminal half broader and less
deeply cut than the basal half. Acorns ⅞–2 inches
long, with a cup 1–2½ inches across, fringed at the
rim. Twigs stout, those on young trees often corky-
ridged. Buds blunt and hairy. Bark gray and deeply
furrowed.
P. 514

3.1e *Quercus borealis* Michx. f. var. *maxima*
(Marsh.) Ashe
RED OAK

Large tree up to a height of 100 feet. Leaves 5–9 inches
long, smooth, firm, glabrous, dull above, usually with
9 (7–11) lobes and with indentations extending about
halfway to the midrib. Acorns ¾–1¼ inches long; the
cup shallow and saucer-shaped. Branchlets and buds
brown and lustrous. Bark dark, furrowed, with ridges
smooth and shiny, appearing striped on the middle and
upper trunk.
Pp. 103, 512-13

3.1f *Quercus shumardii* Buckl.

SHUMARD OAK,
SHUMARD RED OAK

Large tree up to a height of 100 feet.
Leaves 4–7 inches long, glabrous except
for tufts of hairs in the vein angles
beneath, usually with 7 (5–9) lobes, and
with the indentations extending more
than halfway to the midrib. Acorns ¾–1
inch long; the cup deep saucer-shaped,
covering about ¼ of the nut (or deeper
and cup-shaped in var. *schneckii* Sarg.);
scales of the cup long-pointed. Buds
glabrous, gray or brownish. Bark as in
Q. borealis var. *maxima*.
P. 516

3.1g *Quercus coccinea* Muench.
   SCARLET OAK

Tree up to 70 feet in height. Leaves
3–6 inches long, usually 7-lobed
(5–7), lustrous, glabrous except for
tufts of hairs in the vein angles
beneath. Acorns ½–⅞ inch long,
usually with concentric lines around
the apex; the cup covering about
half the nut. Buds brown, hairy
beyond the middle. Bark with shallow
fissures and smooth ridges, sometimes
having a striped appearance.
P. 513

3.1h *Quercus palustris* Muench.   PIN OAK

Tree up to a height of 80 feet, pyramidal when young, becoming open and round-topped when old. Branches slender and numerous, bearing many pinlike spurs; the lower branches pointed downward, the middle ones spreading horizontally, and the upper ones ascending. Leaves 3–6 inches long, usually 5-lobed (5–7), lustrous, with large tufts of hairs in the vein angles beneath. Acorns ½ inch long; the cup shallow and saucer-shaped. Bark on branches and young trunks smooth, that on old trunks with shallow fissures and low smooth ridges.

P. 516

3.1i *Quercus velutina* Lam.

BLACK OAK

Tree up to 80 feet in height. Leaves thick, glossy
above, 4–10 inches long, usually 7-lobed, usually cut
about halfway to the midrib but cut less in leaves
on young trees and low branches; the lower surface
bearing hairs that can be rubbed off. Acorns ½–¾
inch long, enclosed for about half their length;
scales of the cup spreading at the rim. Buds angled
and hairy. Bark very dark, cut into blocks; inner bark
orange-colored.
P. 517

3.1j *Quercus falcata* Michx.

SOUTHERN RED OAK, SPANISH OAK

Tree up to 75 feet in height with large spreading branches. Leaves 4–7 inches long, somewhat rounded at the base, usually 5-lobed (the lobes often scythe-shaped) except in var. *triloba* (Michx.) Nutt., which is 3-lobed; the lower surface densely short-hairy. Acorns about ½ inch long; the cup saucer-shaped, either deep or shallow, and hairy. Buds hairy. Bark with shallow fissures and broad ridges.

P. 513

3.1k *Quercus marilandica* Muench.

BLACK JACK OAK

Small or medium-sized tree up to 40 feet in height with an irregular crown of stout crooked branches. Leaves 5–7 inches long, thick and leathery, lustrous above, hairy beneath, obscurely 3-lobed. Acorns about ¾ inch long; the cup covering ½ or more of the nut; scales hairy and loosely overlapping. Branchlets coarse and hairy; buds angled and hairy. Bark deeply furrowed.
Pp. 514-15

3.11 *Quercus nigra* L.   WATER OAK

Tree up to 60 feet in height, symmetrical, with slender branches.
Leaves 2–4 inches long, glabrous, broad at the apex, 3-lobed or
unlobed. Acorn about ½ inch long; the cup saucer-shaped.
Buds angled and hairy. Bark more or less smooth.
Pp. 515-16

3.2a *Crataegus* spp. (representing several species)
the HAWTHORNS

Usually small trees with dense, wide-spreading branches.
Thorns usually abundant. Buds nearly spherical, with
numerous scales; bundle scars 3.
Pp. 49, 131, 530

3.2b *Crataegus mollis* (T. & G.)
Scheele
RED HAW

Medium-sized tree up to a height
of 35 feet, wide-spreading, sparingly
thorny or thornless. Leaves as in
no. 3.2a.
Pp. 50, 132, 530

3.2c *Crataegus phaeno-pyrum* (L. f.) Medic.
WASHINGTON THORN

Small tree up to a height of 25 feet. Leaves 1½–2 inches long, rounded or heart-shaped at the base. Branchlets slender and thorny.
Pp. 49, 131, 530

3.3 *Pyrus coronaria* L.   WILD CRAB

Small tree with thornlike spur branches. Leaves either lobed or merely doubly toothed. Fully described and illustrated on pages 404-05.

3.4 *Sassafras albidum* (Nutt.) Nees
SASSAFRAS

Usually a small tree but sometimes up to 75
feet in height, with spreading branches and
upturned branchlets, aromatic in all parts.
Leaves 4–6 inches long, 2- or 3-lobed or
unlobed. Branchlets light yellow-green;
true terminal bud present; 1 bundle scar per
leaf scar. Bark on old trunks consisting of
furrows and scaly ridges.
Pp. 26, 108, 140, 525-26

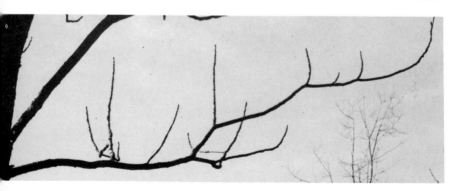

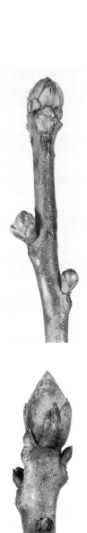

3.5 *Liriodendron tulipifera* L.
TULIP TREE, TULIP POPLAR, YELLOW POPLAR

Tall tree sometimes attaining a height of nearly 200 feet. Leaves 5–7 inches long, squarish, firm, and lustrous. The aggregate fruit cone-like, about 3 inches long, and upright; the individual fruits overlapping on an elongated axis which persists through winter after the separate winged fruits are shed (illustrated: immature in summer and empty in winter). A pair of stipules functioning as bud scales on the terminal bud; stipule scars forming a line encircling the twig at each leaf scar. Bark gray, with regular ridges and furrows on old trunks, on young trunks whitened within the small grooves and nearly smooth.

Pp. 41, 522-23

(Continued)

L. tulipifera
(continued)

3.6 *Morus alba* L.
WHITE MULBERRY

Tree up to 35 feet in height, with a spreading, bushy habit of growth. Leaves 2–4 inches long, glabrous except on the veins beneath, usually with obtuse palmate lobes but often unlobed. Buds with 3–6 scales; bundle scars numerous; end bud false. Pp. 103, 118, 520

Compare *M. rubra*, the red mulberry, pages 382-83.

3.7 *Broussonetia papyrifera* (L.) Vent. PAPER MULBERRY
Tree up to 35 feet in height. Leaves 4–8 inches long, lobed or
unlobed, sandpapery on the upper surface, grayish and densely hairy
beneath. Branchlets hairy; outer bud-scale striped; end bud false;
bundle scars numerous, usually forming an ellipse. Bark greenish
gray.
P. 520

Compare *Morus rubra*, the red mulberry, pages 382-83.

3.8 *Populus alba* L.
WHITE POPLAR
Tree up to 60 feet in height.
Leaves 2–4 inches long, white-
felted beneath and bright green
above. Branchlets and buds white-
woolly. Bark of branches and
upper trunk smooth and white,
base of old trunks dark and
cracked.
Pp. 500-501

3.9 *Platanus occidentalis* L.

SYCAMORE

Massive tree up to a height of 130 feet with
wide-spreading branches and an open head.
Leaves 4–7 inches long, copiously coated
beneath with a fuzz which wears off. Fruit
spherical, about 1 inch in diameter, composed
of achenes, persisting through winter and
breaking apart in spring, each achene supplied
with a tuft of hairs. Buds with a single scale,
covered by an enlarged petiole-base which
leaves a circular scar around the bud; stipule
scars forming a line encircling the twig. Bark
peeling in autumn leaving the branches and
upper trunk smooth and whitish and the lower
trunk scaly.

P. 528

3.10 *Liquidambar styraciflua* L.

SWEET GUM, RED GUM

Tall tree up to a height of 100 feet, pyramidal when young, the crown becoming oblong when old. Leaves 5–7 inches long, star-shaped. Fruit spherical, 1–1½ inches in diameter, composed of crowded 2-beaked capsules. Branches and branchlets often corky-winged. Short spur branches often present. Buds shiny and resinous, with numerous scales edged with hairs. Bark gray and furrowed.

Pp. 29, 527

Part III.

Natural History Accounts of the Species Arranged According to Families

Families are arranged in taxonomic order.
Genera and species are arranged
alphabetically within families.

Taxaceae, Yew Family

Taxus canadensis Marsh.
CANADIAN YEW, AMERICAN YEW
The Canadian yew is a common evergreen shrub of the northern coniferous forest. Its range extends from Labrador and Newfoundland across the southern edge of Hudson Bay south to New England, Pennsylvania, the Great Lakes states, and the high mountains of the southern Appalachians. In Kentucky there are three remarkable colonies, each in a different cool, moist gorge near the western edge of the Pottsville Escarpment, none at high altitude. The Canadian yew here is a northern relict which has persisted since Pleistocene glaciation when it received refuge in valleys and coves south of the ice sheet. Thus here it was contemporary with the mastodons, and a few localities were sufficiently protected from the summer's heat to permit it to survive.

This species is too straggling to merit cultivation; the varieties of *Taxus* grown ornamentally are derived from Asiatic and European species. [Pp. 122, 160]

Pinaceae, Pine Family

Our four species of native pines are confined to soils derived from sandstone and shale in hilly areas of the state and are absent from calcareous regions.

Pinus echinata Mill. YELLOW PINE, SHORTLEAF PINE
In Kentucky this species is usually called yellow pine, while in states to the south, where the longleaf pine grows, it is called shortleaf pine. It is found especially on sandstone uplands in eastern and southeastern Kentucky but is now less common than *P. rigida* and *P. virginiana* largely because it has been extensively logged. It is usually mixed with these other pines or all three are mixed with oaks and hickories. Although in Kentucky the yellow pine does not usually invade an old field as the scrub pine does, it is successful in reforestation projects and such plantings of this

species should be encouraged. It is one of the most valuable timber trees of the state. Its wood, which is used in general construction for both exterior and interior work, is strong, heavy, fine-grained, and hard for a "softwood."

A mature yellow pine is altogether noble in aspect. Its tall straight trunk with a map-patterned bark stands in unquestioned dignity bearing a lofty crown of slender branches. It is handsome in parks and large lawns, and in such places it should be planted more frequently.   [Pp. 154-55]

Pinus rigida Mill.   PITCH PINE

The dark and rugged pitch pine is common on dry slopes and ridges in the eastern Knobs and the Appalachian portion of the state, where it is associated with scrub pine, yellow pine, and xerophytic species of oak. Its coarse-grained knotty wood is of limited value but is durable as mine timbers, for example, and in other rough construction; it is also used for making charcoal. Pioneers used tar from the pitch pine.   [Pp. 112, 152-53]

Pinus strobus L.   WHITE PINE

This monarch of a former empire in the northern states has a relatively minor southern extension in the Appalachian Mountains. Extensive logging of white pine forests began in colonial days, first in New England, then spreading westward and reaching the peak of rapacious cutting in the Great Lakes states in the 1880s and 1890s. Many private fortunes were amassed by destroying the forests of the most valuable timber tree of northeastern America.

White pine is a versatile wood. It is smooth, straight-grained, and relatively free of knots; it is soft and easily worked, light but strong for its weight, and free of warping. With such properties it was used for ship masts, covered bridges, general house construction, window sashes, interior finish work, carved ornaments, and gilded frames. With destruction of the pine forests of the north, lumbermen began to exploit the white and yellow pines of the southern Appalachians, cutting on a big scale by the turn of the present century. Reforestation of white pine should be encouraged although in pure stands it is vulnerable to the attack of a blister rust if the alternate host, either a currant or a gooseberry (*Ribes* spp.), grows nearby. Hence the latter should be eliminated in the vicinity of a white pine plantation.

The white pine is a shade-tolerant, mesophytic species, in Kentucky growing especially in humus soil in coves and on valley slopes. Though occasionally mixed with other pines on slopes, it is more often associated with hardwoods and hemlock. Less frequent in this state than our other pines, it is locally common in scattered suitable habitats in eastern and southern Kentucky, especially near the western edge of the Cumberland Plateau. The largest and most beautiful pine of eastern North America, it is ornamental at any age in parks, lawns, and gardens. The dark blue-green foliage is soft, the tiered branches give a pagoda-like silhouette, and when old the tree is majestic and picturesque.　　　　　　　　[Pp. 150-51]

Pinus virginiana Mill.　SCRUB PINE, VIRGINIA PINE

Before pine was used for pulpwood and before knotty pine became popular for interiors, this species had almost no commercial value. Its many branches coming from the main trunk make numerous knots in wood that is weak at best. Furthermore, with dead branches persisting and with short, somewhat sparse and disheveled needles, it has little to recommend it ornamentally. However, its role in ecology makes it a valuable species.

The scrub pine, often accompanied by pitch pine, will grow in soil too thin, poor, or dry for the survival of most trees. During its occupancy it so improves an area—holding soil and adding humus—that yellow pine, oaks, hickories, and others get started and are on hand to take over when the old scrub pines die. In noncalcareous areas when severely eroded or leached land is abandoned, the scrub pine is the chief tree to invade the weeds and brush, and it becomes the dominant species of the first woodland that follows. Hence this poor-land species makes poor land less poor. Creating a habitat in which more valuable trees can later grow, it is ecologically a pioneer tree in forest succession.

In Kentucky it is abundant throughout the Knobs, Cumberland Plateau, and Cumberland Mountains; it also occurs in the Pennyroyal and Western Coalfields.　　　　　　　　[Pp. 156-57]

Tsuga canadensis (L.) Carr.
EASTERN HEMLOCK, CANADA HEMLOCK

The hemlock is a prominent constituent of the Mixed Mesophytic climax communities in the Appalachian sections of the state. This is a southern extension of the range of a primarily northern species which is one of the dominants in the hemlock—white pine—northern hardwoods forest region. In eastern Kentucky it is frequent on steep, cool, moist slopes and in deep ravines and coves rich with leaf mold, but occurs infrequently in the Green River valley in western Kentucky. It is the most shade-tolerant of any native conifer and requires shade for its seedlings.

Hemlock wood has little value, being coarse-grained, splintery, light, weak, brittle, and not weather-resistant. It is, however, suitable for laths, sheathing under clapboards, crates, and pulpwood, and in the present dearth of superior woods is being used more than previously. Hemlock has always been a source of tanbark; formerly only the lower bark was stripped off, wastefully leaving the dead tree standing. It is for its beauty that the hemlock is most outstanding, whether as a majestic tree soaring over the tranquility of a virgin forest or as an ornamental tree in lawn or garden. In addition to its stately grace when growing alone, it can make a hedge par excellence and lends itself to being thus pruned.   [Pp. 158-59]

Taxodiaceae, BALD CYPRESS FAMILY

Taxodium distichum (L.) Richard BALD CYPRESS
This denizen of the deep swamp forests of the Atlantic and Gulf Coastal Plains and the Mississippi Embayment is at home in Kentucky only along the Mississippi River, the lower Ohio and Green rivers, and their immediate tributaries. Although in the wild it grows only in areas inundated for several months a year, it will thrive in an average lawn or park. The foliage is attractively soft, feathery, and pale green but not dense enough to provide much shade.

Cypress wood is valued for its strength, lightness, durability in the weather, and resistance to moisture. If a cypress swamp is drained when the trees are cut, other trees will invade the area and cypress will not return. There is little or no reforestation with cypress because of its slow growth.

The few remaining cypress swamps in Kentucky should be protected as ecological museums. Also the species deserves respect as one of the few living representatives of an ancient family that includes also the redwoods and sequoias of the West. Millions of year ago, in the Tertiary, members of this family were numerous and spread throughout the northern hemisphere. Now most are extinct and only a few persist in restricted localities. [Pp. 354-55]

Cupressaceae, CYPRESS FAMILY

Juniperus virginiana L.   RED CEDAR
The common name is misleading since this is not one of the true cedars, such as the cedar of Lebanon of the genus *Cedrus,* nor is it closely related to them.

Although probably occurring in every county of the state, it is abundant only in calcareous areas. It is a characteristic species of thin soil on limestone cliffs and ridges and is one of the chief trees to invade worn-out fields and overgrazed, eroded slopes. Therefore ecologically it is a pioneer, either in primary succession on limestone bluffs and ledges or in secondary old-field succession. Its occupancy of an area will build soil and hold moisture to the extent that other trees can later come in and survive. The role of red cedar on calcareous land is comparable to that of scrub pine (*Pinus virginiana*) in acid soil. In either rich or poor soil red cedar springs up in fencerows, where the seeds are dropped by birds which relish the "berries." This so-called "berry" has the same basic structure as a pine cone but has only a few cone scales, which are fleshy and grown together.

The pinkish red wood, being aromatic, is used for clothes closets and chests; being soft, light, and smooth, it is used for pencils; and being durable in the weather and in contact with the soil, it is used for fenceposts. Over thirty horticultural varieties of *Juniperus virginiana* have been developed and are cultivated ornamentally both in the United States and in Europe.   [Pp. 145, 148-49]

Gramineae, GRASS FAMILY

Arundinaria gigantea (Walt.) Chapm.   CANE
The cane is our only woody member of the grass family and our only representative of the bamboo tribe of that family. Today it is found on river banks, flood plains, and valley slopes throughout the state but is usually neither abundant nor dense. However,

accounts written at the time of settlement describe extensive cane lands or canebrakes, and some early maps located thousands of acres of "good cane lands." These extended far back from the streams, especially in central Kentucky, and were taken as an indication of rich land. Cane grew so thick and tall as to be almost impenetrable, and some of the earliest "roads" were the traces where bison had beaten down the cane. The pioneers' cattle fattened on its young shoots as the bison had earlier.   [P. 161]

Liliaceae, LILY FAMILY

Smilax bona-nox L.   BRISTLY GREENBRIER
This large, stout, high-climbing, well-armed vine grows in open disturbed woodland. It is widely distributed but more frequent in calcareous than in noncalcareous areas.   [Pp. 137, 165, 193]

Smilax glauca Walt.   SAWBRIER, CATBRIER
Creating a tangle which impedes walking, the sawbrier is common in old abandoned fields, thickets, and clearings. It usually grows in somewhat acid soil or, if in a calcareous area, it is in leached or eroded ground.   [Pp. 68, 136, 163, 192]

Smilax hispida Muhl.   HISPID GREENBRIER
This stout, high-climbing vine of second-growth woods and thickets is frequent and widely distributed.   [Pp. 69, 137, 164, 192]

Smilax rotundifolia L.   GREENBRIER
This greenbrier, a large climbing vine with vicious spines, often creates a tangle in clearings and second-growth thickets. It is common in most sections of the state.   [Pp. 137, 166, 193]

Salicaceae, WILLOW FAMILY

Populus alba L.   WHITE POPLAR
Introduced from Europe, the white poplar was formerly planted as an ornamental tree and is a frequent escape along roadsides and near old dwellings throughout Kentucky. Although the white branches and lower leaf-surfaces give an interesting contrast with

other trees, this species is not recommended because its roots are shallow and produce numerous sprouts. [Pp. 486-87]

Populus deltoides Marsh. COTTONWOOD
The cottonwood is fairly common on flood plains and alluvial bottomlands of rivers and large creeks in most sections of Kentucky except the southeast. [Pp. 393-94]

Populus gileadensis Rouleau BALM-OF-GILEAD
This is probably a hybrid between *P. deltoides* and *P. balsamifera* of the northern states. It was formerly planted widely and, though sterile, spread from cultivation by sprouts. It is found infrequently today. [P. 392]

Populus grandidentata Michx. LARGE-TOOTH ASPEN
The large-tooth aspen, abundant in the northern states and Canada, is found infrequently in northern and eastern Kentucky in upland second-growth woodlands and thickets. [Pp. 388-89]

Populus heterophylla L.
SWAMP COTTONWOOD, DOWNY POPLAR
The swamp cottonwood is common in swamps and alluvial bottomlands in the western half of the state. [Pp. 390-91]

The Genus *Salix*, the WILLOWS

The willows constitute a large genus of nearly 300 species worldwide, of which the greatest number grow in cold-climate areas of the northern hemisphere. Most species are shrubs rather than trees, and in arctic and alpine habitats many are only a few inches high. Precise identification of species is often difficult and is complicated by hybridization.

The slender flexible branches of several species have been used in both Europe and the United States for basket-making. In many the twigs snap off easily where they join a larger branch. The ease with which they break in a storm is an advantage as well as a disadvantage because, since they readily form roots from detached twigs lying on moist ground, this aids in covering a bank with vegetation. Willows thus perform a valuable service in holding stream banks.

Salix alba L.   EUROPEAN WHITE WILLOW
Introduced from Europe and escaping from cultivation, this tree may frequently be found in low ground along roadsides and along streams near roadsides.   [P. 395]

Salix amygdaloides Anders.   PEACH-LEAF WILLOW
A northern species reaching its southern limit here, this willow is rare in Kentucky.   [P. 395]

Salix caroliniana Michx.   CAROLINA WILLOW
This southern willow is found infrequently along stream banks in scattered sections of Kentucky.   [P. 272]

Salix discolor Muhl.   PUSSY WILLOW
The pussy willow, essentially a northern species, is infrequent strictly in the wild in Kentucky. However, it has been extensively planted for its attractive staminate catkins appearing in earliest spring and has escaped from cultivation, thus extending its range. The catkins are most furry and kittenlike when immature, before they become yellow with pollen. The branches may be cut in late winter and catkin development forced indoors. Roots develop easily on the cut stems, and persons with pussy willows like to pass on cuttings to friends.   [Pp. 106, 268-69]

Salix fragilis L.   CRACK WILLOW, BRITTLE WILLOW
This introduced native of Europe sometimes escapes.   [P. 395]

Salix humilis Marsh.
UPLAND WILLOW, PRAIRIE WILLOW
This small shrub may grow in dry ground as well as lowland clearings and other somewhat moist situations. It is frequent in the Knobs, Mississippian Plateau, and Cumberland Plateau, and probably occurs in other regions of the state with the possible exception of the Inner Bluegrass.   [Pp. 106, 271]

Salix interior Rowlee   SANDBAR WILLOW
Easily recognized and colony-forming, this willow grows on bars in streams, in other alluvia, and on pond margins. It is fairly frequent throughout most of the state.   [Pp. 105, 270]

Salix nigra Marsh.   BLACK WILLOW
This is our only large willow tree that is native, and it is common on stream and pond margins throughout the entire state. Its mass of shallow roots makes an excellent soil binder. Although its wood and branches have some commercial uses, the tree's greatest value is its service to the land while it lives.   [Pp. 105, 396-97]

Salix rigida Muhl.   HEART-LEAF WILLOW
This species is fairly frequent along slow streams in the Knobs, Outer Bluegrass, and Inner Bluegrass, and probably occurs elsewhere in the state.   [P. 272]

Salix sericea Marsh.   SILKY WILLOW
The silky willow is probably the most beautiful of our large shrubby species. It is widespread and frequent, especially on banks of small streams in open wooded areas.   [Pp. 106, 267]

Salix tristis Ait. [*S. humilis* var. *microphylla* (Anders.) Fernald]
DWARF UPLAND WILLOW, DWARF PRAIRIE WILLOW
This small shrub grows occasionally in dry ground but more often in lowland woods and clearings. It is frequent especially in the Cumberland Plateau, Knobs, and Mississippian Plateau.   [P. 271]

Myricaceae, Wax-Myrtle Family

Comptonia peregrina (L.) Coult.   SWEET-FERN
This boreal shrub, common from Nova Scotia to Saskatchewan and throughout the northern states, extends southward in the Appalachians. In Kentucky it is known to occur only on the sandy shores of the South Fork of the Cumberland River.   [P. 293]

Juglandaceae, Walnut Family

The Genus *Carya*, the *HICKORIES*

Of the fifteen species of *Carya* in North America, Kentucky has nine. It is almost an American genus, for the hickories of Europe have been extinct since the Ice Age and the only other species extant is one in China.

Hickories grow very slowly but can attain a height of 100 feet and a diameter of 3 feet. Their wood is heavy, tough, flexible, and strong, said to be stronger than the same weight in steel, and more elastic. Because the wood is resilient and shock-resistant and because it can take friction and strain, it makes the best axe handles and skis; for the same reasons wagon makers of the past demanded it for hubs, singletrees, and other parts, and today it is still used in trotting-horse sulkies. Pecan and other hickories are also used in furniture making. Hickory wood is excellent fuel, and in most species a cord has approximately the same thermal units as a ton of coal. Green hickory, with its aroma and long-lasting embers, cannot be surpassed for smoking meats. The trees unfortunately are subject to insect damage, especially from the hickory bark beetle, and logs are often attacked by wood-boring beetles. The wood decays quickly when exposed to the elements.

Of our nine species, *C. glabra, C. laciniosa, C. ovata,* and *C. tomentosa* are the most outstanding in wood properties; the wood of *C. illinoensis* is lighter and less strong, and *C. aquatica* and *C. cordiformis* are inferior to all the others.

Carya aquatica (Michx. f.) Nutt.   WATER HICKORY
This species, rare in Kentucky, grows in swamps which are inundated for considerable periods. In this state it is known to occur only along the Mississippi River and in McLean County. [P. 344]

Carya cordiformis (Wang.) K. Koch   BITTERNUT HICKORY
As the name implies, the nuts are inedible and are usually even too bitter for squirrels. Found in mesophytic situations, it grows less slowly than the other species. It is widely distributed in the state and is one of the most common hickories in the Bluegrass region.   [Pp. 342-43]

Carya glabra (Mill.) Sweet   PIGNUT
This is a common constituent of oak-hickory forests and can endure poor dry soil, although in such situations it grows extremely slowly. It is common and widely distributed in Kentucky but is less frequent in the Inner Bluegrass than in other areas. The nuts are not palatable.   [Pp. 350-51]

Carya illinoensis (Wang.) K. Koch   PECAN
In Kentucky the pecan, which is the largest of all species of *Carya,*

grows wild on the rich bottomlands along the Mississippi, lower Ohio, and lower Green rivers.

The pecan is the most delectable of all American nuts, and in the Deep South there are extensive orchards of its various horticultural varieties, which are grafted on wild stock. The species will grow and become a noble shade tree for the lawn in almost any part of Kentucky, but most of the nuts fail to mature except in the western section, where it is native. [Pp. 340-41]

Carya laciniosa (Michx. f.) Loud.
BIG SHAGBARK HICKORY, BIG SHELLBARK HICKORY, KINGNUT
The big shagbark grows on alluvial bottomlands and gentle mesophytic slopes, and since such areas are now usually in cultivation, fewer of this species exist today than of those species found on dry hills and ridges. It is nevertheless the most frequent hickory in the Inner Bluegrass, is frequent in south-central and western Kentucky, but is rare in eastern Kentucky. Its nuts are the largest of any hickorynuts and are as palatable as those of *C. ovata*, but the excessively thick shell makes them difficult to crack. [Pp. 348-49]

Carya ovalis (Wang.) Sarg.
SWEET PIGNUT, SMALL-FRUITED HICKORY
Though widely scattered in the state this species is infrequent, much less frequent than *C. glabra*, to which it is closely related. Its nuts are edible but very small. [P. 352]

Carya ovata (Mill.) K. Koch
SHAGBARK HICKORY, SHELLBARK HICKORY
Although occurring throughout Kentucky, the shagbark is most common in the hilly portions of the state, where it is a prominent constituent of oak-hickory forests. It is noteworthy for its wood properties and its palatable nuts. [Pp. 100, 346-47]

Carya pallida (Ashe) Engl. & Graebn. PALE HICKORY
Although closely related to the common *C. glabra*, this species is infrequent. It is found in several counties of the eastern and southern Knobs and in a few localities in the Cumberland Mountains. Unlike the pignut, it has edible nuts. [P. 352]

Carya tomentosa Nutt. MOCKERNUT, WHITE HICKORY
The mockernut is frequent in oak-hickory woodlands and is widely distributed, although less frequent in the Inner Bluegrass than in other sections. The nuts are edible if one is willing to crack a thick shell to obtain a small kernel. [P. 345]

Juglans cinerea L. BUTTERNUT, WHITE WALNUT
Growing on ravine slopes and in other mesophytic situations, the butternut is widespread in Kentucky but is only fairly frequent. The species is not flourishing; in fact, most mature trees seen are dying or half-dead, in sharp contrast to those in the Ohio valley described by Michaux in 1810 (*North American Sylva*), which were 10-12 feet in circumference 5 feet above the ground.

The oily kernel is palatable when fresh but soon becomes rancid. Young trees that are still healthy bear nuts; however, wind easily breaks the brittle branches and soon there are signs of injury by fungi and insects. The wood, which has been used for furniture and interior finish, is light brown, satiny and lustrous, soft, and light in weight. [Pp. 100, 336-37]

Juglans nigra L. BLACK WALNUT
The black walnut was originally abundant in the mixed forests of rich bottomlands and moist fertile slopes throughout Kentucky. Pioneers considered it one of the indicators of good land, and such land was cleared early. Today it is still widespread in the state but young trees are more often seen in dooryards and fence-rows and along roadsides than in woodlands. The nuts are flavorful, and a mature tree is stately in a lawn. It is a majestic tree, formerly growing up to 150 feet high and 4 to 6 feet in diameter, but today a tree 100 feet high and 3 feet in diameter is a rare specimen, still standing only because it is being specifically preserved.

Black walnut is America's foremost cabinet wood: hard, strong, durable, fine-grained, and finishing with a beautiful luster. It is superior to any other wood for gunstocks, being light in proportion to its strength and having less jar or recoil than any other. Walnut wood today is in great demand and short supply; it is so scarce that lumbermen seek it in door-to-door canvassing of farms. In contemporary furniture-making most walnut is cut as veneering, and little solid walnut is to be found except in antique pieces. However, a century and a half ago in Kentucky it was often used as structural timbers in houses and barns, and sometimes it was even used in fences and as railroad ties. Plantings of black walnut should indeed be made for future harvest of timber.   [Pp. 100, 238-39]

Betulaceae [Corylaceae], BIRCH FAMILY

Alnus serrulata (Ait.) Willd.   COMMON ALDER

The alder is a large shrub growing in swamps and on stream banks, usually in somewhat acid soil. In such habitats it is frequent in all noncalcareous sections of Kentucky, infrequent in the Mississippian Plateau, rare in the Outer Bluegrass, and apparently absent from the Inner Bluegrass.   [Pp. 102, 273]

Betula lenta L.   SWEET BIRCH, CHERRY BIRCH

This tree is called sweet birch because of the wintergreen aroma of the bark, twigs, and leaves, and is called cherry birch because the bark resembles that of the wild black cherry. (It has also been called black birch, a name which should be discouraged because the scientific name of another species of birch is *Betula nigra*.) It is a northern species with a southern extension in the Appalachian Mountains. In Kentucky it is restricted to the Cumberland Plateau and Cumberland Mountains, where it is frequent on steep mesophytic banks and cliffs of forested coves and valleys. It is a handsome forest tree, and in early spring before leaves appear it becomes delicately beautiful for a few days when the long catkins hanging from graceful branches are golden with pollen.

The wood is hard, strong, and close-grained, finishing with a good sheen. It has a variety of uses, including furniture, in which it can be made to resemble mahogany. Because it grows slowly, however, it requires about a century and a half before it interests the lumbermen. The wood is also distilled for wood alcohol, and the bark and twigs on distillation yield an aromatic oil which is chemically the same as the oil of the true wintergreen (*Gaultheria procumbens*). However, most of the oil of wintergreen on the market today is synthetically produced.   [Pp. 432-33]

Betula lutea Michx, f. (including var. *alleghaniensis* [Britt.] Ashe)
YELLOW BIRCH

The yellow birch is a northern species with a southern extension in the Appalachian Mountains. In Kentucky it grows in the mixed mesophytic forests of coves and deep ravines. It is found especially in the southeastern mountains, in the Cumberland Plateau, where it is less frequent than *B. lenta,* and in a few scattered localities in the southern part of the state. With hard, strong, satiny wood it is the chief timber birch and one of the most valuable timber trees of the northern states; it supplies much lumber for furniture and interior finish. [Pp. 101, 434-35]

Betula nigra L. RIVER BIRCH

The river birch is frequent along stream margins and in swamps in most sections of Kentucky except the Bluegrass. Though appearing a bit unkempt with its ragged bark, it is nevertheless graceful; its wood is hard, strong, and close-grained but is seldom marketed. It performs a real service in holding the banks of streams that are subject to flooding. What a woeful misconception some persons have had in clearing river banks to hasten the draining of flood waters! In so doing they have greatly increased erosion and thereby compounded the total problem. [Pp. 101, 430-31]

Carpinus caroliniana Walt.
AMERICAN HORNBEAM, BLUE BEECH, IRONWOOD

This tree is interesting for the uniqueness of its smooth, sinewy trunk. Growing along creek banks and as an understory tree in mesophytic forests, it is frequent and distributed throughout the state. Pioneers used its hard strong wood in hand-wrought tools, such as rake teeth, mallets, cogs, and handles, but since the tree is small and usually crooked, it is not used today. However, this does not mean it has no value. As a part of the natural biota of a mixed deciduous forest community, it has a role in the organization of the community; for instance, it provides food for several species of birds and mammals and nesting sites for birds which choose low trees. [Pp. 100, 436-37]

Corylus americana Walt. AMERICAN HAZELNUT

This shrub grows in a variety of habitats but especially in woodland borders, where it often forms thickets. In either dry or moist situations, it is frequent throughout most of Kentucky although apparently absent from the Inner Bluegrass. Providing cover, nesting sites, and food for wildlife, it is excellent in fencerows—those little habitats which farmers are tempted to remove. In growing native plants and harboring birds, fencerows are helpful in combatting crop-destroying insects. [Pp. 102, 274]

Ostyra virginiana (Mill.) K. Koch
HOP-HORNBEAM, IRONWOOD

The hop-hornbeam is an understory tree, growing especially in oak woods on dry hillsides. It is scattered throughout the state but is never abundant. Its wood is harder than oak, ash, or hickory and is surpassed in hardness only by dogwood. It is too small to be of much commercial value, rarely growing over 25 feet in height or 1 foot in diameter, but in the past it was used by local artisans to fashion tools where great strength was required. It is a hardy tree, little injured by insects or disease, and although not showy it contributes to the forest community. Besides providing food for wildlife it helps in the enrichment of dry hillsides by adding humus, holding soil, and retaining moisture. [Pp. 100, 438-39]

Fagaceae, BEECH FAMILY

Castanea dentata (Marsh.) Borkh. AMERICAN CHESTNUT

Once a grand and mighty tree frequently 100 feet tall and over 4 feet in diameter, the chestnut in Kentucky was most common in the Appalachian sections, extended westward across the state chiefly in noncalcareous areas, but was absent from the Bluegrass. Formerly a prominent constituent of both dry and mesophytic forests, the species is now seen only as a few standing skeletons, a few sprouts, or a rare small tree which is doomed sooner or later.

The chestnut blight, a fungus disease accidentally brought from Asia, in 1904 began its deadly work on our American chestnuts, which had no resistance to the foreign disease. Spreading rapidly, the blight almost exterminated the species within thirty years. Crossing with a blight-resistant Chinese chestnut has yielded a blight-resistant hybrid which has been back-crossed with the American chestnut, hopefully to combine resistance with the superior qualities of the American species.

Old-timers recall the delicious roasted nuts. In many Victorian houses chestnut wood may still be seen as interior trim. The wood is light, soft, strongly patterned, and satiny. Since it possessed a remarkable resistance to decay in the weather and in contact with the soil, it was widely used for fences and railroad ties. Even after the bark had peeled off trees long dead, lumbermen continued harvesting the wood. [Fp. 104, 114, 442-43]

Castanea pumila (L.) Mill.
CHINQUAPIN, DWARF CHESTNUT
An obscure relative of a vanquished monarch, this small tree, sometimes scarcely more than a shrub, continues in its lowly station to produce diminutive chestnuts, tasty and edible by man but used chiefly by wildlife. It grows in pine and oak-pine woods in eastern Kentucky but is generally rare, being more plentiful on Pine Mountain than elsewhere. We would be wise to plant it extensively for the benefit of wildlife such as grouse and bobwhite quail, for our own eating pleasure, and for the role of a small tree in landscape design. [Pp. 104, 114, 444-45]

Fagus grandifolia Ehrh. AMERICAN BEECH
The beech retains the smooth surface of its bark because the outside continues to grow in diameter as the wood increases and thus does not peel off as in most trees. This unfortunately attracts initial carvers—modern Orlandos and Rosalinds—who can return years later and see that their inscriptions have expanded.

This stately tree is shade-tolerant and grows in mesophytic climax forests. It is found in all regions but is most frequent in the eastern half of the state. Though rare in the Inner Bluegrass, it does occur in every Bluegrass county, especially in the Kentucky River gorge. The early settlers believed that the beech indicated good soil, much of which they plowed, but considered its wood second-rate. Though the wood has a variety of uses today, it is still not described with any superlatives. Beechnuts were the chief food of the ill-fated and extinct passenger pigeon, and today they are still in the diet of grouse, wild turkey, finches, grosbeaks, squirrels, chipmunks, and others. A good nut crop, however, usually occurs only about one year in three. [Pp. 104, 440-41]

The Genus *Quercus*, the *OAKS*

Each continent has its oaks, and altogether the world has nearly three hundred species of them. There are sixty in the United States, and nineteen are native to Kentucky. The oak is often called the king of trees, and it is a legendary symbol of strength, grandeur, and venerable age. Many ancient and historic oaks still stand in England, and in the United States many historic trees are oaks, marked with plaques and protected by fences. A white oak, estimated to be now over 300 years old, is mentioned in an 1805 survey of Thomas Lincoln's land and still stands at Abraham Lincoln's birthplace near Hodgenville, where it is known as the Boundary Oak.

Most of our oak species are good timber trees. Although the wood differs somewhat from species to species, some features are characteristic of all oak wood. It has large vessels formed only in early spring, and such a ring of pores is separated from the next ring by a band of dense hard cells formed during the remainder of the growing season. Its rays are larger than those of other woods and are conspicuous in surface view on boards cut from the center of the trunk. In most lumberyards species of oak are not distinguished; the wood is simply "white oak" or "red oak," and in each category species differ in quality.

Not only do oaks supply food for squirrels, but the squirrels in turn help to plant a new generation of forest trees when they do not return to dig up all the acorns they bury.

Quercus alba L.   WHITE OAK

This most magnificent of oaks probably occurs in every county of Kentucky and grows in a variety of habitats: dry hillsides, wet flats, and mesic situations. It is one of the ten most prominent species in the Mixed Mesophytic forest climax: it is one of the dominants in upland oak, oak-chestnut, and oak-hickory forests; and it is associated with sweet gum and pin oak on valley flats. It is less common in the Inner Bluegrass than in the hilly sections of the state. Michaux in 1810, in his *North American Sylva*, predicted that from the increase in population and the impoverishment of the soil the white oak would become scarce where it then prevailed and that it would replace the species which then composed the forests in richer ground. We note today that when the rich mixed mesophytic forests in eastern Kentucky are cut and left to nature, they are replaced by oak forests in which white oak is one of the dominants; and an oak forest dominated by white oak, when cut and left to nature, is replaced by oak and oak-pine forests—the oaks being species predominantly more xerophytic than white oak. Thus we commend Michaux's accuracy of forest analysis.

The wood of the white oak is strong, tough, hard, heavy, durable, and beautiful. It combines the good qualities of several other good timber trees, and even though it may rank second or third in particular features, the combination makes it altogether an incomparable wood in the variety of its uses—from shipbuilding to whiskey barrels to flooring and furniture. Top-grade white oak lumber comes from trees over 100 years old, and the supply of the old patriarchs is running out. The species has a potential life span of 500–800 years and may reach a height of over 100 feet and an even greater spread.

White oak trees are ornamental in a lawn but, being difficult to transplant, are most successfully planted as acorns or small trees. Since they grow slowly, anyone who plants a white oak is planting for posterity. Whether in lawn or forest this species has both dignity of form and beauty of detail. The rich verdure of summer starts as the pink-and-silver young growth of spring, and from a bright crimson in autumn it passes into bronze for winter.

The acorns are the most palatable and the least bitter of any of the oaks and are favorites of squirrels and other mammals and birds which eat mast. [Pp. 456-57]

Quercus bicolor Willd. SWAMP WHITE OAK
The swamp white oak is widely scattered over the state but is only fairly frequent and usually not numerous where it occurs. It is most often associated with sweet gum and pin oak on wet flats but also grows in other moist ground. The wood is excellent— hard and strong—and the small amount to be marketed passes as "white oak." [Pp. 454-55]

Quercus borealis Michx. f. var. *maxima* (Marsh.) Ashe [*Q. rubra* L.] RED OAK
This is the southern variety of the "northern red oak." Fairly common and probably occurring in every county of the state, it grows in somewhat mesophytic oak forests, neither in swamps nor on the driest ridges, and is a constituent of the Mixed Mesophytic

association. The red oak is a stately tree, handsome for lawns, streets, and parks. It is called red from the color of its wood; its leaves do not turn red in autumn. It grows more rapidly than *Q. alba,* and the wood is high grade though weaker, coarser, less heavy, and less durable than white oak.　　　　　[Pp. 103, 464-65]

Quercus coccinea Muench.　SCARLET OAK

As the last tree to turn in autumn, the scarlet oak closes out its annual career in a blaze of glory, contrasting strikingly with the green of its associated pines. It is the most xerophytic of our oaks, growing especially with pines and chestnut oak in noncalcareous soils of ridge crests and south and west hillsides. It is common in the Cumberland Mountains, Cumberland Plateau, and Knobs, and also occurs in similar habitats in other regions of the state except the Inner Bluegrass. It is a beautiful tree, and its value in ornamental planting has not been adequately appreciated in this state. It will grow in all situations except swampy ground and, if planted, will flourish in rich limestone land, where it does not naturally occur. The wood of the scarlet oak, which is heavy and strong, is sold as red oak.　　　　　[Pp. 468-69]

Quercus falcata Michx.
SOUTHERN RED OAK, SPANISH OAK

Kentucky is near the northern limit of the range of the southern red oak, also ineptly called Spanish oak. Occurring in all regions except the Bluegrass, it is frequently associated with scarlet and chestnut oaks on dry uplands and sometimes with pin oak and sweet gum on low flats. The wood is slightly inferior to that of other red oaks; the bark, being especially rich in tannins, has long been used in tanning leather.　　　　　[Pp. 474-75]

Quercus imbricaria Michx.　SHINGLE OAK

This species acquired its common name because the wood splits easily and early settlers used it for making shingles. While it occurs in all regions of the state, it is most common in the Knobs and very frequent in the Outer Bluegrass and Pennyroyal. It grows in a variety of situations which are ecologically in successional stages rather than in climax forests: swampy flats, stream margins, and dry uplands. It deserves to be used in ornamental planting more than it has been in Kentucky.　　　　　[Pp. 368-69]

Quercus lyrata Walt. OVERCUP OAK

A tree of the swamps, the overcup oak is restricted to the western half of the state and is infrequent even there. The wood is stronger than white oak but is less beautiful; however, no merchantable amount occurs in Kentucky.   [Pp. 458-59]

Quercus macrocarpa Michx. BUR OAK

The bur oak is the most characteristic tree in the Bluegrass landscape. It is common in the Inner Bluegrass, frequent in the Outer Bluegrass and Pennyroyal, and rare or absent in other sections of Kentucky. The species is characteristic of savannas, those parklike grassy openings with scattered trees intermediate between forest and prairie; it does not grow in dense forests because its seedlings cannot tolerate shade. The stronghold of the bur oak is west and northwest of Kentucky, where forest and prairie climates merge.

The fact that there are numerous bur oaks over 200 years old in the Bluegrass, many 300–400 years old, is ecologically significant in interpreting the original vegetation here before white man modified it. The gently rolling interstream areas were apparently savanna and not true forest, although the rainfall has long been adequate for forest. It would seem that this constituted a relict community which persisted from an earlier, probably interglacial, drier time. Vast herds of bison would have helped to prevent a return to forest; also, especially in the open so-called "Barrens" in the Mississippian Plateau, the occasional burning of the area by Indians to encourage grass and attract game would have contributed. Today many Bluegrass pastures with their grand old bur oaks are yielding to urban expansion, and in the remaining pastures and country lawns the old patriarchs are not reproducing themselves because the seedlings are mowed down. Planting bur oaks should be encouraged; although they grow slowly like most oaks, they are more easily transplanted than several others. Without bur oaks there would be no truly typical Bluegrass scene.

The wood is hard, strong, tough, and durable, and resembles white oak. It has been used in shipbuilding, interior finish, general construction, and railroad ties.   [Pp. 462-63]

Quercus marilandica Muench. BLACK JACK OAK

We are indebted to the scrubby, crooked black jack oak, seldom over 20 feet tall, for growing where most trees will not grow. It is fairly frequent on thin, dry, sterile soil on ridge crests and eroded hills. The species occurs in all regions of the state except the Bluegrass. [P. 476]

Quercus michauxii Nutt.
SWAMP CHESTNUT OAK, BASKET OAK, COW OAK
The swamp chestnut oak is a large and handsome southern species relatively infrequent in Kentucky and found chiefly in the western half of the state. It grows in swamp forests with sweet gum and pin oak. The wood is tough, strong, and durable, and is used for implements, railroad ties, and heavy construction. Since the wood will split into tough ribbons, it has been used for strong baskets and hence is often called basket oak. [Pp. 452-53]

Quercus montana Willd. [*Q. prinus* L.]
CHESTNUT OAK, MOUNTAIN CHESTNUT OAK,
ROCK CHESTNUT OAK
The chestnut oak is a dominant species in upland oak forests. It grows especially in noncalcareous soil and is most abundant on dry slopes and ridges in eastern Kentucky, where it is associated with white oak, scarlet oak, and pines. It is common in the Western Coal Field and occurs in other regions with the apparent exceptions of the Bluegrass and the Jackson Purchase. The bark has the highest tannin content of any oak. The wood is dark, hard, heavy, tough, and durable, and has been used for railroad ties and heavy construction. [Pp. 448-49]

Quercus muehlenbergii Engelm.
CHINQUAPIN OAK, YELLOW OAK
The chinquapin oak, the limestone counterpart of the mountain chestnut oak, is a dominant species on calcareous uplands. It is abundant in the Bluegrass region, common in the Mississippian Plateau, and infrequent in other regions. It is a truly handsome tree which deserves planting in our parks and lawns. Unfortunately most of our nurseries have not seen fit to propagate it and make it available for planting. The wood has properties and uses similar to those of *Q. montana* but the bark has less tannin. [Pp. 450-51]

Quercus nigra L. WATER OAK
The water oak grows in swamps and alluvial bottomlands in western

Kentucky but is rare. It is sometimes planted on lawns as a shade tree and as such is highly ornamental. [P. 477]

Quercus palustris Muench. PIN OAK
Because of its graceful and symmetrical form, good autumn color, and relatively rapid growth the pin oak is one of the most widely planted trees on streets and lawns throughout Kentucky. Natively it is common in wet, poorly drained ground such as swamps, valley flats, sinkholes, and shallow depressions in alluvium; it is one of the dominant trees in swamp forests. In the wild it occurs in all regions except apparently the Inner Bluegrass but is most abundant in the Knobs, Western Coal Field, and Jackson Purchase. Because the trunk produces more small horizontal branches than most oaks, the wood has many knots which make it inferior to other red oaks for lumber. [Pp. 470-71]

Quercus phellos L. WILLOW OAK
This southern species extends into southern Kentucky and the Jackson Purchase. Here it is frequent on poorly drained bottomlands, where it is associated with sweet gum and pin oak. As an ornamental tree having delicate foliage, beautiful symmetry, and rapid growth, it may be grown in lawns and parks all over Kentucky. In the southern states, where it is common, it is a valuable timber tree. [Pp. 370-71]

Quercus prinoides Willd. CHINQUAPIN OAK
This oak was reported growing on rocky slopes in several localities in Kentucky a century ago and may or may not remain in the state. It is a shrub, usually 3–4 feet in height but sometimes taller, bearing runners which produce large clumps.

Quercus shumardii Buckl. (including var. *schneckii* Britt.)
SHUMARD OAK, SHUMARD RED OAK
The tall and stately Shumard oak grows in rich, moist, well-drained soil. It is common throughout the Inner and Outer Bluegrass regions, absent from the Appalachian sections, and infrequent elsewhere in the state. It resembles the red oak (*Q. borealis*) in some respects and the scarlet and pin oaks (*Q. coccinea* and *Q. palustris*) in others; lumbermen do not distinguish its wood from that of *Q. borealis*. [Pp. 466-67]

Quercus stellata Wang. POST OAK
This species is known as post oak because the early settlers, finding the wood durable in contact with the soil, used it for fenceposts. Since the heavy branches may be crooked and ungainly and the leaves are coarse and stiff, it is not recommended for ornamental planting. However, let not its virtues go unpraised. It grows in poor, thin, eroded soil and on dry rocky ridges where many species would never survive, and here, by holding existing soil and helping to build more, it prepares the way in nature's plant succession for other oaks and hickories. And even an old post oak may, in its lack of symmetry, be picturesque. In Kentucky this species occurs in all regions; it is common wherever there is much poor rocky ground and scarce where there is little of such habitat.
[Pp. 460-61]

Quercus velutina Lam. BLACK OAK
Also called quercitron or yellow oak from the orange inner bark which yields a dye, the black oak grows in upland woods where it is associated with either white or scarlet oak. Though rare in the Inner Bluegrass, it is common in most of the state. The wood, marketed as "red oak," is inferior to the true red oak. [Pp. 472-73]

Ulmaceae, Elm Family

Celtis laevigata Willd.
SUGARBERRY, SMOOTH HACKBERRY
This predominantly southern species is frequent in low ground in the western half of Kentucky.   [Pp. 376-77]

Celtis occidentalis L. HACKBERRY
The hackberry is distributed over the entire state but unevenly so. It is abundant in the Bluegrass, where it commonly springs up in fencerows, along roadsides, and in old fields; it is infrequent in the Cumberland Mountains and Plateau and is frequent elsewhere.

A full-grown hackberry 50 feet tall, round-topped, slender-twigged, and graceful, is beautiful, but being usually thought of as plebeian it does not receive the appreciation it deserves. Its tough, flexible, and free-splitting wood also has had rather humble uses (a favorite for tobacco sticks among an earlier generation of Bluegrass farmers, who split such sticks by hand), but since it has an attractive pattern and takes a good polish, it could have more aristocratic uses. [Pp. 380-81]

Celtis tenuifolia Nutt. DWARF HACKBERRY
This scrubby little tree with crooked branches grows in dry, usually calcareous, ground. It is common in the Bluegrass region and the Mississippian Plateau, rare in the Cumberland Plateau and Mountains, and infrequent in other sections of the state. [Pp. 378-79]

Planera aquatica (Walt.) J. F. Gmel. WATER ELM
This small tree is fairly frequent in swamps of western Kentucky. Its fruits are eaten by ducks. [P. 422]

Ulmus alata Michx. WINGED ELM
This southern species extends as far north as the Inner Bluegrass and is distributed throughout the southern and western parts of the state. It grows on dry ridges, slopes, and bluffs and also in moist bottomlands. On bluffs it is a small straggly tree, but in bottomlands it may grow up to 40 or 50 feet in height with a trunk diameter of 2 or more feet. The species attains its best development in the valleys of the southern states west of the Mississippi River. [P. 423]

Ulmus americana L. AMERICAN ELM, WHITE ELM
The American elm is frequent throughout the state, especially along streams and in moist woods in coves and lowlands. Also, in good soil such as that in the Bluegrass region it is a common invader of old fields.

This tall, gracefully spreading tree with branches suggesting a fountain of foliage has been one of America's favorite shade trees for lawns and streets, especially in the northern states. Along avenues its branches make vaulted arches, and a home beneath an arching elm seems protected by its beneficence. Under its domelike crown many an early council was held. At Boonesborough in May of 1775 it was a great elm tree beneath which the first legislature in Kentucky gathered. The first public service of worship in Kentucky was held under this elm during the legislative assembly and was conducted by John Lythe, an Anglican clergyman who was one of the delegates.[1] In the United States elms probably out-number oaks as "historic trees."

However, many a noble elm has fallen before a new and fatal disease, and the prognosis for the species is gloomy. Hence young elms should no longer be included in landscape planting. The Dutch elm disease, first observed in Holland and later in England, probably entered the United States with English elm burls to be used for veneer. They contained the elm bark beetle which carries the fungus responsible for the disease.   [Pp. 109, 424-25]

Ulmus rubra Muhl.   SLIPPERY ELM, RED ELM

The slippery elm is so named because of the mucilaginous inner bark of trunk, branches, and twigs. In folk medicine this layer of inner bark is moistened and used as a poultice for allaying in-flammation, and is also steeped in boiling water for use as a medicinal beverage. The tree is occasionally called red elm because of the reddish heartwood.

This species never attains either the size or the grace of the American elm, and it too is susceptible to the Dutch elm disease. Frequent throughout Kentucky, it grows both on dry slopes and in moist, well-drained bottomlands. The wood is hard, strong, and durable in contact with the soil and has been used for cheap furniture, wheel hubs, implements, fenceposts, and railroad ties.

[Pp. 109, 426-27]

Ulmus serotina Sarg.   SEPTEMBER ELM

This species flowers in the fall instead of the early spring when other elms flower. It is a southern species, nowhere common; in Kentucky it is widely scattered, occurring on alluvial terraces in only a few localities.   [Pp. 109, 423]

Ulmus thomasi Sarg.   ROCK ELM, CORK ELM

This is a northern species which has corky wings on the twigs. It is rare in Kentucky, less frequent than the winged elm, *U. alata*, a southern species with corky wings. It grows on dry limestone slopes.   [Pp. 428-29]

---

[1] Frances K. Swinford and Rebecca S. Lee, *The Great Elm Tree: Heritage of the Episcopal Diocese of Lexington* (Lexington, Ky.: Faith House Press, 1969), pp. 1-2.

Moraceae, MULBERRY FAMILY

Broussonetia papyrifera (L.) Vent. PAPER MULBERRY
The paper mulberry is a native of Asia which was introduced into the United States and is fairly frequent in Kentucky. It may be found as an escape near cities, especially in urban waste areas. In Asia the inner bark has been used for making paper. [P. 486]

Maclura pomifera (Raf.) Schneid.
OSAGE ORANGE, HEDGE APPLE
The osage orange, a native of east Texas northward into Arkansas and Oklahoma, was introduced into the eastern states for hedge planting. In Kentucky not many such hedges remain, but the species has escaped and may be a thorny pest on roadsides, in pastures, and in other open places; it is most common in the Bluegrass region. It can become a tree 50 feet tall and equally widespreading. The wood, which is hard, strong, and flexible, is used by modern archers for bows, as it was by early Indians. Other names for the tree are bois-d'arc, bodark (a corruption), and bowwood. [Pp. 362-63]

Morus alba L. WHITE MULBERRY
This native of Asia is the mulberry which feeds the silkworm. It is an attractive small tree which has been cultivated and is occasionally seen as an escape in Kentucky. [Pp. 103, 118, 485]

Morus rubra L. RED MULBERRY
Our native mulberry grows rapidly in thickets, fencerows, woodland borders, and on roadsides, and is frequent throughout the state. Although it is not an outstandingly ornamental tree, it should be encouraged in order to attract songbirds, many of which eat the fruit. Ripening in summer, the fruit is important to squirrels before nuts mature. [Pp. 103, 118, 382-83]

Santalaceae, SANDALWOOD FAMILY

Pyrularia pubera Michx. BUFFALO-NUT, OILNUT
The buffalo-nut is a straggling shrub parasitic on roots of various trees from which it obtains water and minerals. It is fairly frequent

in forests of the Cumberland Plateau and Mountains. The plant contains an acrid oil which is most concentrated in the fruit and the endosperm of the seed. [Pp. 107, 252]

Loranthaceae, MISTLETOE FAMILY

Phoradendron flavescens (Pursh) Nutt. MISTLETOE
The mistletoe is an evergreen parasitic shrub, frequent and widely distributed over the state. This popular Christmas decoration lives on branches of many species of trees such as black walnut, American elm, hackberry, black locust, honey locust, sour gum, and over a dozen others. Deforming but not killing the branch on which it grows, it obtains water and minerals from the xylem of the host and manufactures sugar in its own green leaves. The berries are eaten by birds, which distribute the parasite. [Pp. 146, 162]

Aristolochiaceae, BIRTHWORT FAMILY

Aristolochia durior Hill DUTCHMAN'S-PIPE
Aristolochia tomentosa Sims PIPE-VINE
Both of these twining vines are high-climbing. The Dutchman's-pipe grows in mesophytic woods in southeastern and southern Kentucky, and the pipe-vine grows in swamps and alluvial woodlands of western Kentucky. Neither is frequent. [Pp. 68, 191]

Polygonaceae, SMARTWEED FAMILY

Brunnichia cirrhosa Gaertn.
BUCKWHEAT VINE, LADIES'-EARDROPS
This large vine is common in swamps and lowland thickets in western Kentucky. [Pp. 107, 194]

Menispermaceae, MOONSEED FAMILY

Calycocarpum lyoni (Pursh) Nutt. CUPSEED
Found infrequently, the cupseed climbs to the treetops in rich floodplain woods in the western half of the state. [P. 197]

Cocculus carolinus (L.) DC. CAROLINA SNAILSEED
The snailseed is a southern semiwoody twiner with seeds suggesting the coiling of a snail's shell. Of limited distribution in Kentucky, it is fairly frequent in moist woods and thickets and on limestone cliffs near streams in the Inner Bluegrass and in southern and western Kentucky. [Pp. 123, 195]

Menispermum canadense L. MOONSEED
This semiwoody twining vine is frequent throughout the state in moist thickets and woodland borders. Its blue-black fruits, resembling wild grapes, are poisonous. [Pp. 80, 136, 196]

Ranunculaceae, Buttercup Family

Xanthorhiza simplicissima Marsh. SHRUB YELLOWROOT
This small slender shrub with erect stems is infrequent although locally plentiful along stream margins in the Cumberland Plateau and Mountains. [Pp. 107, 116, 251]

Magnoliaceae, Magnolia Family

Members of this family were among the earliest flowering plants on earth, flourishing in Europe, Asia, both western and eastern North America, and Greenland during the Cretaceous Period. Today they are restricted to eastern Asia and eastern North America, plus one species in Mexico. The genus *Liriodendron*, formerly with about sixteen species, now has only two: ours and one in China. There are still many species of *Magnolia*, most of them Asiatic.

Liriodendron tulipifera L.
TULIP TREE, TULIP POPLAR, YELLOW POPLAR
Kentucky, Indiana, and Tennessee each chose the tulip tree as its state tree. It is the tallest hardwood species in North America, attaining a height of 200 feet with a straight trunk that may be 80–100 feet to the lowest limb and may have a diameter of 8–10 feet. Michaux (*North American Sylva*, 1810) said that in its wide range in eastern North America it was most abundant in Kentucky, and nowhere else did he find the tulip tree so tall and so great in

diameter. He considered it one of the most magnificant productions of the temperate zone.

Its greenish yellow and orange flowers account for both the specific epithet and the preferred common name. "Yellow poplar," a lumberman's term, is a misnomer because the species is not related to the true poplars, which have far inferior wood.

This beautiful and stately tree occurs in every county in Kentucky. It is one of the chief trees of the Mixed Mesophytic forest and is a dominant in many such communities. It is—or was— abundant in deep, rich, well-drained soil of coves and valleys. The pioneers considered it an indicator of good soil, and to cultivate the land they cleared away and burned more than they used in their houses and barns. Commercial logging of the "yellow poplar" increased till it reached mammoth proportions in the 1880s and 1890s.

The wood is light in weight, soft, easily worked, and adaptable. Its many uses have ranged from the dugout canoes of Indians and early explorers to paper pulp of today, and have included exterior construction, interior finish, and furniture.

The tulip tree is a superior shade tree for lawn and street wherever there is adequate soil moisture and richness. It is extensively grown in England and France as one of the most popular of American trees. [Pp. 41, 482-84]

Magnolia acuminata L.
CUCUMBER-TREE, CUCUMBER MAGNOLIA
Of our four magnolias the one with the smallest leaves and smallest flowers makes the largest tree. The cucumber-tree, so named because of the appearance of its fruit when young and green, may grow up to 80 feet in height. Although its greenish flowers may go unnoticed, the tree is beautiful and is ornamental in lawns and parks. Natively it is frequent on forested mountain slopes in eastern and southern Kentucky. Its wood is similar to that of the tulip tree. [Pp. 41, 114, 356-57]

Magnolia fraseri Walt.
FRASER'S MAGNOLIA, MOUNTAIN MAGNOLIA
In Kentucky this lovely tree is restricted to the southeast where it grows as an understory tree in the Mixed Mesophytic association in rich protected coves. [Pp. 42, 116, 358]

Magnolia macrophylla Michx. LARGE-LEAF MAGNOLIA
Its great leaves, the largest in the North American sylva, and its fragrant flowers to the same scale create an effect like nothing else in a temperate forest. On first sight one can hardly believe one's eyes. In autumn and winter after the fall of the giant leaves, which are whitened beneath, the forest floor appears to be strewn with newspaper. This magnolia grows on rich wooded mountain slopes in the Cumberland Plateau and Mountains and in the Green River valley of Edmondson County, but is only locally frequent. It is most plentiful in the Cumberland Mountains and the ravines of the western edge of the Cumberland Plateau in the outcrop of the Rockcastle conglomerate.   [Pp. 42, 115, 359]

Magnolia tripetala L. UMBRELLA MAGNOLIA
The umbrella magnolia grows on mesophytic wooded slopes; it is frequent throughout eastern Kentucky and less frequent in the south-central and southwest-central counties. Although less striking than its scarcer relatives, this attractive tree with beautiful though ill-scented flowers still merits praise.   [Pp. 42, 115, 360]

Calycanthaceae, CALYCANTHUS FAMILY

Calycanthus fertilis Walt.
CALYCANTHUS, SWEET SHRUB, CAROLINA ALLSPICE
This species, with aromatic twigs, leaves and flowers, grows along river banks in McCreary County, but is rare.   [Pp. 43, 209]
   A more fragrant species, *C. floridus* L., was one of the favorite shrubs in our grandmothers' gardens. Its dark red flowers with the odor of ripe strawberries would become increasingly sweet on wilting. This cultivated *Calycanthus* is a native of the Appalachian Mountains and was recorded in Bell and Harlan counties in 1870. It may still be in our state's wild flora.   [P. 209]

Annonaceae, CUSTARD-APPLE FAMILY

Asimina triloba (L.) Dunal. PAPAW
The papaw is a small tree or large shrub belonging to a family which is predominantly tropical. Often forming thickets, it grows

in a variety of habitats, both wooded and open, and is common throughout the state. The fruit, is soft, sweet, rich, and custardy.
[Pp. 43, 120, 255, 361]

Lauraceae, Laurel Family

This is the family of the true laurel, a Mediterranean evergreen species first used by the ancient Greeks and better known in the wreaths which crowned victorious Romans. Our so-called mountain laurel is not a true laurel and does not belong to this family. Kentucky's two representatives of the *Lauraceae* are deciduous.

Lindera benzoin (L.) Blume SPICEBUSH
The spicy aroma from a broken twig, crushed leaf, or berry of the spicebush is more pungent and to most persons more pleasing than that of any other aromatic woody plant in our flora. It is frequent in shady valleys and mesophytic woods throughout the state. Though never showy, it is always beautiful. From an unassuming winter aspect of graceful slender twigs and an early prefoliage flowering, it develops a smooth rich verdure which is accented by red berries in late summer and becomes a clear yellow in autumn. It grows rapidly in rich moist soil and is useful as a background shrub in ornamental planting. [Pp. 108, 133, 253]

Sassafras albidum (Nutt.) Nees SASSAFRAS
Sassafras means many things to many people. A follower of folk traditions will dig the roots for brewing sassafras tea; a child may search the leaves for righthand and lefthand "mittens"; an autumn color enthusiast is thrilled by the brilliance of its scarlet and orange foliage, while birds in fall relish its fruits; and a winter hiker may admire the olive green upturned twigs and break one for its spicy aroma and taste. A plant geographer or paleontologist sees it as a relict from the geologic past, for, although only two species of sassafras remain in the world today (this one in eastern United States and another in eastern Asia), there are fossils of sassafras species throughout the world.

Persons familiar with bushy sassafras thickets, commonly growing at the edge of woods and invading abandoned fields in all parts of Kentucky, may overlook the fact that it can be a large tree.

The pioneers believed that the aromatic wood, if used in bedsteads and poultry houses, would discourage insects. Explorers along the east coast as early as the late sixteenth century carried sassafras roots and bark to Europe because of reputed medicinal properties, and it was one of the first American trees intoduced into Europe. Although of no therapeutic value it is still cultivated there occasionally as an ornamental tree. Its beauty is too little appreciated at home where it is common.   [Pp. 26, 108, 140, 480-81]

Saxifragaceae, Saxifrage Family

Hydrangea arborescens L.   WILD HYDRANGEA

The hydrangea is frequent on moist wooded cliffs and ravine slopes across the state. This species is widely cultivated in a form which resulted from the selection of plants having more showy sterile flowers in a cluster than small fertile ones.   [Pp. 88, 231]

Itea virginica L.   VIRGINIA-WILLOW

This pretty little shrub, also called tassel-white and sweet-spires, grows in swampy woods and along streams in southern Kentucky from east to west, but is infrequent.   [Pp. 72, 276]

Philadelphus hirsutus Nutt. and *P. inodorus* L.
MOCK-ORANGE

Several foreign species of mock-orange and several hybrids are used in ornamental planting. Our two native species, both infrequent, are found on cliffs and in woodland borders in southern and southwestern Kentucky.   [Pp. 43, 220]

Ribes cynosbati L.   PRICKLY GOOSEBERRY

This little shrub grows on rocky wooded slopes, especially above creeks, in widely scattered localities in the state, but is only fairly frequent.   [Pp. 95, 294]

Ribes missouriense Nutt.   MISSOURI GOOSEBERRY

The Missouri gooseberry is found in central and western Kentucky on rocky wooded creek banks and in woodland borders, but is infrequent.   [P. 294]

Hamamelidaceae, WITCH-HAZEL FAMILY

Hamamelis virginiana L. WITCH-HAZEL

An oddity indeed is the witch-hazel. From the time of Hallowe'en witches through November little yellow flowers with slender twisted petals appear on the twigs after leaves have fallen. The hard dry capsules, which do not mature until a year later, are interesting also as they explosively discharge their seeds, shooting them 10 to 20 feet away on a warm, sunny autumn day following a frosty night. Cultivated species of witch-hazel introduced from other countries flower in late winter.

The witch-hazel obtained its name probably from the "water witches" who would sometimes choose its forked branches allegedly to locate ground water. It has long been the source of a pleasant but inert essence extracted from the dried leaves and twigs for use in lotions.

It is a large shrub, frequent in woodland borders and on ravine slopes and stream banks in all parts of Kentucky. In ornamental planting it is useful in a shrub border in the shade. [Pp. 44, 275]

Liquidambar styraciflua L. SWEET GUM, RED GUM

The sweet gum grows especially on swampy flats where it is associated with pin oak, but also on stream banks where it is associated with river birch and sycamore. Apparently absent in the wild from the Inner Bluegrass and infrequent in the Outer Bluegrass, it is either frequent or common in the rest of the state.

The balsamic resin which oozes from the tree is used in medicines, perfumes, and incense and is commercially extracted in the states to the south of us, where the trees produce more of the substance. The sweet gum yields one of the chief cabinet woods in use today. The heartwood is pink or rosy-reddish, and the relatively large sapwood is white. Since it has an attractive pattern and takes stain well, it is often used to imitate mahogany, cherry, and other woods.

The sweet gum is an attractive lawn tree, especially in autumn when its star-shaped leaves become wine-colored—rosy or purplish red or even purple. However, when grown in rich calcareous soil its coloration is less intense. [Pp. 29, 490-91]

Platanaceae, Plane Tree Family

Platanus occidentalis L.   SYCAMORE
Abundant along streams both large and small, the sycamore probably occurs in every county. It reaches its greatest size in rich
bottomlands, and in girth is the largest hardwood species in North
America. In primeval America many were giants, such as the one
measured by Michaux in 1802 on the north bank of the Ohio,
being 47 feet in circumference 4 feet above the ground. Very
large sycamores are usually hollow.

The wood, which is moderately hard though not strong or
decay-resistant, has had numerous uses, chief of which is the
butcher's block because it does not split with repeated hacking.
It is light-colored and when quarter-sawed has a satiny or moiré
pattern and texture attractive in paneling and furniture.

The beauty of the tree lies in its trunk and branches, whitish
and dappled with gray-green and tan. The sight of such branches
against a bright blue sky is one of the joys of a sunny winter day.
For planting, the tree is good for large spaces but not for a city
lawn or street both because the leaves are coarse and because their
lower surface has a fuzz which gives hay fever to allergic persons
if they are close to the leaves.

The American sycamore is a relative of the European plane tree,
but the sycamore of Amos and Zacchaeus in the Bible was a
species of fig. [Pp. 488-89]

Rosaceae, Rose Family

Amelanchier arborea (Michx. f.) Fernald
SERVICEBERRY, SARVIS, SARVIS TREE,
JUNEBERRY, SHADBUSH
This most widespread species of *Amelanchier* in the United States
has different common names in different localities. In many places
it is known as Juneberry because its fruits mature earlier than most
edible fruits. In the eastern states it received the appellation of
shadbush because it flowers early when the shad "run." But in the
southern Appalachians this species and *A. laevis* are known as
service tree or serviceberry, pronounced "sarvis." This is an
interesting local retention of an Elizabethan English pronunciation.

It is said that this was called service tree in the mountains because its early flowering coincided with memorial services held after the end of winter to honor those who died during the season when travel up the hollows was too difficult for all who wished to pay final respects.

The beauty of this understory tree is appreciated in leafless woods, where it is conspicuous at a distance because of its graceful white racemes blooming before any other forest tree with showy flowers. It is frequent in eastern and southern Kentucky, fairly frequent in western Kentucky, rare in the Outer Bluegrass, and apparently absent from the Inner Bluegrass. It will grow in any locality and should be propagated and grown widely for both its beauty and the attraction of its fruit for birds.   [Pp. 44, 134, 398-99]

Amelanchier intermedia Spach.   JUNEBERRY, SHADBUSH
This species has been recorded from northern Kentucky.

Amelanchier laevis Wieg.   SMOOTH SERVICEBERRY
This species grows in southern Kentucky, both the southeast and the southwest, but is rare.   [Pp. 44, 398]

Aronia arbutifolia (L.) Ell. [*Pyrus arbutifolia* (L.) L. f.]
RED CHOKEBERRY
Our largest and most beautiful species of chokeberry, found infrequently in the swamps of western Kentucky, is now being cultivated for ornamental planting. Its red berries are eaten by many birds.   [Pp. 82, 132, 278]

Aronia melanocarpa (Michx.) Ell.
[*Pyrus melanocarpa* (Michx.) Willd.]
BLACK CHOKEBERRY
This little shrub with small apple-like flowers is fairly frequent on sandstone banks and acid swampy flats in eastern and southern Kentucky.   [Pp. 82, 134, 277]

Aronia prunifolia (Marsh.) Rehder
[*Pyrus floribunda* (Lindl.) Spach.]
PURPLE CHOKEBERRY
This species has been recorded from southeastern Kentucky but is rare.   [Pp. 82, 278]

The Genus *Crataegus*, the *HAWTHORNS*

Species of hawthorns are many, complex, and difficult to separate. Since identification of each of the approximately two dozen in Kentucky is only for the specialist, hawthorns in this book primarily for the layman are treated collectively except for three easily identified species.

A few hawthorns can become medium-sized trees, most are small trees, and some are shrubs. They are found in cut-over areas, abandoned farmlands, woodland borders, and roadsides. Old World species have for centuries been used in English and continental hedgerows. Our native hawthorns are equally well adapted for such use, taking trimming well, but have seldom been so planted. Such a hedge not only would be beautiful but would provide nesting places for birds that help combat farmers' insect pests.

Crataegus crus-galli L. COCKSPUR THORN
This species, fairly frequent or frequent in most sections of the state, can be distinguished readily from other hawthorns and hence is listed separately.   [Pp. 49, 131, 415]

Crataegus mollis (T. & G.) Scheele   RED HAW
This is the most common hawthorn in central Kentucky and is also frequent in other parts of the state. It is included here as a representative of a large number of species.   [Pp. 50, 132, 478]

Crataegus phaenopyrum (L. f.) Medic.
WASHINGTON THORN
This is one of the most exquisite of American hawthorns and is easily distinguished. Because of its beauty it was introduced into English gardens in the seventeenth century and is still cultivated in England, France, and Germany. It was dubbed Washington thorn when some cultivated stock from Washington, D.C., was taken to Pennsylvania.

Natively in Kentucky it is rare and scattered, but birds cause its frequent escape from cultivation.   [Pp. 49, 131, 479]

Physocarpus opulifolius (L.) Maxim. NINEBARK
In Kentucky this shrub is apparently restricted to the areas of Ordovician and Mississippian limestone outcrop: the Inner and

Outer Bluegrass regions, the Mississippian Plateau, and smaller areas near the Pottsville Escarpment. It grows on both cliffs and rocky creek bottoms and is fairly frequent.   [Pp. 71, 295]

The Genus *Prunus*: the PLUMS, CHERRIES, and PEACH

PLUMS   All four species of wild plums in Kentucky form thickets in clearings and along woodland borders, roadsides, and fencerows, and die when taller-growing trees have overtopped and shaded them. They are exquisite in early spring when they become a mass of fragrant white flowers, which on a sunny day formerly hummed with bees (DDT has reduced the bee population). In summer they provide tangy fruit, delicious for preserves and jellies, as well as provender for wildlife: rabbits nibble the juicy fruit when it falls and mice in winter make holes in the stones to extract the seed.

Prunus americana Marsh.   WILD PLUM
This species is common and widespread.   [Pp. 45, 121, 408]

Prunus angustifolia Marsh.   CHICKASAW PLUM
This is smaller and more shrubby than the other species. It is infrequent in Kentucky in comparison with its abundance farther south, but occurs in the central, southern, and southwestern parts of the state.   [Pp. 45, 121, 279, 407]

Prunus hortulana Bailey
HORTULAN PLUM, WILD GOOSE PLUM
Similar to *P. munsoniana*, this species is infrequent.   [Pp. 45, 409]

Prunus munsoniana Wight & Hedrick
WILD GOOSE PLUM
This plum is frequent in the Bluegrass regions, both Inner and Outer, but infrequent elsewhere in the state.   [Pp. 45, 121, 409]

CHERRIES and PEACH

Prunus mahaleb L.   PERFUMED CHERRY
This is a small tree imported from Europe as a grafting stock for cultivated cherries. It is now established in the wild and is fairly frequent in scattered localities in Kentucky.   [Pp. 46, 411]

Prunus persica (L.) Batsch PEACH
The cultivated peach sometimes escapes and may be found on roadsides. [Pp. 46, 410]

Prunus serotina Ehrh. WILD BLACK CHERRY
The wood of the wild black cherry ranks second only to black walnut as the finest cabinet wood in the United States, but in Kentucky it holds first place in popularity. It is warm-colored, hard (though not strong), and close-grained, finishing with a silky sheen. Cherry furniture made over a century ago often contains boards wider than any living wild cherry tree. Other former uses included carriages and early Pullman and trolley cars. Today the cherry that is cut goes into precision instruments, musical instruments, show cases, backings used in the printing trade, and other articles, besides furniture and veneer for paneling.

Very little good cherry timber remains because forest conditions are necessary for the trees to grow tall, straight, and knot-free. Most mesophytic forests in which they grew were cleared early, since the situations made good farmland, and in the few remaining forests the large cherry trees have been removed due to the demand for their wood. Today the species is common, probably occurring in every county, but rarely of good timber quality. The trees grow especially along roadsides and fencerows and in other open areas where birds drop the seed; in such situations they are too crooked and too knotty to be of commercial value. Even these crooked trees with their graceful branches are beautiful in a lawn though they are unsuited for street planting because of the cherries that fall. Unfortunately the tree's aesthetic qualities are diminished in those springs when there is a heavy infestation of tent caterpillars.

Since livestock can be killed by eating cherry leaves, farmers sometimes remove cherry trees from pastures. However, pruning the low branches will eliminate the danger unless a branch breaks off; even then livestock are not likely to eat it if good grass is available. Hence the danger is not great. [Pp. 71, 135, 412-13]

Prunus virginiana L. CHOKE CHERRY
A small tree, sometimes scarcely more than a shrub, the choke cherry in May is laden with racemes which are dense with white flowers. Beauty is its value. In Kentucky it occurs infrequently in widely scattered localities. [Pp. 72, 129, 280, 414]

Pyrus angustifolia Ait. WILD CRAB, NARROW-LEAF CRAB
This species of wild crab-apple is known in Kentucky only in the western part of the state, where it occurs in both the Land Between the Lakes and the Jackson Purchase region. [Pp. 48, 406]

Pyrus communis L. PEAR
Occasionally the cultivated pear spreads into thickets and roadsides.
[Pp. 47, 402-03]

Pyrus coronaria L. WILD CRAB
A wild crab-apple is sheer loveliness with its enchantingly fragrant, delicate pink flowers, and indeed it deserves to be planted for its beauty. As a bonus, the tangy fruit may be used for jelly. It grows in clearings and woodland borders, and though widely scattered is not common. [Pp. 48, 404-05]

Pyrus ioensis (Wood) Bailey PRAIRIE CRAB, WILD CRAB
The prairie crab, which grows in the western part of the state, is rare in Kentucky. [Pp. 48, 406]

Pyrus malus L. APPLE
The apple sometimes occurs as an escape from cultivation, and old trees often persist in an old home-site long after the house has disappeared. [Pp. 47, 400-401]

Rosa canina L. DOG-ROSE
Introduced from Europe and formerly cultivated, the dog-rose may occasionally be found in old pastures and along roadsides. [P. 239]

Rosa carolina L. CAROLINA ROSE, PASTURE ROSE
This pretty little rose, pink and delightfully fragrant, grows in dry ground and is frequent at the edge of woods, in open woods, and in old fields throughout the state. [Pp. 53, 130, 239]

Rosa eglanteria L. SWEETBRIER, EGLANTINE
The sweetbrier, a native of Europe, may occasionally be found as an escape from cultivation. [P. 239]

Rosa multiflora Thunb. MULTIFLORA ROSE
Introduced from Asia, this large sprawling shrub has been widely planted as a farm hedge and is now spreading from seed. Small

white flowers are followed by numerous fruits relished in winter by many birds. Also the shrubs provide excellent wildlife cover and nesting sites. [Pp. 53, 130, 238]

Rosa palustris Marsh. SWAMP ROSE
The swamp rose is a tall erect shrub which grows only in wet ground such as swamps, ditches, and banks of sluggish streams. It is widely distributed and is fairly frequent. [Pp. 53, 240]

Rosa setigera Michx. CLIMBING ROSE, PRAIRIE ROSE
Either a climber or sprawling shrub, this rose is the progenitor of several cultivated climbing roses. It grows in clearings, old fields, and fencerows in somewhat moist ground and is frequent throughout Kentucky. [Pp. 52, 184]

The Genus *Rubus*, the RASPBERRIES, DEWBERRIES, and BLACKBERRIES

In all species of *Rubus* the stems are biennial: unbranched the first year, developing lateral branches and flowering the second year, and dying at the end of the second season; the roots are perennial. The fruits are aggregate, with many small drupelets inserted on a receptacle. In the raspberries the receptacle becomes hard and the fruit slips off from it; in dewberries and blackberries the receptacle is juicy, being the center of the edible fruit. Dewberries have trailing stems whereas blackberries and raspberries have erect or arching stems.

In raspberries the characters are constant and our two species can be easily identified. However, in both dewberries and blackberries the taxonomy is complex; variation is probably due to polyploidy, hybridization, and environmental factors, and species are difficult to separate. Precise identification of these groups is for the specialist, and even one *Rubus* specialist may differ from another regarding the separation of species. It is outside the scope of this book to draw the fine lines between species in dewberries and blackberries.

RASPBERRIES

Rubus occidentalis L. BLACK RASPBERRY
Our native black raspberry, the source of many horticultural vari-

eties, is delicious and flavorful even in its wild state. It grows in partial shade in somewhat moist soil; it is widely distributed and frequent.   [Pp. 51, 119, 241]

Rubus odoratus L. FLOWERING RASPBERRY
The flowering raspberry, which has purple flowers and dry inedible fruit, grows in gorges and on moist wooded cliffs in the Cumberland Mountains and Cumberland Plateau. It is relatively infrequent.   [Pp. 52, 292-93]

DEWBERRIES. There are between five and ten species of dewberries in Kentucky, depending on the taxonomist naming them.

Rubus enslenii Tratt. SOUTHERN DEWBERRY
Rubus flagellaris Willd. NORTHERN DEWBERRY
These species and their close relatives constitute the "common dewberries." They are common and distributed over the state in old fields, on roadsides, and at the edge of woods.   [Pp. 50, 120, 185]

Rubus hispidus L. SWAMP DEWBERRY
This species with its close relatives can easily be distinguished from the group of common dewberries. It grows in swamp forests and wet meadows. Though infrequent it is locally plentiful in southern and eastern Kentucky.   [Pp. 51, 185]

BLACKBERRIES. The highbush blackberries, with stems erect or arching and 2½–9 feet long, are abundant in old fields where they are one of the dominants in the shrub stage of old field succession. In Kentucky there are between five and twenty species, depending on whether the reporting taxonomist is a "lumper" or a "splitter." *R. alleghaniensis* Porter, together with its coterie of close relatives, is probably the most abundant of the common blackberries.   [Pp. 51, 119, 242]

Spiraea alba DuRoi MEADOWSWEET
The lovely meadowsweet is known here only in wet meadows of western Kentucky, where it is not common.   [Pp. 82, 290]

Spiraea japonica L. JAPANESE SPIRAEA
An escape from cultivation, the Japanese spiraea is locally estab-

lished on cliffs and cut-over hillsides in several widely separated areas in eastern and southeastern Kentucky.   [Pp. 81, 291]

Spiraea tomentosa L.   STEEPLEBUSH, HARDHACK
The spire-shaped inflorescence accounts for one common name, and the tough wiry stem for the other. It is frequent in sunny, wet, flat, poorly drained ground in various sections of the state except the Bluegrass, and is most frequent in the Knobs.   [Pp. 81, 290]

Leguminosae, Legume Family

Amorpha fruticosa L.   INDIGO BUSH, FALSE INDIGO
The indigo bush is found primarily on alluvial banks of rivers but is infrequent. The genus name is Greek for "without form," alluding to the fact that each flower has but one petal.   [Pp. 73, 244]

Cercis canadensis L.   REDBUD
With a rose-red calyx, the opened flowers cover the bare twigs with purplish pink. Though often an understory tree in open oak woods, it is most plentiful in cut-over areas in calcareous soil, where entire hillsides may display masses of orchid pink against a dark green background of cedar. It is common throughout the state and is planted ornamentally in lawns and gardens.   [Pp. 58, 374-75]

Cladrastis lutea (Michx. f.) K. Koch   YELLOW-WOOD
This handsome tree with graceful, drooping panicles of white flowers is often planted in lawns, where it is highly prized. In the wild it is rare, growing especially on the limestone cliffs of the Kentucky River in the Inner Bluegrass region but also found sparingly in southeastern Kentucky.   [Pp. 57, 330-31]

Gleditsia aquatica Marsh.   WATER LOCUST
In Kentucky the water locust is known to occur only in swamps in the Jackson Purchase.   [P. 330]

Gleditsia triacanthos L.   HONEY LOCUST
The honey locust, with attractively lacy foliage, is usually thickly beset with long branched thorns but may be thornless; in the latter form it is a desirable ornamental tree. Growing in old fields,

pastures, and other open places, it is common from the Bluegrass westward through the state and is infrequent in eastern Kentucky. The sweet pods are eaten by cattle and other animals which thus distribute the seed. The wood is outstandingly strong and durable but is seldom cut, probably because of the thorns. [Pp. 536-37]

Gymnocladus dioica (L.) K. Koch
KENTUCKY COFFEE-TREE
The coffee-tree, occurring in open woods and grassy areas in all limestone sections of Kentucky, is common only in the Inner Bluegrass. The early settlers used the roasted seed as a somewhat unpalatable coffee substitute. Its large twice-compound leaves give a lacy aspect in summer and, after falling, leave in winter a ruggedly picturesque silhouette without small twigs. [Pp. 326-27]

Robinia hispida L. ROSE-ACACIA, BRISTLY LOCUST
This beautiful shrub, native to southeastern Kentucky but rare in the wild, is extensively cultivated and has occasionally become established as an escape. [Pp. 58, 243]
The related *R. viscosa* Vent., the clammy locust, which is a small tree, is also cultivated and may occur wild in Kentucky.

Robinia pseudo-acacia L. BLACK LOCUST
Throughout Kentucky the black locust is common in thickets, pastures, old fields, and roadsides and is particularly abundant in the Bluegrass region.
Although an old tree may be a bit ragged due to wind, lightning, or sleet having broken some branches, in May any locust tree is a thing of beauty. Pendent racemes of fragrant flowers perfume the air nearby and make the whole tree from a distance appear creamy white against a blue sky. Since it is a common tree, springing up readily in common places, and since it has plebeian uses—for fenceposts, railroad ties, and mine props—instead of parlor employment, the locust in America does not receive the appreciation it deserves. However, in Europe it is one of the most widely cultivated of American trees, admired for its beauty and respected for its timber value. It was introduced into France at the beginning of the seventeenth century, and in the early nineteenth century London nurseries sold over a million of the trees. Europe today has several horticultural varieties. Known in England

as false acacia, it is a beautiful flowering tree grown in the inimitable English gardens; yet at home it is virtually without honor.

The locust is useful in erosion control and grows rapidly, much more rapidly than any other tree with extremely hard wood, and by harboring nitrogen-fixing bacteria on its roots it benefits the whole natural community associated with it. It is the strongest and most durable of North American woods and one of the hardest. It converts sapwood to heartwood the most quickly of any tree. Unfortunately it is subject to attack by the locust borer, which renders most American locusts useless as boards, almost all of which would be faulty. However, this insect does not occur in Europe, where the wood can be sawed and used, for example, as beams and occasionally as furniture, in which it takes a high polish.   [Pp. 58, 332-33]

Wisteria macrostachya Nutt.   WISTERIA

Most of the cultivated wisterias are Asiatic species, which may persist at an old house site, although our native species is occasionally planted. It grows in moist ground, widely scattered in the western half of the state, and is rare in the wild. This wisteria is sometimes considered a variety of *W. frutescens* (L.) Poir.

[Pp. 59, 190]

Rutaceae, Rue Family

Ptelea trifoliata L.   HOP-TREE, WAFER-ASH

The thin waferlike fruit was once used as a substitute for hops. Although the bark and flowers are ill-smelling (the flowers are pollinated by carrion flies), this feature is not strong enough to make the shrub objectionable. The rich glossy foliage, greenish yellow flowers, and clusters of round flat fruits are attractive, and the shrub is cultivated in England. It is frequent in ravines and moist thickets in the Bluegrass, infrequent elsewhere in the state.

[Pp. 88, 250]

Xanthoxylum americanum Mill.   PRICKLY ASH

The berry-like fruits, which have a heavy lemony odor, remind us that this shrub belongs to the same family as the citruses. The bark also is aromatic; both bark and berries have been used medicinally. It is widely distributed, infrequent but locally plentiful, forming thickets in dry open woods or borders of woods.   [P. 237]

Simaroubaceae, QUASSIA FAMILY

Ailanthus altissima (Mill.) Swingle
TREE-OF-HEAVEN, AILANTHUS
This Chinese tree reached America via Europe, where it was introduced with the hope of establishing a silk industry. The silkworms failed but the tree became naturalized as a woody weed on both continents. It is found chiefly in waste places in and near cities but also rarely in woods.

The flowers of the male tree are strongly ill-scented, causing it to be called "stink tree," but the flowers of the female tree are unscented. Its fast-growing roots may heave sidewalks and penetrate basements, but the tree does have some virtues. It can live where other trees cannot survive, withstanding smoke and dust; sometimes it is the only green thing in a dump, a back alley, or a hard-packed tenement yard.   [Pp. 87, 117, 334-35]

Anacardiaceae, CASHEW FAMILY

Rhus aromatica Ait. FRAGRANT SUMAC
This attractive small shrub, showy with clusters of bright red fruit in June, grows on limestone cliffs and other thin soil above limestone. It is common in the Bluegrass region and Mississippian Plateau, rare elsewhere, and apparently absent from the Cumberland Plateau and Mountains.   [Pp. 85, 128, 248]

Rhus copallina L. WINGED SUMAC, SHINING SUMAC
The winged sumac is one of the dominant shrubs in old fields and clearings in noncalcareous soil on poorly drained flats and eroded hillsides. It is common and widespread but apparently absent from the Inner Bluegrass. Its glossy leaves are richly colored in autumn.
[Pp. 28, 85, 128, 246]

Rhus glabra L. SMOOTH SUMAC
This is a common shrub all over Kentucky, invading old fields and clearings in a variety of situations. Its wine-red panicles of fruit are showy from late summer into winter, and its leaves are among the first to turn scarlet in the fall.   [Pp. 86, 128, 245]

Rhus radicans L. POISON IVY
This species is also sometimes called poison oak, although the latter name more properly belongs to the next species. It may be trailing, shrubby, or high-climbing on the tallest trees, to which it clings by aerial roots; several varieties have been named. It is common, even abundant in some areas, and doubtless occurs in every county. It grows along roadsides and in fencerows, thickets, and woods, more in disturbed woods than in original forest. Unfortunately it is on the increase; a mature plant produces a large quantity of berries which, besides falling on the ground, are eaten by birds and the seeds are thus widely distributed.

The offending "poison" is an oil which in very minute quantity will cause dermatitis in susceptible persons. The dermatitis results from touching any part of the plant in any season or from touching something that has rubbed it; it may also be caused by infinitesimal droplets of oil in smoke when poison ivy is burning. It never results merely from "looking" at the plant or walking near without touching it, as some persons claim. The oil, insoluble in water but soluble in alcohol, can be removed from the skin with alcohol, especially if followed by strong soap or detergent in hot water. (Note that the mere application of alcohol will dissolve and spread the oil; the purpose is to *remove* it.) If one is unaware of having touched poison ivy until dermatitis develops, the same removal technique should be followed before any palliative substance is applied because the causative agent is still present. Spreading of the dermatitis results from the dispersion of the remaining oil; hence removal is paramount. The longer the oil remains the more difficult it is to remove. Juice from the stems of our two species of jewelweed (*Impatiens capensis* and *I. pallida*), when rubbed on the skin, is effective in both preventing and alleviating irritation from poison ivy.

Every possible effort should be made to curb this obnoxious plant. Spraying with 2-4-5-T or amitrole in late spring or early summer is effective, but the utmost care must be taken to spray only the poison ivy because desirable plants always seem to die more easily. No herbicide use should ever be turned over to anyone who is careless or indiscriminate or who does not know which plants to destroy and which to protect. A person not allergic to poison ivy who could dig, pull, or otherwise destroy the pest could be a "poison ivy specialist"! [Pp. 87, 186-87, 249]

Rhus toxicodendron L. POISON OAK
This is a southern species which in Kentucky is found infrequently
in the southern part of the state. [Pp. 87, 249]

Rhus typhina L. STAGHORN SUMAC
The forking, leafless, velvety branches in winter resembles a stag's
antlers when they are "in velvet." The large pyramid-shaped
panicles of fruit are also conspicuous all winter. The staghorn,
which is our largest species of sumac, is frequent in northern and
northeastern Kentucky, infrequent from east-central to west-central
Kentucky, and absent elsewhere in the state. It is found in clearings and borders of open woodland. [Pp. 86, 129, 247]

Aquifoliaceae, HOLLY FAMILY

Ilex decidua Walt. SWAMP HOLLY, POSSUM-HAW
This deciduous holly is frequent in swampy woods, pond borders,
and wet flats in the western half of the state. [Pp. 96, 124, 281]

Ilex montana T. & G. MOUNTAIN WINTERBERRY
Another deciduous holly, this species is found in mountain forests,
both on summits and in gorges, in eastern Kentucky but is infrequent. [Pp. 96, 125, 282]

Ilex opaca Ait. AMERICAN HOLLY
Our most beloved and most Christmasy of Christmas greens has
been decimated by pickers butchering the trees, usually on another's
land, in order to supply the market. No species, certainly not such
a slow-growing one, can withstand so relentless an attack. It grows
in rich moist woods and gorges, most often in sandstone. In such
situations in eastern and southern Kentucky it was formerly frequent; it has always been less frequent in the southwestern part
of the state. It is shade-tolerant, and its usual associates are hemlock and rhododendron.

The planting of holly on our homegrounds should be encouraged
and increased. It is beautiful all year, and if at Christmastime we
do the pruning necessary to keep the tree dense and shapely, we
have our Christmas decoration free and have not further diminished
the supply of wild holly. The question often arises as to whether

one needs two holly trees, male and female, in order to have berries. A tree with staminate flowers only can never produce berries; a tree with pistillate flowers has also some complete flowers with stamens and pistils, and such a tree can produce some berries alone but will produce a greater quantity if its flowers are more thoroughly pollinated. [Pp. 95, 124, 170]

Ilex verticillata (L.) Gray WINTERBERRY
The winterberry, a species of holly, is fairly frequent in swamp thickets, swamp forests, and margins of slow streams in eastern and southern Kentucky. Its profusion of bright red berries persisting on bare branches till midwinter makes it a desirable shrub for planting in moist situations. [Pp. 96, 125, 282]

Celastraceae, Staff-Tree Family

Celastrus scandens L. BITTERSWEET
Bittersweet is a twining woody vine found at the edge of woods and along fences in a variety of soil situations; though widely distributed throughout the state, it is most frequent in central Kentucky. It is valued for its bright orange and red fruits which last till midwinter. [Pp. 73, 125, 204]

Euonymus americanus L.
STRAWBERRY-BUSH, HEARTS-A-BURSTING-WITH-LOVE
This shrub is especially attractive in autumn with its unusual fruit, which is the source of the common names. It is frequent on valley flats, stream banks, and moist ravine slopes in most sections of the state although it is rare in the Bluegrass. [Pp. 97, 126, 168, 232]

Euonymus atropurpureus Jacq. WAHOO, BURNING BUSH
The wahoo, a tall treelike shrub, grows in a variety of situations, wooded and open, moist and dry. It is widespread in the state and most common in the Inner and Outer Bluegrass regions. In autumn after leaf-fall it is showy with brilliantly colored fruits, which are more abundant in sun than in shade. [Pp. 97, 126, 233]

Euonymus fortunei (Turcz.) Hand.-Mazz. WINTERCREEPER
An introduced evergreen climber and creeping shrub, the winter-

creeper sometimes escapes from cultivation and becomes established.   [P. 168]

Euonymus obovatus Nutt.
RUNNING STRAWBERRY-BUSH, RUNNING EUONYMUS
This little trailing shrub is frequent in rich woods in the Bluegrass region but is scattered and infrequent elsewhere in the state. We recommend its propagation for use as a ground cover in ornamental planting under trees.   [Pp. 98, 126, 181]

Pachistima canbyi Gray   PACHISTIMA, MOUNTAIN-LOVER
This small evergreen shrub is plentiful on limestone bluffs in Carter County; it is not known to occur elsewhere in Kentucky.
[Pp. 98, 176]

Staphyleaceae, Bladdernut Family

Staphylea trifolia L.   BLADDERNUT
The bladdernut has graceful racemes of white flowers in spring and pale green, inflated, pendent capsules, resembling Japanese lanterns, all summer. This attractive shrub grows in rich moist woods, usually on steep slopes; it is widely distributed and frequent, most frequent in the Bluegrass.   [Pp. 74, 208]

Aceraceae, Maple Family

Acer negundo L.   BOX ELDER
Though in leaf not suggesting a relationship to the maples, the peasant box elder does show in its winged, key-shaped fruits a connection with these more aristocratic relatives. Quick-growing and short-lived, the branches break easily and the heartwood decays fast. The wood, being soft, weak, brittle, light in weight, and nearly white, has limited uses and little value. The box elder is common in moist open areas and abundant on stream banks and floodplains throughout the state.   [Pp. 110, 308-09]

Acer nigrum Michx. f.
BLACK MAPLE, BLACK SUGAR MAPLE
The black maple is closely related to the sugar maple (*A. saccharum*)

Clethraceae, White Alder Family

Clethra acuminata Michx. MOUNTAIN PEPPERBUSH
This is a lovely summer-flowering shrub found in eastern Kentucky,
usually on sandstone. It is frequent on wooded cliffs and steep
mesophytic slopes of gorges and ravines in the Cumberland
Mountains and Plateau, and is rare in the Knobs. [Pp. 75, 287]

Ericaceae, Heath Family

All members of the family grow in acid soil.

Epigaea repens L. TRAILING ARBUTUS
Note that the scientific name means "creeping upon the earth."
The popularity of the beautiful fragrant flowers of trailing arbutus
has worked to its detriment. It can be destroyed easily by breaking,
and attempts to transplant it are usually unsuccessful, at least
after a year or two. It should be protected in its own habitat, which
is sandy acid soil in open pine or oak woods on hillsides and
ridges. It is still fairly frequent in eastern and southern Kentucky,
although less plentiful than formerly. [Pp. 55, 174]

Gaylussacia baccata (Wang.) K. Koch HUCKLEBERRY
This is the true huckleberry, common in dry open pine and oak
woods in the Knobs, Cumberland Plateau, and Cumberland Mountains. The black berries are edible though not as delicious as
blueberries, which in the mountains are often called "huckle-
berries." [Pp. 76, 141, 261]

Gaylussacia brachycera (Michx.) Gray BOX-HUCKLEBERRY
In Kentucky this exquisite, tiny evergreen shrub with small glossy
leaves, beautiful flowers, and edible fruits grows only in a few
southeastern counties but may be locally plentiful. It is found
in sandstone areas, usually in pine and oak-pine woods on cliffs and
slopes. [Pp. 76, 141, 175]

Kalmia latifolia L. MOUNTAIN LAUREL
Mountain laurel laden with pale pink flowers is one of the great
beauties of the mountains; the garden-minded English consider

condition it is more vulnerable to storm damage; it takes less storm to break a major portion of the tree than would have been required to break the original branches.

The species is common throughout Kentucky.   [Pp. 312-13]

Acer saccharum Marsh. SUGAR MAPLE
One of our most beautiful forest trees, the sugar maple is spectacular in autumn with its clear yellow foliage sparked with bright red, making a cloudy day seem like a sunny one. It is a common member of mesophytic forests, probably occurring in every county although less common in western Kentucky. It is one of our finest lawn trees but does not fare well in urban air pollution.

The wood of the sugar maple is hard, close-grained, heavy, and strong. Its uses include furniture, violins, croquet mallets and balls, and gymnasium floors. The grain may be plain or fancy.

Although Kentucky's climate does not favor a high yield of maple sugar to be extracted commercially, as does the New England climate, nevertheless many persons in an earlier day tapped the trees in their woods for family use and for local sales. In fact the cash seemed so good that sometimes they improvidently "killed the goose that laid the golden egg" by overtapping the same trees year after year.   [Pp. 25, 110, 310-11]

Acer spicatum Lam. MOUNTAIN MAPLE
This understory shrub characteristic of boreal forests extends into the southern states in cool ravines in the high Appalachians. In Kentucky it was reported a century ago in four counties of the Cumberland Plateau but is now known to occur only in Carter County.   [Pp. 74, 230]

Hippocastanaceae, HORSE-CHESTNUT FAMILY

Aesculus discolor Pursh   RED-AND-YELLOW BUCKEYE
This small tree or large shrub of the South is rare in Kentucky, where it is known to occur only in the Jackson Purchase region.
    [P. 60]

Aesculus glabra Willd. OHIO BUCKEYE
The Ohio buckeye, so named by Michaux in 1810, is also plentiful in some parts of Kentucky. In second-growth woods and thickets,

often on dry slopes, it is common in the Inner and Outer Bluegrass regions, and fairly common in the Mississippian Plateau and western Kentucky, but is absent from most of eastern Kentucky. It is the first tree to become green in spring and, beginning to yellow in midsummer, it is the first to lose its leaves in fall. Since the seeds are poisonous, the tree is unpopular with farmers. The wood has the same properties as those described under the yellow buckeye but is used less because this species does not grow as tall and straight. [Pp. 59, 298-99]

Aesculus octandra Marsh.
YELLOW BUCKEYE, SWEET BUCKEYE
The yellow buckeye is one of the most characteristic constituents of the Mixed Mesophytic forest climax in eastern Kentucky and does not range far beyond the extent of this climax. It is common in the Cumberland Mountains, Cumberland Plateau, and eastern Knobs; it occurs infrequently in the Outer Bluegrass and the eastern part of the Mississippian Plateau.

Buckeye wood is weak, soft, and of little value. However, since it is light in weight and does not split readily, it is used for artificial limbs. In an earlier day it was hollowed out for shoulder yokes, and buckeye logs were hollowed into troughs to catch maple sap.
[Pp. 60, 300-301]

Aesculus pavia L.   RED BUCKEYE
This small tree or large shrub, frequently cultivated for its showy flowers, is rare here in the wild. It was reported a century ago in several central counties and more recently has been found on wooded banks of the Licking River in Rowan County and in southwestern Kentucky. [Pp. 60, 297]

Rhamnaceae, BUCKTHORN FAMILY

Berchemia scandens (Hill) K. Koch   SUPPLE-JACK
This high-climbing vine of Coastal Plain affinities has been found in Kentucky only on loess bluffs of the Mississippi River. [P. 194]

Ceanothus americanus L.   NEW JERSEY TEA
This small summer-flowering shrub grows in dry open woods and is fairly frequent in all parts of the state. Its leaves were used as a tea substitute during the American Revolution. [Pp. 75, 283]

Rhamnus caroliniana Walt. CAROLINA BUCKTHORN
A native not adequately appreciated, the Carolina buckthorn should be propagated and grown ornamentally. The foliage is rich, lustrous, and dark green, beautiful all summer, and the fruit is brilliantly rose-red in September. This tall shrub or small tree is fairly frequent in open woods in most sections of the state but is less frequent in eastern Kentucky.   [Pp. 99, 127, 284, 418]

Rhamnus lanceolata Pursh LANCE-LEAF BUCKTHORN
This species grows in calcareous soil and is frequent in the Inner and Outer Bluegrass regions.   [Pp. 99, 135, 285]

Vitaceae, GRAPE FAMILY

Ampelopsis arborea (L.) Koehne PEPPER-VINE
The pepper-vine, essentially a Coastal Plain species, grows wild in alluvium and other wet ground in western Kentucky but is infrequent. It has been cultivated in all parts of the state because of its rapid growth and sometimes escapes, even occasionally becoming a pest.   [P. 191]

Ampelopsis cordata Michx. HEART-LEAF AMPELOPSIS
This high-climbing, tendril-bearing vine is fairly frequent in wooded valleys and floodplain thickets of central, southern, and western Kentucky. The fruit is a favorite of several species of songbirds.
          [P. 198]

Parthenocissus quinquefolia (L.) Planch.
VIRGINIA CREEPER, FIVE-LEAF IVY
Throughout Kentucky the Virginia creeper is abundant in thickets and woods, where it climbs to the treetops by means of tendrils bearing adhesive disks. It has value as an ornamental vine which will rapidly cover fences and walls. Its berries are favorites of many birds.   [Pp. 135, 188-89]

The Genus *Vitis*, the GRAPES

Although wild grapes provide excellent wildlife food, the vines greatly damage the trees on which they grow. In contrast to vines such as the Virginia creeper, which cling to the trunk, the tendrils of grapes twist around branches, and the grape leaves thus cover the tops of the trees. The resulting shading of the tree's leaves curtails the growth of the tree, and many branches die; also a tree top-heavy with a large grape vine will break in a sleet storm or windstorm to which an unimpeded tree would not have fallen victim.

Over a hundred horticultural varieties of grapes have been developed from American species.

Vitis aestivalis Michx. SUMMER GRAPE

The summer grape grows in thickets and open woods and is common in all parts of Kentucky except the Inner Bluegrass, where it is infrequent. The variety *argentifolia* (Munson) Fernald is more common than the typical variety. [Pp. 109, 202]

Vitis baileyana Munson BAILEY'S GRAPE

This species, combining the leaf shape of V. *cordifolia* with the cobwebby hairs of V. *aestivalis*, has been found in a swamp in Rowan County. Though rare, it is to be expected elsewhere in the state.

Vitis cinerea Engelm.
GRAYBARK GRAPE, SWEET WINTER GRAPE

This species grows in moist alluvial soil in southern and western Kentucky but is infrequent. Early settlers called it pigeon grape before the extinction of the passenger pigeon. [P. 201]

Vitis labrusca L. FOX GRAPE

The fox grape is the progenitor of more cultivated varieties (including Concord and Catawba) than all other American species of grape. It grows in thickets and clearings in moist ground in widely scattered sections of Kentucky but is not frequent. [P. 202]

Vitis palmata Vahl CATBIRD GRAPE

This colorful vine is common in swamps and wet thickets in western Kentucky. [P. 201]

Vitis riparia Michx. RIVERBANK GRAPE

This species is infrequent but occurs on the banks of the Ohio River in several counties. [P. 200]

Vitis rotundifolia Michx.   MUSCADINE
The muscadine is a southern grape which in Kentucky has been found only in the southeastern counties. Here it is frequent in open woods.   [P. 203]

Vitis vulpina L.   FROST GRAPE
Growing in a variety of habitats, the frost grape is abundant throughout the state and is our most common grape. [Pp. 136, 200]

Tiliaceae, LINDEN FAMILY

The Genus *Tilia*, the BASSWOODS or LINDENS

Our various species of basswood grow in mesophytic forests in coves and ravines and on north slopes. They are tall stately trees with gracefully downswept branches and are excellent shade trees for the lawn. Some European species are also planted ornamentally, and some American species, especially the white basswood, are planted in Europe. The nectar in the fragrant flowers is a favorite of bees, and bees also often choose a hollow basswood for honey storage.

The wood, soft and light in weight, is easily worked. Some of its uses include woodenware, porch shades, crates, and paper pulp. Indians used its abundant bast fibers for making rope.

T. floridana, *T. heterophylla*, and *T. neglecta* are among the dominants of the Mixed Mesophytic forest climax.

Tilia americana L.   BASSWOOD, AMERICAN LINDEN
This species is predominantly northern in range and is less frequent in the wild here than the other species. However, of American species of *Tilia* planted as shade trees in our area it is the most frequent, not because it is the best but because nurseries have stocked it.   [Pp. 84, 386-87]

Tilia floridana (V. Engler) Small   BASSWOOD, LINDEN
This tree is frequent in mesophytic forests and is widespread in Kentucky.   [P. 385]

Tilia heterophylla Vent.   WHITE BASSWOOD
The white basswood is particularly beautiful when a breeze displays the whitish lower surface of the shimmering leaves. It is a

characteristic species of the Mixed Mesophytic forest climax and is frequent in mesophytic forests in most of the state but rare in western Kentucky. [P. 385]

Tilia neglecta Spach BASSWOOD, LINDEN
This species, or species complex, may have resulted from hybridization between *T. americana* and *T. heterophylla* during the glacial epoch. It is frequent in Kentucky. [P. 387]

Theaceae, TEA FAMILY

Stewartia ovata (Cav.) Weatherby MOUNTAIN CAMELLIA
The lovely mountain camellia is our only representative of the tea family, which is predominantly tropical and oriental and which includes the beverage tea and the camellias of southern gardens. It grows in a few of the southeastern counties, where it is only locally plentiful, usually in rich wooded ravines and gorges. One wonders why a shrub or tree with flowers so exquisite is not more widely propagated and featured. [Pp. 54, 286, 419]

Hypericaceae [*Guttiferae*], ST. JOHN'S-WORT FAMILY

Hypericum densiflorum Pursh BUSHY ST. JOHN'S-WORT
This is a southern species ranging only into southwestern Kentucky, where it is infrequent. [Pp. 54, 213]

Hypericum frondosum Michx. GOLDEN ST. JOHN'S-WORT
With large, showy yellow flowers the golden St. John's-wort is sometimes cultivated as an ornamental shrub. It grows wild on limestone cliffs in southern and southwestern Kentucky, where it is only locally plentiful. [Pp. 54, 214]

Hypericum spathulatum (Spach) Steud.
SHRUBBY ST. JOHN'S-WORT
This is our most common woody St. John's-wort. It is widely distributed and grows in a variety of habitats, usually in woodland borders, either moist or dry. [Pp. 54, 213]

Thymelaeaceae, MEZEREUM FAMILY

Dirca palustris L.   LEATHERWOOD
Although not showy, the leatherwood is an interesting shrub with flexible branchlets that will not break. Indians found its tough bark useful in basket making. It is one of our first shrubs to flower in early spring, but the pretty little flowers often go unnoticed. It is widespread and fairly frequent in Kentucky's woods. [Pp. 108, 254]

Lythraceae, LOOSESTRIFE FAMILY

Decodon verticillatus (L.) Ell.
SWAMP LOOSESTRIFE, WATER-WILLOW
This semiwoody plant is rare in Kentucky, apparently confined to the Purchase region, where it may infrequently be found arching over standing water in cypress swamps.   [Pp. 53, 214]

Nyssaceae, SOUR GUM FAMILY

Nyssa aquatica L.   TUPELO GUM, WATER TUPELO
Common in the swamps of the Deep South, the tupelo gum in Kentucky is restricted to swamp forests of the Jackson Purchase, where it is locally plentiful.   [Pp. 366-67]

Nyssa sylvatica Marsh.
SOUR GUM, BLACK GUM, BLACK TUPELO
Picturesque in winter with a fine tracery of twigs, and beautiful in summer with rich glossy foliage, the sour gum achieves its greatest glory with its brilliant autumn coloration. It has two extremes of habitat: pine and oak woods on dry hills, and sweet gum—pin oak woods on wet flats. It is common in all noncalcareous regions, infrequent in the Outer Bluegrass, and missing from the Inner Bluegrass.

The wood is tough and does not split; though not of great value, it is used where these properties are desirable. It decays easily both in the cut wood and in the tree, where death starts at the top. In an earlier day a hollow sour gum was often cut and used for beehives.   [Pp. 140, 364-65]

Araliaceae, GINSENG FAMILY

Aralia spinosa L.
HERCULES'-CLUB, DEVIL'S-WALKINGSTICK
The stout erect stems bearing large bipinnate leaves and enormous panicles of flowers or berries give an unusual aspect which has attracted cultivation of the Hercules'-club for ornament. However, the spines on stems and branches forbid much handling. Usually growing in fairly moist soil, such as lower slopes at the edge of woods, it is widely distributed in Kentucky and is frequent in most sections except the Inner Bluegrass.   [Pp. 28, 69, 133, 236]

Hedera helix L.   ENGLISH IVY
The English ivy is an introduced ornamental vine commonly cultivated and occasionally found as an escape in rich woods. [P. 169]

Cornaceae, DOGWOOD FAMILY

Cornus florida L.   FLOWERING DOGWOOD
The flowering dogwood is probably our most beautiful small tree. Pure and lovely in its spring white, glowing in its autumn crimson, and bright with red berries in September, it is atractive in all seasons with horizontally spreading branches upturned at the tip. Since the structures that make the tree conspicuous at flowering time are bracts and not petals, they persist longer. It is abundantly cultivated and rightly so; it should be planted even more extensively. It is frequent—was formerly common—as an understory tree in woodlands throughout the state and should be protected in its natural setting to maintain the beauty of the woods for the enjoyment of all. Public opinion should condemn any who would cut for selfish and temporary pleasure these slow-growing and fastwilting branches.

Today the commercial cutting of dogwood lumber is far in excess of its growth rate. Most of this goes into shuttles for the textile industry. Since the wood is extremely hard and resistant to shock, it is sometimes used for golf club heads.   [Pp. 93, 123, 322-23]

The shrub DOGWOODS. The various species of shrub dogwood are less showy and less well known than the so-called flowering dogwood (of course they all have flowers). However, they have value in ornamental planting and are attractive in the wild. They are found in thickets, woodland borders, and open areas, with the exception of the alternate-leaf dogwood (*Cornus alternifolia*), which grows in mesophytic forests.

Cornus alternifolia L. f. ALTERNATE-LEAF DOGWOOD
This is a characteristic shrub of the Mixed Mesophytic forest climax. In rich woods, especially on ravine slopes, it is common in eastern Kentucky, fairly frequent in central, northern, and southern Kentucky, and not reported from the far western part of the state. [Pp. 93, 144, 256]

Cornus amomum Mill. SILKY DOGWOOD
The silky dogwood is widely distributed and fairly frequent on stream banks and in swamps. [Pp. 94, 144, 218]

Cornus drummondi Meyer ROUGH-LEAF DOGWOOD
This species grows in dry situations; it is common in the Bluegrass region, fairly frequent in other calcareous areas, and rare in non-calcareous soil. It is not known to occur in the Cumberland Mountains or Plateau. [Pp. 93, 144, 216]

Cornus foemina Mill. STIFF DOGWOOD
This dogwood grows on stream banks and wet flats, especially in the Knobs, but is infrequent. [P. 219]

Cornus obliqua Raf.
SILKY DOGWOOD, PALE DOGWOOD
The pale dogwood is scattered from east to west and north to south in Kentucky but is infrequent. It grows in swamps, on stream banks, and on dry slopes. [Pp. 94, 144, 219]

Cornus racemosa Lam. GRAY DOGWOOD
The gray dogwood is infrequent and scattered in Kentucky. It is found either in dry situations or on stream banks. [Pp. 94, 145, 217]

Cornus stolonifera Michx. RED OSIER
The red osier is a northern species often cultivated in our area but rare here in the wild. It has been found, however, in thickets on creek banks. [P. 219]

and by some is considered only a variety of that species. It produces the same sweet sap, the wood is of the same quality and appearance, and it is equally slow-growing and long-lived. Since the leaves are coarser and darker, it is perhaps a bit less beautiful but nevertheless is of great value as a shade tree. Like the sugar maple it grows in mesophytic habitats and is widely distributed in Kentucky, but it is less common. [P. 311]

Acer pensylvanicum L. STRIPED MAPLE
This interesting small tree with striped bark is a characteristic understory tree of damp forests in the far north. In Kentucky it is restricted to the highest elevations of the Cumberland Mountain section, where it grows, infrequently, in cool glens. [Pp. 74, 316]

Acer rubrum L. (including var. *trilobum* K. Koch) RED MAPLE
This tree is well-named because there is usually something red about it at all seasons: buds in winter, flowers in earliest spring, fruits in late spring, leaf petioles in summer, and finally scarlet foliage in autumn. It is a good shade tree for lawn or street. It is common in all sections except the Inner Bluegrass, where it is rare and not brilliantly colored in autumn. It grows most often in noncalcareous soil, and its habitat includes dry oak hills, floodplains, sweet gum swamps, and mixed-mesophytic slopes. To the lumberman it is "soft maple" although by the time it reaches a furniture store it may be called "hard maple." The wood is only moderately hard and not strong, but takes a smooth finish. [Pp. 27, 98, 117, 314-15]

Acer saccharinum L. SILVER MAPLE, WATER MAPLE
Growing large in its native habitat of river banks and floodplains, where it is free of man's mutilations, the silver maple is a graceful and beautiful tree. However, it is probably known to more persons when planted on city streets—so planted because of its rapid growth—where it often becomes hollow, maimed, and disfigured. It is our worst victim of tree "butchery." Since the wood is brittle and branches break easily, a homeowner with a silver maple is persuaded by a self-styled "tree surgeon" (not a reputable, professionally trained one) to have the branches cut back. The ends, several inches in diameter, cannot heal over, decay sets in, and since silver maple wood decays fast when exposed, soon the main branches and trunk become hollow. Then in its weakened, hollow

it to be one of the loveliest of all the American flowering shrubs.
An examination of the flower reveals an extraordinary pollinating
mechanism as well as beauty. Each of ten stamens has its anther
fitting into a little pocket in the corolla, with its filament arched
and under tension. When a bee lights in a flower and touches a
filament, the stamen suddenly springs up, dusting the insect with
pollen which can then be carried to the stigma of another flower.
The stamens are limp after they have been tripped. This mechanism can be demonstrated by touching a tense filament with a
pencil point.

If it has acid soil, mountain laurel will grow in sun or shade,
in moist or dry ground, on mountaintops, rocky slopes, and sides
of ravines. In Kentucky it is most common on a sandstone outcrop.
It grows throughout eastern Kentucky and in the sandstone area
surrounding the Western Coalfield. The leaves are poisonous but
browsing livestock rarely eat them. Honey made from the flowers
is poisonous to man.   [Pp. 55, 173]

Lyonia ligustrina (L.) DC.
PRIVET-ANDROMEDA, MALE-BERRY
This shrub grows in swampy woods and on swampy stream banks;
it is infrequent but is scattered from eastern and southeastern to
southwestern Kentucky.   [Pp. 84, 288]

Oxydendrum arboreum (L.) DC.
SOURWOOD, SORREL TREE
In midsummer the sourwood bears graceful sprays of flowers resembling lilies-of-the-valley. These flowers are favorites of bees,
and sourwood honey in the southern Appalachians is sought by
epicures and connoisseurs. Its summer beauty is rivalled or surpassed by its crimson foliage in autumn.

Outside its natural range, which is the southeastern quarter of
the United States, the sourwood is considered one of the most
ornamental of trees and as such is cultivated in Europe, and in
both northwestern and northeastern United States. However, in
Kentucky it is not planted as much as its beauty merits. In nature
it is usually an understory tree although it may be larger. It is
common in woods, usually oak, in noncalcareous soil; it is found
throughout eastern Kentucky and in the Pennsylvanian outcrops
in and near the Western Coalfield.   [Pp. 79, 420-21]

The Genus RHODODENDRON

Rhododendron is a large and ornamentally significant genus divided into two subgenera, the true rhododendrons with evergreen leaves and the azaleas with deciduous leaves. Species in both groups are native to eastern and central Asia and eastern North America. Numerous cultivated varieties have been developed from both oriental and American species, many through hybridization. Spectacularly beautiful, they are popular in parks and gardens in both this country and Europe. All require acid soil.

Evergreen Species of *Rhododendron*

Rhododendron catawbiense Michx.
PURPLE RHODODENDRON, MOUNTAIN ROSEBAY
Though abundant in the mountains to the south of us, the purple rhododendron is rare in Kentucky and is found only in the Cumberland Mountains and a few adjacent counties.   [Pp. 61, 171]

Rhododendron maximum L.
GREAT LAUREL, GREAT RHODODENDRON
Thought of the great rhododendron brings to mind the music of a mountain brook or of tinkling water falling from an overhanging ledge, the fragrance of moist humus on sandstone, and the picture of great spherical clusters of flowers in the coolness of a forest cove when summer's heat nears its highest.

This large evergreen shrub, growing in forested, moist, well-drained, acid soil, is distributed through the Cumberland Plateau and Mountains. It may be locally plentiful, occasionally forming almost impenetrable thickets. As with the mountain laurel, honey made from its flowers is poisonous.   [Pp. 61, 172]

Deciduous Species of *Rhododendron*: AZALEAS. The common name "wild honeysuckle," sometimes locally applied to the azaleas, should be discouraged because they are not related to the honeysuckles and because we have true wild honeysuckles.

Rhododendron arborescens (Pursh) Torr. SMOOTH AZALEA
This usually white-flowered species, growing in swampy woods and on stream banks in the Cumberland Mountains, is rare in Kentucky.

Rhododendron calendulaceum (Michx.) Torr. FLAME AZALEA
The flame azalea, an **outstandingly** attractive flowering shrub, is

found on oak-wooded ridgetops in the Cumberland Mountains and the southern half of the Cumberland Plateau but is no longer frequent. Such beauties are protected by law in our national parks, national forests, and state parks; elsewhere let public opinion so condemn the despoilers that no one would dare to break a branch or dig a plant. [Pp. 63, 260]

Rhododendron cumberlandense E. L. Braun   RED AZALEA
The spectacular red azalea grows in the Cumberland Mountains and a few adjacent southeastern counties. It is found in open oak woods and woodland borders in somewhat mesophytic situations and is becoming less frequent. [Pp. 64, 259]

Rhododendron nudiflorum (L.) Torr.
PINXTER-FLOWER, PINK AZALEA
The flowers, usually pink, appear before the leaves. This lovely species grows on cliffs and in either moist or dry open woods; it is scattered throughout the Cumberland Plateau and Cumberland Mountains but is infrequent. [Pp. 62, 258]

Rhododendron roseum (Loisel.) Rehder   ROSE AZALEA
The beautiful fragrant rose azalea grows in open oak woods in the Cumberland Plateau and Mountains but is found less frequently than formerly.
A certain woman, seeing some of these lovely flowering shrubs from a car, gathered the branches as decoration for a special event; the next year when the same annual event rolled around, she returned and expressed surprise that there were no flowers on the bushes. Thus, until the shrub grew sturdy new branches that would produce flower buds, no other passers-by were permitted the enjoyment of some beauty that was rightfully theirs. [Pp. 62, 257]

Rhododendron viscosum (L.) Torr.   CLAMMY AZALEA
This species was reported in southeastern Kentucky many years ago, but may have been exterminated in the state. [P. 64]

Vaccinium alto-montanum Ashe
MOUNTAIN DRYLAND BLUEBERRY
Despite a name that might indicate otherwise, this species of blueberry is not restricted to high mountains. It grows in open woods

on noncalcareous rocky hills and slopes in eastern and southern Kentucky but is not frequent. The edible berries have an excellent flavor. [Pp. 143, 264]

Vaccinium arboreum Marsh. FARKLEBERRY
The farkleberry is a tall, irregular, beautiful shrub with thick glossy leaves and is especially attractive when laden with flowers. The black berries are inedible. It is fairly frequent in open oak woods on noncalcareous hills and bluffs in southern and western Kentucky. [Pp. 77, 262]

Vaccinium constablaei Gray
CONSTABLE'S HIGHBUSH BLUEBERRY
Our largest blueberry, 6–15 feet tall, bears bright blue berries of excellent flavor. It is found in the Cumberland Mountains and Cumberland Plateau but is infrequent. [Pp. 79, 143, 265-66]

Vaccinium pallidum Ait. LOWBUSH BLUEBERRY
A small shrub under 3 feet tall, this is our most common blueberry. It is abundant in oak-pine and oak (especially chestnut oak—scarlet oak) woods on dry hills throughout eastern Kentucky and the Western Coalfield. [Pp. 78, 142, 264]

Vaccinium simulatum Small HIGHBUSH BLUEBERRY
This highbush blueberry, 5–10 feet tall, is fairly frequent in upland oak and pine woods, in swampy pine woods, and on shaly slopes and sandstone bluffs above streams throughout eastern Kentucky. [Pp. 79, 143, 265-66]

Vaccinium stamineum L. DEERBERRY, SQUAWBERRY
With inedible fruits following pretty flowers, the deerberry grows in dry oak and pine woods in acid soil. It is common in most regions of the state except the Bluegrass and the limestone areas of the Mississippian Plateau. [Pp. 77, 261]

Vaccinium vacillans Torr. LOWBUSH BLUEBERRY
This little blueberry is frequent in open oak and pine woods on uplands and in borders of swampy woods in the acid soils of eastern Kentucky and the edge of the Western Coalfield.
[Pp. 78, 142, 263]

Sapotaceae, Sapodilla Family

Bumelia lycioides (L.) Gaertn. f.
BUCKTHORN BUMELIA, SOUTHERN BUCKTHORN
This tall erect shrub or small tree is found infrequently in the
Pennyroyal and the Jackson Purchase.   [Pp. 70, 255, 371]

Ebenaceae, Ebony Family

Diospyros virginiana L.   PERSIMMON
The persimmon occurs throughout the state. It is found in dry
woodlands and grassy openings but is most common forming
thickets in abandoned fields and fence corners.

Although the unripe fruit is highly astringent, the ripe fruit is
very sweet with a food value approaching that of the date. It can
be eaten raw or made into puddings; the Indians made a persimmon
bread. It is an important wildlife food eaten by bobwhite quail,
raccoons, foxes, skunks, opossums, and deer. Neither deer nor
domestic stock will browse the leaves.

The persimmon belongs to a genus and family that are largely
tropical. Its genus, which includes ebony, has been on earth since
the Cretaceous Period and is still widespread. The dark heartwood
of our persimmon, resembling ebony and exceeded in hardness in
North America only by dogwood and ironwood, is not formed until
the tree is a century old. It is used largely for golf club heads; the
sapwood is used for shuttles and shoe lasts.   [Pp. 99, 122, 372-73]

Styracaceae, Storax Family

Halesia carolina L.   SILVERBELL
When in flower the silverbell is laden with pendent, white, bell-
shaped flowers, and when the flowers fall the ground beneath is
white as if covered by snow. It is often cultivated ornamentally,
and a tree so beautiful should be planted even more. In the wild it
grows as an understory tree in rich mesophytic woodland; it is rare
in this state but has been found in both southeastern and southwestern Kentucky.   [Pp. 56, 289, 416-17]

Styrax americana Lam. SNOWBELL
This graceful shrub with pendent, white, bell-shaped flowers on slender branches is fairly frequent in swampy woods in western Kentucky. [Pp. 56, 289]

Styrax grandifolia Ait. LARGE-LEAF SNOWBELL
This species of snowbell, frequent in woodlands of the Deep South, is rare in Kentucky and is known to occur only in the Jackson Purchase region. [Pp. 56, 289]

Oleaceae, OLIVE FAMILY

Chionanthus virginicus L. FRINGE-TREE
The fringe-tree, bearing fringelike clusters of white flowers, has long been a favorite in gardens and lawns. It grows wild in a variety of habitats—including open woods on ridgetops, valleys, and moist wooded ravine slopes—in eastern and southern Kentucky, where it is sometimes locally plentiful. [Pp. 57, 140, 210]

Forestiera acuminata (Michx.) Poir. SWAMP PRIVET
The swamp privet is found infrequently on river banks and in swamp forests of western Kentucky. [Pp. 111, 139, 234]

Forestiera ligustrina (Michx.) Poir.
UPLAND FORESTIERA
This species has been found in dry rocky ground in western Kentucky but is rare. [Pp. 111, 139, 234]

Fraxinus americana L. WHITE ASH
The white ash, frequent in all sections of Kentucky, is the most common ash both here and in all of the eastern United States. It grows in a variety of soils, usually in somewhat mesophytic situations. Since it grows fastest in open woods, it flourishes in second-growth woodland. Also it is a good ornamental shade tree.

The white ash is one of our leading commercial hardwoods. The wood is hard, strong, outstandingly tough, and somewhat elastic, not breaking under strain. With such properties it is suited for baseball bats, tennis rackets, hockey sticks, polo mallets, and tool handles; it has also been used for furniture. [P. 303]

F. americana var. *biltmoreana* (Beadle) J. Wright
BILTMORE ASH
This variety has the same habitat, range, and uses but is less
frequent than the typical white ash. [P. 303]

Fraxinus pennsylvanica Marsh. RED ASH
This ash is relatively infrequent in Kentucky but is widely scattered,
occurring usually on wooded slopes. The wood, softer and weaker
than that of the white ash, is less valuable but still goes to the
lumber market. It is less ornamental than other ashes. [P. 306]

F. pennsylvanica var. *subintegerrima* (Vahl) Fernald
GREEN ASH
The green ash is frequent in swampy woods and fairly frequent on
river floodplains and creek banks. It is a better ornamental shade
tree for lawns than the red ash, and the wood is of better quality.
However, it is less hard, tough, strong, and elastic than the more
valuable white ash, and is heavier; it has similar uses. Most oars
and canoe paddles today are made of green ash instead of the
more expensive white ash. [P. 306]

Fraxinus quadrangulata Michx. BLUE ASH
The blue ash may be found in any part of the state where limestone
outcrops but is common only in the Inner Bluegrass region. Along
with the bur oak it is a characteristic tree of the typical, long-
established bluegrass pastures. It is also plentiful on the limestone
cliffs of the Kentucky River in the Inner Bluegrass.
 The wood has the same properties as that of the white ash
except that it is heavier. It is now too scarce to reach the market
often, but when it does, it is not distinguished from white ash.
In the early days of homebuilding in the Bluegrass region, prior
to the Victorian period, blue ash was the chief wood used for
flooring and stair treads. [Pp. 111, 304-05]

Fraxinus tomentosa Michx. f. PUMPKIN ASH
In Kentucky the pumpkin ash is restricted to the swamps of the
west. Inferior to white ash, the wood was not used until recently
when the latter became scarcer and more expensive. [P. 307]

Ligustrum spp. PRIVET
Several foreign species of *Ligustrum* are in cultivation here and some escape, such as *L. vulgare*, *L. ibota*, and others.
[Pp. 83, 139, 174, 211]

Apocynaceae, Dogbane Family

Trachelospermum difforme (Walt.) Gray
CLIMBING DOGBANE
The small, semiwoody climbing dogbane clambers over river banks in southern Kentucky, both southeastern and southwestern, but is not common. Its "Dr. Jekyll and Mr. Hyde" leaves of two shapes account for its specific epithet.   [Pp. 80, 183]

Bignoniaceae, Trumpet-Creeper Family

Bignonia capreolata L. CROSS-VINE
One may first become aware of the presence of a cross-vine in the woods by seeing the ground strewn with red and yellow funnel-shaped flowers; then one may have to look to the tops of tall trees to see whence they fell. The leaves of this high-climbing vine are green or bronze all winter and, in pairs, make a distinctive pattern against a tree trunk to which they cling. The cross-vine is frequent in open woods all over Kentucky but most common in calcareous soil on river banks and cliffs and in ravines.   [Pp. 67, 167, 180]

Campsis radicans (L.) Seem.
TRUMPET-VINE, TRUMPET-CREEPER
This large and vigorous vine bearing orange and scarlet flowers, a favorite of hummingbirds, is sometimes cultivated. It can be attractive growing wild, for instance on a fence, but in old fields and thickets it can become a troublesome woody weed. It is common all over the state.   [Pp. 67, 178,-79]

Catalpa bignonioides Walt.
SOUTHERN CATALPA, INDIAN BEAN
Indigenous to the South, this species is often planted and sometimes escapes in Kentucky. It is similar to *C. speciosa*.   [Pp. 66, 317]

Catalpa speciosa Warder
CATALPA, NORTHERN CATALPA, CIGAR-TREE
Native to alluvial forests in western Kentucky, this species has been widely planted over the state and sometimes escapes. With large and showy clusters of white flowers it is suitable as an ornamental tree in parks and large lawns. Since the wood is durable in contact with the soil, though soft, coarse-grained, and not strong, it is often used for fenceposts. [Pp. 66, 318-19]

Paulownia tomentosa (Thunb.) Steud.
ROYAL PAULOWNIA, PRINCESS-TREE, EMPRESS-TREE
The royal paulownia, a native of the Orient, has been planted ornamentally and has become locally established as an escape in mesophytic woodlands in different sections of the state, including Pine Mountain, the Outer Bluegrass, and others. It is fast-growing and valued for its large, fragrant, lilac-colored flowers produced before the leaves; however, it is a coarse-looking tree, and the long-persistent capsules are unattractive. Countless small winged seed are disseminated far and wide by the wind. [Pp. 66, 320-21]

Rubiaceae, MADDER FAMILY

Cephalanthus occidentalis L. BUTTONBUSH
With a globose cluster of flowers full of nectar and attractive to bees, this shrub is also known as globe-flower and honey-balls. It is widely distributed in the state and is common in swamps, pond borders, and margins of sluggish streams. [Pp. 70, 117, 215]

Caprifoliaceae, HONEYSUCKLE FAMILY

Lonicera dioica L. WILD HONEYSUCKLE
This straggling, inconspicuous vine has pretty flowers and interesting leaves. It grows on steep wooded banks, principally in central and eastern Kentucky, but is infrequent. [Pp. 65, 127, 182]

Lonicera flavida Cockerell YELLOW HONEYSUCKLE
Similar to the preceding, this honeysuckle is found infrequently in the Bluegrass region. [Pp. 65, 127, 182]

Lonicera japonica Thunb.   JAPANESE HONEYSUCKLE
Introduced into cultivation as a semievergreen vine with deliciously fragrant flowers, the Japanese honeysuckle has become not only naturalized but a common and highly obnoxious pest. Where it escapes into thickets and woodlands, it festoons the trees and makes a tangled mat over all small growth, completely obliterating it; this prevents any possibility of new vegetation, such as young timber trees, getting started.   [Pp. 65, 169, 181]

Lonicera prolifera (Kirchn.) Rehd.   WILD HONEYSUCKLE
This species, similar to *L. dioica* but less frequent, grows on limestone cliffs in the Bluegrass region.   [Pp. 65, 182]

Lonicera sempervirens L.   TRUMPET HONEYSUCKLE
Indigenous to the southern states and possibly to Kentucky, the red-flowered trumpet honeysuckle is sometimes found here as an escape from cultivation.   [Pp. 57, 182]

Sambucus canadensis L.   COMMON ELDER, ELDERBERRY
Beauty is often unappreciated when it is common and wild. Such is the elderberry, widespread and common in alluvial bottoms, open places in wet woodland and fencerows in moist ground. Its lacy flowers are exchanged for purple-black berries borne on rose-red stalks that are attractive even after the berries have been eaten by birds or gathered by man for jelly or wine.   [Pp. 89, 133, 207]

Sambucus pubens Michx.   RED-BERRIED ELDER
This species, characteristic of the far north, is a Pleistocene relict in our area remaining in only a few localities in the Cumberland Mountains and Cumberland Plateau.   [Pp. 89, 133, 206]

Symphoricarpos orbiculatus Moench.
BUCKBERRY, CORALBERRY
This old-field shrub is found in overgrazed, eroded, or abandoned fields and pastures. It is widely scattered, locally plentiful, and most abundant in the Outer Bluegrass.   [Pp. 127, 212]

Viburnum acerifolium L.   MAPLE-LEAF VIBURNUM
Lovely in flower, this little viburnum nevertheless is gayest in its autumn foliage of rose, purple, and magenta. Frequent in meso-

phytic woods and ravines in dry woods, it is found in most sections of the state, although it is apparently missing from the Inner Bluegrass and the Jackson Purchase and is rare in the Outer Bluegrass.

[Pp. 90, 137, 229]

Viburnum cassinoides L.   WITHE-ROD

Essentially a northern species with a southern range extension in the Appalachian Mountains, the withe-rod in Kentucky is found fairly frequently in the Cumberland Mountains and Plateau, where it grows in swampy woods, river bank thickets, and other moist situations. It is an attractive shrub for the garden and will thrive in moderately moist ground.   [Pp. 91, 222]

Viburnum dentatum L.   ARROW-WOOD

This species of arrow-wood is found fairly frequently in swampy woods and on mesophytic slopes in central and eastern Kentucky. It is a good shrub for ornamental planting.   [Pp. 92, 138, 226]

Viburnum lentago L.   NANNYBERRY

The nannyberry is often planted where a large shrub is desired, but in the wild it is rare in Kentucky. Most of its range is to the north of us.   [Pp. 91, 138, 222]

Viburnum molle Michx.   KENTUCKY VIBURNUM

The Kentucky viburnum, beautiful and suitable for cultivation, grows on cliffs, rocky banks of creeks, and moist slopes. It is widely scattered but most frequent in the Bluegrass.   [Pp. 92, 139, 228]

Viburnum nudum L.   POSSUM-HAW, SWAMP-HAW

This species is restricted to western Kentucky, where it is frequent in swamps, roadside ditches, and margins of sluggish streams.

[Pp. 91, 221]

Viburnum prunifolium L.   BLACK-HAW

This large shrub or small tree is frequent on wooded slopes and in woodland borders throughout Kentucky. [Pp. 91, 138, 223, 324]

Viburnum rafinesquianum Schult.   ARROW-WOOD

This species of arrow-wood is infrequently found on wooded slopes, usually limestone, in central and eastern Kentucky.

[Pp. 92, 138, 227]

Viburnum recognitum Fern.   ARROW-WOOD
This arrow-wood, similar to V. *dentatum* and included in the *dentatum* complex, is found on wooded stream banks, but is scattered and infrequent in Kentucky.

Viburnum rufidulum Raf.   SOUTHERN BLACK-HAW
The southern black-haw is very frequent in all limestone regions, especially the Inner Bluegrass, but is infrequent in noncalcareous areas. This is such a beautiful large shrub or small tree, having thick, highly lustrous leaves as well as lovely flowers, that one wonders why our nurserymen have overlooked propagating and promoting it for ornamental planting.   [Pp. 90, 138, 224-25, 324]

Suggested References for
Continued Study

The earliest comprehensive work on North American trees was by François Michaux, three volumes published in Paris in 1810–1813 under the title *Histoire des Arbres*, soon translated into English and published in several American editions as *The North American Sylva*. Although not widely available even in some of the later editions, it is rewarding whenever accessible.

The most complete treatment of North American trees is *The Silva of North America*, 14 volumes, by Charles S. Sargent (Boston: Houghton Mifflin Company, 1890–1902). A condensed single volume by Sargent is *Manual of the Trees of North America*, second edition (Boston: Houghton Mifflin Company, 1922). A. H. Graves, *Illustrated Guide to Trees and Shrubs* (New York: Harper, 1956) may also be helpful.

Books concerning woody plants of adjacent states which are also useful in Kentucky include:

Braun, E. Lucy. 1960. *The Woody Plants of Ohio*. Columbus: Ohio State University Press.

Coker, William C., and Totten, Henry R. 1945. *Trees of the Southeastern States*. Third edition. Chapel Hill: University of North Carolina Press.

Deam, Charles C. 1931. *Trees of Indiana*. Fourth edition. Indianapolis: Indiana Department of Conservation, Division of Forestry.

———. 1932. *Shrubs of Indiana*. Indianapolis: Indiana Department of Conservation, Division of Forestry.

Several comprehensive published floras of nearby states may also be helpful:

Mohlenbrock, R. H. 1959. *A Flora of Southern Illinois*. Carbondale: Southern Illinois University Press.

Radford, A. E.; Ahles, H. E.; and Bell, C. R. 1964. *Manual of the Vascular Flora of the Carolinas*. Chapel Hill: University of North Carolina Press.

Strausbaugh, P. D., and Core, E. L. 1952–1964. *Flora of West*

Virginia. Parts 1–4. Morgantown: West Virginia University Bulletin.

The following standard botanical manuals cover all of Kentucky's flora, both woody and herbaceous:

Fernald, M. L. 1950. *Gray's Manual of Botany*. Eighth edition. New York: American Book Company.

Gleason, H. A. 1952. *New Britton and Brown Illustrated Flora of the Northeastern United States and Adjacent Canada.* 3 volumes. New York: New York Botanical Garden.

———, and Cronquist, A. 1963. *Manual of Vascular Plants of Northeastern United States and Adjacent Canada.* Princeton: D. Van Nostrand Company.

A valuable reference in forest ecology is *Deciduous Forests of Eastern North America* by E. Lucy Braun (Philadelphia: Blakiston Company, 1950).

For natural history we suggest A *Natural History of Trees of Eastern and Central North America* by Donald Culross Peattie (Boston: Houghton Mifflin Company, 1948), and *Trees of the South* by Charlotte Hilton Green (Chapel Hill: University of North Carolina Press, 1939).

Illustrated Glossary

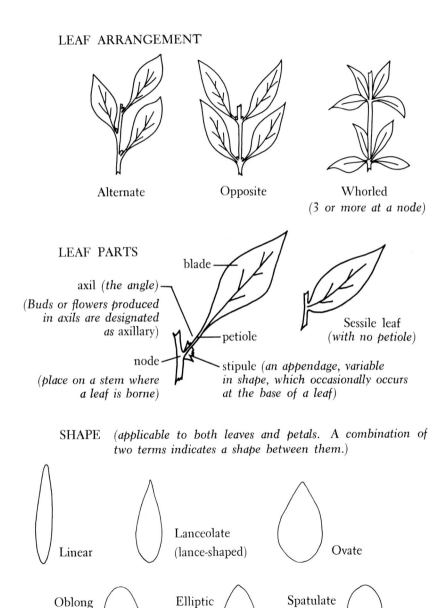

LEAF ARRANGEMENT

Alternate

Opposite

Whorled
(3 or more at a node)

LEAF PARTS

blade

axil (the angle)
(Buds or flowers produced
in axils are designated
as axillary)

petiole

Sessile leaf
(with no petiole)

node
(place on a stem where
a leaf is borne)

stipule (an appendage, variable
in shape, which occasionally occurs
at the base of a leaf)

SHAPE (applicable to both leaves and petals. A combination of
two terms indicates a shape between them.)

Linear

Lanceolate
(lance-shaped)

Ovate

Oblong

Elliptic

Spatulate

VENATION *(vein pattern)*

 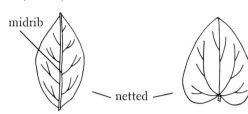

midrib

netted

Parallel
*(main veins running
from base to apex)*

Pinnate
*(main veins extending
from the midrib)*

Palmate
*(main veins radiating
from the base)*

SIMPLE LEAVES *(Blade undivided)*

Entire
(smooth-margined)

Toothed

Pinnately lobed

Palmately lobed

COMPOUND LEAVES *(Blade divided into leaflets)*

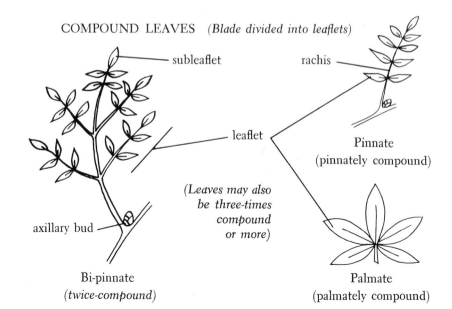

subleaflet

rachis

leaflet

*(Leaves may also
be three-times
compound
or more)*

axillary bud

Pinnate
(pinnately compound)

Bi-pinnate
(twice-compound)

Palmate
(palmately compound)

FLOWER SYMMETRY

Radial symmetry

(Can be cut into 2 equal halves in many ways provided the plane of cutting passes through the center)

Bilateral symmetry

(Two-sided. Only 1 plane of cutting will divide it into 2 equal halves)

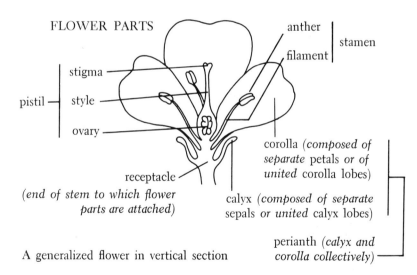

FLOWER PARTS

anther | filament | stamen

stigma

pistil — style

ovary

receptacle

(end of stem to which flower parts are attached)

corolla *(composed of separate petals or of united corolla lobes)*

calyx *(composed of separate sepals or united calyx lobes)*

perianth *(calyx and corolla collectively)*

A generalized flower in vertical section

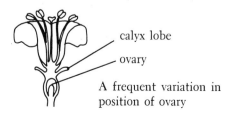

calyx lobe

ovary

A frequent variation in position of ovary

INFLORESCENCES *(flower clusters)*

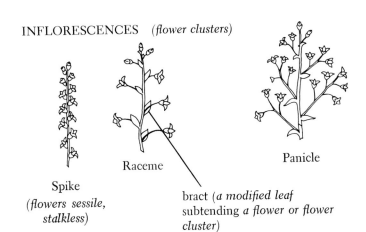

Spike
*(flowers sessile,
stalkless)*

Raceme

bract *(a modified leaf
subtending a flower or flower
cluster)*

Panicle

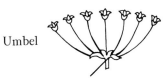

Umbel

involucre *(a compact group of bracts)*

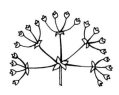

Compound umbel

Cyme
*(central flower
matures first)*

Compound cyme

Catkin
*(a scaly-bracted spike,
usually drooping,
usually having
unisexual flowers
without corollas)*

Corymb

Flowers whorled

WINTER TWIGS

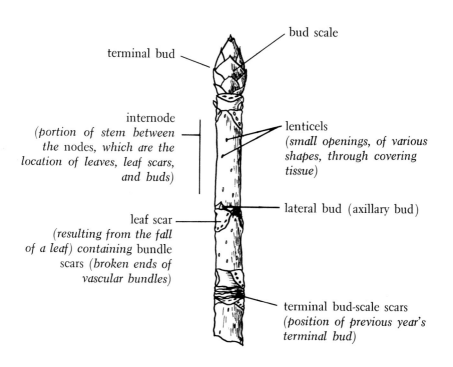

terminal bud

bud scale

internode
*(portion of stem between
the* nodes, which are the
*location of leaves, leaf scars,
and buds)*

lenticels
*(small openings, of various
shapes, through covering
tissue)*

lateral bud (axillary bud)

leaf scar
*(resulting from the fall
of a leaf) containing* bundle
scars *(broken ends of
vascular bundles)*

terminal bud-scale scars
*(position of previous year's
terminal bud)*

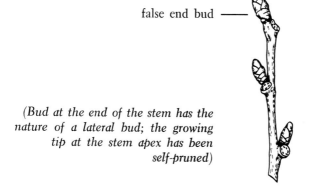

false end bud

*(Bud at the end of the stem has the
nature of a lateral bud; the growing
tip at the stem apex has been
self-pruned)*

MISCELLANEOUS TERMS

Glabrous. *Without hairs*

Glandular. *Having minute, roundish secreting structures, sometimes associated with hairs*

Glaucous. *Having a thin, whitish, powdery coating*

2-ranked. *Having leaves in two vertical rows down the stem*

FRUIT TYPES

Dry fruits, splitting at maturity:

Capsule. *Developed from a compound pistil, often containing more than one locule (compartment) and splitting along two or more lines*

Pod. *Developed from a simple pistil, having only one locule (compartment), and splitting along two lines*

Dry fruits, not splitting at maturity:

Achene. *Small and one-seeded*

Nut. *One-seeded, hard and bony*

Fleshy fruits:

Berry. *A fleshy fruit in which the seeds (not enclosed in stones) are embedded in the pulp*

Drupe. *A so-called stone fruit, having the seed enclosed in a hard covering surrounded by the fleshy pulp*

Pome. *An apple-type fruit, crowned by sepals and having a papery or hard core at the center containing several seeds*

ECOLOGICAL TERMS

Association. *A major climax unit of a formation, such as the Mixed Mesophytic association or the Oak-Hickory association of the deciduous forest formation*

Climax. *The final result of succession: a self-perpetuating community with no further development possible under existing climatic or physiographic conditions*

Community. *Any vegetational unit regardless of rank or stage in development*

Formation. *A major vegetational unit, such as deciduous forest, grassland, etc.*

Mesic. *Descriptive of a moderately moist habitat*

Mesophytic. *Descriptive of plants or plant communities of medium moisture requirements*

Relict. *A species or community which has survived from an earlier geologic time*

Second-growth forest, secondary forest. *A forest coming in after disturbance*

Succession. *A series of stages consisting of the replacement of one community by another as the result of progressive development*

Virgin forest. *A forest which has reached maturity through natural processes without any influence of man's activities*

Xeric. *Descriptive of a dry habitat, with low moisture and often with a high evaporation rate*

Xerophytic. *Descriptive of plants or plant communities adapted to a dry habitat*

Index to Scientific
& Common Names